Home, work and class consciousness

MARILYN PORTER

Home, work and class consciousness

MANCHESTER UNIVERSITY PRESS

Copyright © Marilyn Porter 1983

Published by
Manchester University Press
Oxford Road, Manchester M13 9PL

British Library cataloguing in publication data

Porter, Marilyn
    Home, work, and class consciousness
    1. Labor and laboring classes — Great Britain
    2. Social classes — Great Britain
    I. Title
    305.5'62   HD8395

    ISBN 0-7190-0899-9

Library of Congress Cataloging in Publication Data

Porter, Marilyn, 1942–
    Home, work, and class consciousness.
    Bibliography: p.
    .Includes index.
    1. Working class women—England—Bristol (Avon)—
Attitudes. 2. Housewives—England—Bristol (Avon)—
Attitudes. 3. Labor and laboring classes—England—
Bristol (Avon). 4. Division of labor. I. Title.
HQ1600.B7P67   1982   305.5'62   82-20854

Printed in Great Britain by
Butler & Tanner Ltd,
Frome and London

CONTENTS

ACKNOWLEDGEMENTS

This book has been a long time in the making, and my debts of gratitude are consequently large.

First and foremost there are the men and women of Bristol who gave me their time and attention so generously. Without them there would have been no book.

The Women's Movement first propelled me into activity and has subsequently been my main source of political and intellectual support and inspiration.

There are too many colleagues and friends who have given me unstinting support and help to name. Especial thanks are due to Theo Nichols, Miki David and Bob Reiner, who bore the brunt in more ways than one. Jackie West, Anna Pollert, David Morgan, Sue Webb and Liz Stanley were all vital sources of encouraging criticism.

I would also like to thank those institutions which gave me the employment I needed to support this study, and especially Manchester University and the Memorial University of Newfoundland, which provided such generous and stimulating intellectual atmospheres.

Doris Macey and Valerie Ryan triumphantly and speedily translated my appalling handwriting into legible typescript.

Finally I would like to thank my children, Fenella and Luke, who gave me unswerving love and encouragement but are delighted it is finished; Julie Downes, Ginny Duggan, Kate Pollard and Wendy Gilchrist, who also lived with it; and Tony Thomas, who provided a mystified but indispensible alternative.

INTRODUCTION

The sexual division of labour is so obvious and universal that even feminists have sometimes taken it for granted. As a concept it has not been subjected to the same rigorous scrutiny as such terms as 'patriarchy', 'reproduction', 'domestic mode of production' or even 'domestic labour'. Indeed, very often the debates rested on the assumption that we all knew that there was a sexual division of labour, and that, at least, was unproblematic. A recent example is Michèle Barrett's lucid and definitive survey of the theoretical problems of Marxist feminism (M. Barrett, 1980). 'Sexual division of labour' merits twenty-five entries in the index, but nowhere does she investigate it as a concept with the same seriousness that she devotes to other ideas.

I am not especially critical of this, for it seems to me that one of the values of the term is precisely that it does describe a marked and known reality. After all, Talcott Parsons outlined in 1955 a sexual division of labour that we would all recognise today.

> The adult feminine role has not ceased to be anchored primarily in the internal affairs of the family, as wife, mother and manager of the household, while the role of the adult male is primarily anchored in the occupational world, in his job and through it by his status giving and income-earning functions for the family. [1955, pp. 14–15]

There is even a certain scorn in some feminist references to the idea of sexual 'spheres' of wage work (production) and the sphere of the family (reproduction) which leads to a kind of dualism.[1] But in her influential piece in *Beyond the Fragments* S. Rowbotham (1980) suggests that the two spheres are 'bridged by ideology and the state', and it is precisely that bridging which is the subject of this study.

The idea of the sexual division of labour and its extension into the two 'worlds' of men and women also enables us to circumvent the thorny problem of the relationship between the subordination of women and their place in the family. We know that in practice and historically there is an intimate relationship. As J. West has put it:

> ... the family has persisted as the site for the basic reproduction of labour power. It is the institution within which most commodities and services are consumed, which provides for the mediation of the wage, and whose material responsibilities and relations of dependency and support are reinforced by the state. [1980, p. 175]

Other writers (V. Beechey, 1977, 1978; L. Bland *et al.*, 1978) have argued that this relationship determines the conditions under which women operate outside the family, 'for women as wives are situated in a state of permanent transition between two modes of labouring, the capitalist and the family mode' (L. Bland *et al.*, 1978).

Pauline Hunt, in another recent contribution, has argued for 'the underlying integration of the family unit and social production, in the sense that each sphere constitutes the conditions and existence of the other ... the contradiction between the apparent separation, but actual integration of the domestic and industrial arena' (1980, p. 2). Pauline Hunt's book is an invaluable contribution to the exploration of the 'experiences of contradiction' in the lives of men and women focusing on the primary division of roles into home-maker or breadwinner. Much of her material is paralleled in my own findings, but this study addressed itself more explicitly to the political and ideological consequences of that division. In the last paragraph of her book Pauline Hunt indicates what needs to be done in order to relate such work explicitly to the labour movement and to the women's movement and also to develop a more adequate theory of class consciousness. Let us now begin that task.

Women are not a class,[2] nor even a homogeneous group. They have many different kinds of experience as wives, as mothers, as daughters, as young girls and as old women. 'Middle-class' women and 'working-class' women have very different experiences in a class society. Here I am obviously particularly concerned with working-class women who are wives and mothers, a concern that springs from the operation of the concept of the sexual division of labour within a Marxist problematic.

The term 'sexual division of labour' signals an understanding that the main reality for men and women is both materially and ideologically different. The reasons for that, the origins and the universality of the phenomenon, its consequences for and place within capitalist society can be analysed within other concepts — 'patriarchy' and 'reproduction' spring to mind.[3] The sexual division of labour enables us to leave those problems on one side for the moment and explore the consequences of the reality for experience. The sexual division of labour is one of responsibility more than activity. The prime responsibility for all the 'reproductions' analysed by Edholm *et al.* (social reproduction, reproduction of the labour force and human or biological reproduction; 1977, p. 104) clearly lies with women, and this has profound consequences for *all* women, whether or not they are married and have children. The experience of single women ('spinsters'), lesbians and childless couples bears constant witness to the socital expectation of conformity. It was therefore logical to choose to talk with women who had apparently conformed to this norm.[4] That they were working-class had to do with the Marxist orientation of the study. There is a real sense in which capitalist relations bear most heavily on those who sell their labour at the raw edge of capitalist relations. It is arguable, of course, that those in marginal positions, or outside the economy — the unemployed, the aged, outworkers and public service workers — are much worse off in material terms. But what is of more interest to us here is the quality of the relationship between worker and capitalist, and the way in which that direct relationship is understood by and mediated to those working-class women who are removed from that direct relationship.

This study, then, is an examination of how the sexual division of labour operated — materially and ideologically — in the lives of twenty-five working-class couples living and working in Britain in the early 1970s. The husbands all worked as production workers or foremen in a medium-size fibre-making firm that I have called 'Hampers Ltd'. The wives were all primarily occupied in looking after their homes and dependent children in Bristol.

The situation of these largely home-bound women seemed to me to be not just typical, but the paradigm situation of all women — married or not, with children, or without, working or not. For the expectation that they are, were, will be or should be in this situation affects both the way women think of themselves and how society regards them. More than this, it is part of the objective reality of their lives.

Origins

The original impetus for the study came from an awareness that both Marxist theory and even the best studies of 'images of society' or of working-class consciousness were wholly involved in the analysis of 'productive work' and productive workers. And by that they meant men engaged in male-dominated work processes (e.g. steel, cars, chemicals). This was back in 1973/4, before feminists and fellow-travellers had organised their sustained attack on overt sexism and the covert sexism of the omission of women. The study began as part of that campaign. Working-class men, employed in factories, struggling for dignity amid the 'degradation' of selling their labour, constructing their ideas in struggle and occasionally breaking into open conflict with management — these had all been carefully and sensitively described.[5] I was also impressed by that group of studies which focused more broadly on working-class images of society, and which drew its inspiration from the work of David Lockwood[6] and others. But these too examined the ideas that men had in the work context, as if that was their only significant experience.[7]

Most of the men, I observed, were married. Many had children. They did not live wholly in the encapsulated vacuum of the factory, in fact they spent only a third of their lives there. They had to go elsewhere to reproduce their labour power so that they could return to work the next day. In a word, they went home. But at home there were wives. What were *they* doing? What were they thinking? How did they understand the work that consumed so much of their husband's energy? Did they share his militancy when they went on strike?

To begin with, then, I wanted to know how, if at all, the consciousness of working-class women differed from that of working-class men, and whether the differences related to differences in their experience. None of the studies I have mentioned dealt with men's life at home, much less with the women who shared it: nor did those few studies of industrial conflict (e.g. A. Gouldner, 1954; T. Lane and K. Roberts, 1971[8]).

Working men's wives have appeared fleetingly from behind their husbands: brawny frames, either in confirmation of their husband's ideological position or as part of the backcloth of the community structure. (Other working-class women, the unmarried, daughters or mothers, get even less attention.) In fact these studies had only taken over the conventional wisdom of sociology, which said (with some inherent contradiction) that: (a) women think as their husbands do — an assumption that was usually the result of the conflation of politics with the study of voting preferences (e.g. W. G. Runciman, 1966; A. Shostak, 1969; R. F. Hamilton, 1967) — and (b) that women are more 'conservative' than men (e.g. R. F. Hamilton, 1967; L. Rainwater, 1959; B. M. Berger, 1960). This latter assumption tended, *ipso facto*, to cause them to be neglected by those writers mainly interested in *radical* potential.

There was, and is, little conclusive evidence for assumption (b). Even if it were proved it would still raise a number of questions, for it is as important to determine the factors that generate and sustain a *conservative* consciousness as to identify those that generate and sustain a radical consciousness. In any event, more recent work on *men's* consciousness had indicated that the whole matter was much more complicated than had previously been allowed. People's ideas — men's as well as women's — were too fragmentary and incomplete to fall into neat, predetermined categories (M. Bulmer, 1975; T. Nichols, 1974; S. Aronowitz, 1973; R. Sennett and J. Cobb, 1974).

In theory, assumption (a) was more problematic, because it flew in the face of the funcamental axiom that experience and consciousness are connected (E. Bott, 1959, p. 159; M. Bulmer, 1975). Women do not have the same experience of society as men do — even those who work outside the home — and, *a fortiori*, women who are primarily occupied at home with young children do not have the same experience as their husband at work, and certainly they do not have direct experience of *his* work. It did not therefore seem legitimate merely to assume that their ideas would be identical to their husbands' (even if they voted for the same candidate at elections).

Working-class men share their homes with working-class women, and those women cannot be assumed to be silent, passive or without social experience of their own. If imagery and consciousness arise from social experience, then, in so far as their social experience differs from the men's, so will their imagery and consciousness. The easy assumption that women — especially wives — will merely echo what their husbands say contradicts a central tenet of the work on images of society.

The omission of women's experience and images from both Lockwood's typology and the subsequent work indicates that the original insight that men's experience was all of a piece, and that all elements in it should be considered significant, has been ignored. Instead the focus reverted to the eight hours a day a man spends at work. I felt that the sixteen hours a day he spends elsewhere were as significant in the formation of his ideology, and that this 'home' experience, as well as that of his wife, merited at least as much consideration if we were to understand the totality of working-class consciousness.

This 'omission' of women is gradually decreasing. There are more studies on women each month. Yet a new kind of ghettoism is growing up. Studies on women — yes, studies on men that genuflect in the direction of women, but still not studies that use our developing insights into women to reform our view of *men's* ideas and practice.

In addition I was becoming increasingly absorbed by the problems of the mediation of both experience and ideology. Ideology is constructed, but not in isolation. It is the *social* nature of experience that makes it relevant. How, then, *did* people socially construct their ideology; how did they mediate it to others — significant working-class others who had not shared all or part of their social experience? The nature of contradiction became pivotal. Pauline Hunt has correctly observed that 'where an idea is held in common by a group of people [it] has the effect of making these people unaware of the contradiction contained in their situation' (1980, p. 180).

Process

This, then, was the initial framework of the study — essentially still an exercise in what Margherita Rendel has called 'completing the record'. But the material itself soon ensured that the study transcended that role. In concentrating on the sexual division of labour I found I was uncovering a much more fundamental fracture than I had realised. It became increasingly clear that not only was much of the practice of people's lives organised around this principle, but so was their ideology — and this was not surprising. For in looking at how experience structures ideology I was finding that gender-differentiated experience played a crucial part in the structuring of gender-differentiated ideology. Necessarily it followed that working-class men and women were approaching class consciousness by largely separate routes.

Another aspect of the material that became important (and which I have had largely to neglect in the present volume) was the partiality of both 'men's' and 'women's' worlds. Neither experience nor the consequent ideology included a third 'public' world of power, politics and most of the accepted ingredients of the potential for a full *class* consciousness. Both men and women laid tentative claims to parts of this public world — often in contradictory ways. At the end of the book we shall be able to see something of how the experience of being men and women differentiates approaches to these wider concerns; and how that differentiation cuts across the construction of full class consciousness.

Method

A fuller discussion of the methods I used and the problems I encountered can be found in Appendix I. Here I want to draw attention to a central theme in the study that dictated my approach — the specificity and reality of people's experience, and the key part it played in its mediation to ideology. This concern, coupled with a conviction that contradictions were more revealing than bland coherence, dictated an exploratory tentative study with a relatively small group of people and using the time-honoured qualitative methods of participant observation and in-depth interviews.

I therefore chose a medium-size factory in a large provincial city. Hampers Ltd made cardboard boxes (or fibreboard, to use the correct and grander term). The firm had begun as an ancillary to the tobacco industry. After the war it branched out into many other kinds of packaging. During the late '60s, as a result of several take-overs and mergers, it became a small part of a vast industrial empire. Five hundred and forty men and a few women worked in the plant, and they lived mainly in two districts to the south of the city. The only special feature of the factory was that one of the two main unions in it — the Tobacco Workers' Union (TWU)[10] — had been in dispute a few weeks before I began my study. From this workplace I chose twenty-five men — from similar work-related categories that 'images of society' studies used — foremen and stewards, and rank and file from both unions. This much was dictated by my original 'completing the record' aim. All these men were married. None of the wives worked full-time and all had at least one dependent child under sixteen. They were, in fact, paradigm housewives — a choice that arose from the state of feminist theory in 1974. But I shall argue later (in Chapter 5) that these 'paradigm women', married, economically dependent on their husband's earnings and primarily occupied at home with the domestic responsibilities of house, husband and children, constitute a theoretically important focus for us now.

For a year, then, I talked to these twenty-five couples, fifty men and women, together and separately, at home and at work. I taped many of the conversations, and it is the analysis of these tapes that provides the bulk of the material that follows.

Terms and concepts

It will already be clear that the sexual division of labour is an organising concept in the study. What should be stressed here is that I do not mean it to refer only or even mainly to the material sexual division of labour — who *does* what — but more to the ideological sexual division of labour: what women and men think, and how they interpret their experience in relation to the differential nature of that experience.[9] The sexual division of labour thus becomes a tool that we can use to unlock some of the mediation[11] and contradictions that occur between men's and women's worlds.

By sexism and sexist ideology I refer to the ideology and practice that point not merely to a difference between men and women but to a significant division, one which asserts the superiority of men. It also assumes that the male perspective is the 'normal' one, that male priorities are taken as given, and that the assertion of women's claims is seen as deviant.

Where I have used 'women's work' rather than domestic labour it is because I wished to dissociate the usage from the now well trodden domestic labour debate,[12] and with it any implication that I might be making theoretical claims for it. I also wanted to use a term that covered not only the whole area of women's responsibilities at home but also their place in the labour market and in society generally. It is, broadly, the practice of being a woman.

While I have used the word 'feminist' quite freely to refer to writers from within the Women's Liberation Movement who would explicitly accept that designation, I have not applied it to ideas or standpoints held by the women in this study.

The concept of 'feminism' is still very diffuse. It is associated with notions of women's 'oppression' or women's 'liberation' – themselves not very clearly defined. Of the many who claim to be 'feminists' few have ventured a complete definition. I shall take one example. Juliet Mitchell's 'baseline' definition of feminism is to 'see women as a distinct and oppressed social group'.[13] A few pages later this neutral platitude is filled out:

> Feminism is a method of analysis as well as the discovery of new material. It asks new questions as well as coming up with new answers. Its central concern is with the social distinction between men and women, with the fact of this distinction, with its meaning and with its causes and consequences ... feminism transforms the ideological notion that there is a biological opposition between the sexes which determines social life, and says instead that there is a contradiction in the social relations between men and women. This contradiction is never static as a biological opposition would be, but it shifts, moves and is moved and is therefore one force among others that effects social change, and the movement of human history. [J. Mitchell and A. Oakley, 1976, p. 14]

This is a clear, if personal, interpretation. It is less than appropriate when applied to the working-class women in this study. Although many of them were deeply concerned about the social distinction between men and women, they would not use the term 'feminist'. Nor, according to Juliet Mitchell, should they. In the concluding essay to the same book (pp. 380–1) she insists that the term be reserved for those women who make 'conscious protest ... against their position' and admits that this does specifically exclude 'the massive contributions of working class women to its formation'.

So I have made use of the term 'women's consciousness' to describe those ideas, attitudes and responses that seemed to indicate a conscious awareness of what it is to be a woman in society. I have avoided prejudging the interpretation the women put upon their experience. I have simply indicated their *awareness*, and their attempts to construct an ideology from their experience as women. I have also used the term in order to relate it to other 'partial consciousnesses' — 'factory consciousness' (H. Beynon, 1974), 'trade union consciousness' (V. Lenin, 1902). In any attempt to discern the makings of true class consciousness these 'partial consciousnesses' are of absorbing interest. One of the aims of the study is to try to locate 'women's consciousness' within this process.

And, finally, a definition of those two pivotal words — 'consciousness' and 'ideology'. Definition robs them of the richness of their association with other images, yet I have used them specifically and not interchangeably. As I have used the word, 'ideology' is a set of ideas that derives from an external source — hegemonic ideology, trade union ideology. It comprises an explanation of perceived experience. The 'constructed ideology' of any individual is a patchwork of ideas assembled to answer questions imposed by experience. Consciousness is understanding. Full class consciousness is the complete 'Marxist' understanding of one's position in the social formation and the ability to unite with others to change it. It is internally created in a dialectical relationship with experience. 'Partial consciousness' is the result of real understanding of *part* of one's experience, e.g. factory consciousness, trade union consciousness, women's consciousness. 'Imprisoned consciousness' is latent understanding that is prevented by experience and ideology from being articulated, and 'arrested' consciousness is an understanding that cannot be developed because of adverse experience or ideology.

Outline

The first chapter, 'Experience of home and work', supplies the indispensable background information to the study — the parameters of experience, historically, geographically and socially, of the people involved. I also raise questions and contradictions that will be pursued in the rest of the book — what does all this mean for the people concerned and how does it work out in their ideas?

In the second chapter, 'The strike: a problem in experience', I take a recent event in these people's lives — a strike in the factory where the husbands worked — and examine its impact on them, and its implications for their ideas. In particular I look at the very different effects on participants (stewards and rank and file) and on non-participants (the other workers not on strike and the wives of all the men at home). This example serves as a touchstone by which to compare other 'experiences' and their effect on other ideas.

In the third chapter, 'Women, men and experience', I look at a different kind of experience — the personal experience of four married couples and the ways in which the husbands' and wives' ideas are related to their different experience of marriage, home and family. The couples are chosen to highlight important aspects that are similar to, or contrast with, the other couples in the study.

The next chapter, 'Men's world: work at the factory', explores the chasm between the two 'worlds' of work and home: men and women. Here we look at the men's experience of their jobs at the factory, their interpretation of it, and the effects of their work on their family life. I pay particular attention to those aspects of their jobs that directly affected their wives, and to the wives' understanding of, and response to, their husbands' 'world'.

Chapter 5, 'Women's world: work at home', takes the other 'world' — women's world at home. We note that the theme is the sexual division of *labour*, and focus on the *work* women do in and for the home, and on its consequences for their ideas. A parallel is drawn between the 'sectional consciousness' of strikers and the sectional consciousness of women in a 'man's world'. Here again I have paid attention to the husbands' understanding of what goes on at home — how it affects them and how they interpret it.

In 'Ideology and consciousness' we return to the common experience of public events, local or national, removed from the direct experience of either the men or the women and felt by them to be remote and uncontrollable. This kind of experience is mediated to them through ideological understandings and representations which are ultimately based on their different experiences, and this affects the way in which they understand them.

Finally, in 'Women, men and politics' the discussion in Chapter 6 is extended to draw together the main themes of the book. Here we look at class and gender consciousness in action, using one woman's experience as pivotal. We look too at the extension of ideas that are rooted in experience in the more tentative area of general politics, and suggest ways of treating the findings of the book to illuminate the contradictions of political consciousness.

What follows, then, is an attempt to present some of the experience of these people's lives, and to see how far that experience is structured by gender. By looking at men's and women's ideas we learn something of the complex ways in which experience is translated into ideology, and how interaction and contradiction are key constituents in the way people *construct* their ideology. The notion of the sexual division of labour offers us a way of understanding how women come to rather different understandings of the world. It also offers us a way of inscribing sexual divisions on an understanding of the workings of class and class consciousness.

Notes

1 E. Wilson, in *Feminist Review*, No. 4 (1980), discusses this tendency in connection with the work of J. Mitchell (1971, 1976) and Z. Eisenstein (1979), among others.
2 This, of course, is still the subject of some debate. Assertions that they are have included feminist writers such as S. Firestone (1970) and more recently C. Delphy (1977). This has often been in response to male writers such as A. Giddens (1973) or F. Parkin (1971), who have defined women as marginal to the class system or as 'placed' within it by their position in the family, i.e. via their *male* relatives. However, most feminists agree that simply to *conflate* the two concepts of sex and class weakens both, and there is a growing body of writing that insists that while women can have an identity as a subordinate group they cannot, *per se*, constitute a class. See, for example, J. West (1978), P. Hunt (1980), M. Barret (1980), L. Bland *et al.* (1978).
3 See M. Barrett (1980), S. Rowbotham, *New Statesman* (December 1979), S. Alexander and B. Taylor, *New Statesman* (January 1980), R. McDonough and R. Harrison (1978), G. Rubin (1975) and V. Beechey (1979) for recent contributions that have been particularly relevant to the formation of these concepts.
4 For a further discussion of the primary definition of *all* women as housewives whether or not they go out to work see M. Porter in J. West (ed.) (forthcoming), and Chapter 5 below.
5 See, e.g., H. Beynon (1974), T. Nichols and H. Beynon (1979), S. Terkel (1975), G. Palm (1977) and H. Braverman (1974).
6 Especially his seminal article 'Sources of variation in working class images of society', *Sociological Review*, vol. 14, No. 3 (1966).
7 Even so-called 'community studies' tended to focus on occupational communities or single-industry towns, e.g. G. Salaman (1974), N. Dennis *et al.* (1956).
8 More recently accounts of the notorious dispute at Grunwick's, involving as it did a mainly female workforce, were forced to take some account of their experience as women, but they did this in a less than satisfactory way, e.g. J. Rogaly (1977) and J. Dromey and G. Taylor (1978).

 9   See, for example, B. O'Laughlin (1974), L. Bland *et al.* (1978).
10   The other major union active in Hampers was the Society of Graphical
     and Allied Trades. TWU's presence dated from the time when Hampers
     had been a wholly employed in making cigarette and tobacco boxes.
     SOGAT had been introduced in 1967.
11   The concept of ideological mediation is not adequately covered by the
     idea of 'translation', although basically that is what happens. What it
     draws attention to is the process of *negotiation* whereby both the
     conveyor of the ideas and the receiver are active agents in construing
     exactly what is transferred.
12   See the recent useful summary by E. Kaluzynska in *Feminist Review*,
     No. 6 (1980).
13   Ed. J. Mitchell and A. Oakley (1976), p. 9, and for a full discussion
     Chapter 12.

ONE

THE EXPERIENCE OF HOME AND WORK

The twenty-five couples in this study were typical; that is to say, there was nothing unusual about them or their lives as industrial manual workers, or the wives of industrial manual workers, in Britain in the early 1970s. They had no distinguishing characteristics, no unique disadvantages. The firm the men worked for was not especially large or dangerous or badly run, and the town they lived in was an unexceptional medium-size conurbation, a little more pleasant than most, perhaps, but similar to many others.

Yet the people were also particular people. They lived in a certain place at a certain time and the men worked for a certain firm. These concrete circumstances are a vital ingredient in this book. We are concerned centrally with the construction of ideology and consciousness from experience — and that experience is actual and specific. The ideas that people have cannot be seriously considered apart from the experience in which they are grounded.

This chapter serves two purposes. On the one hand it demonstrates the typicality of the people in the study. The brief account of them will impress the reader only by its sheer ordinariness. It will also — and this is perhaps more important — sketch in the background to their lives. They did not live in a vacuum, and the reader should have a certain familiarity with the specific context of Hampers Ltd and south Bristol in 1974. The chapter also points towards a question: what is there about men's and women's different experience that might create differential responses to different areas of experience? With that question in mind let us introduce some aspects of their experience.

Marriage and family

All were married couples with dependent children, and the wives were not in full-time work. Thus it was a highly restricted sample, especially as so many women work full-time even when their children are small.[1] However, even these stringent limitations allowed a considerable range in age of couples, ages of children, length of marriage, etc. (Table 1.) The average

Table 1   Average age of couples (years)

TWU stewards	43·8	Wives 40·5
SOGAT stewards } SOGAT workers }	35·6	Wives 35·0
Foremen	34·6	Wives 31·5
TWU workers	31·6	Wives 28·8
All	36·5	34·0

age of the men was 36·5 years; that of the women, 34·0. Foremen, SOGAT stewards and SOGAT workers stayed close to this mean, but the TWU steward couples were considerably older and the TWU worker couples were younger.

The SOGAT men were all much the same age — but the stewards had wives who were closer to them in years and therefore older than the wives of SOGAT rank and file. Probably the most significant point is the relatively greater age of the TWU stewards and the considerable gap between them and those of their members in this sample, which may account for the greater ease that they had in exerting their authority. It is also possible that it was the younger men joining Hampers who became dissatisfied with TWU and therefore introduced and joined SOGAT in 1967.

We should, perhaps, also note that the SOGAT stewards' wives (who tended to be most radical) were the only group of wives to be virtually the same age as their husbands. All the others were, conventionally, married to men three or four years older than themselves.

The age of the TWU stewards was also connected with the large number of them who lived near the town centre in Bedminster. It reflected, at least in part, a stage of life. Bedminster was the most desirable place to live, and many of the younger couples longed to move there eventually. It was also reflected — for obvious reasons — in the age of their children. More TWU steward couples than other groups had children old enough to be 'off their hands'. Which, in its turn, allowed the wives to return to full-time work if they had not already done so.

The twenty-six couples had seventy-five children and two pregnancies, i.e. 2·97 per family — slightly above the national average (which was 2·38 in 1977). Of these children thirteen were under five (two not yet born), thirty-four were at infant or junior school, thirteen were at secondary school, and fifteen were above school-leaving age (although some were still at school or in training). What this amounted to, among other things, was a greater opportunity among some groups for wives to work outside the home than among others. It also made for differences of stress on problems of dinners, isolation, play groups and school problems in the different groups.[2]

We should also consider the length of the marriages. They were long — in view of the divorce statistics, *very* long. It certainly opens up the possibility that only very stable couples would volunteer for this kind of study.[3] The figures are summarised in Table 2. If this is related to Table 1 it will be seen that the trend to marry young was strongest among the foremen.

Table 2   Length of marriage (years)

TWU stewards	19·1
SOGAT stewards	14·6
SOGAT workers	11·8
TWU workers	11·0
Foremen	8·4

Two families had additional members — the Smiths had their orphaned nephew and the Youngs lived with her mother. The Davieses with their six adopted children were also exceptional. There was only one second marriage (the Sykeses'). What is perhaps most surprising about this 'normality' is the high proportion (over a quarter) of the sample who had *themselves* come from broken homes — most often through the death of one or both parents.

Home: south Bristol

Most of the people were Bristol-born and bred. Their parents had lived there. Most of their brothers and sisters had remained in the town, and they had every expectation that their own children would settle there. The few outsiders had come not in search of money but because they had married Bristol women, or by chance.

The city, with a population of half a million, is large, but not one of the huge conurbations. In fact it just failed to achieve metropolitan status in the local government reorganisation of 1974. One's impression is of a large market town, reinforced by the tidy ruralness that comes right up to the boundaries. Bristolians value this proximity to 'the country', laying stress on 'pastoral virtues' of smallness, quietness and a slow pace of lfe. Tobacco is probably the nearest to a 'traditional' industry in the town, but other large employers include aircraft manufacture, engineering, printing and, increasingly, microtechnology. Apart from an outburst of rioting in 1831 (and more recently) there have been few instances of organised working-class militancy, and indeed outside the large engineering complexes few Bristol people have any experience of active unionism. The working class inherit a very different tradition from, say, that of a Yorkshire mining village, or a Lancashire mill town.

Most of the sample lived close to the factory. Of the twenty-six couples, twenty-three lived in a triangle lying south-east of Hampers, between Bridgwater and Wells roads, and within a two-mile radius (see map). Within the triangle there are four distinct localities – Bedminster; Knowle; Bedminster Down and Highbridge; and Withywood and Hartcliffe. Most people knew the area well, being born and brought up south of the river. The majority had lived in the older, inner districts like Bedminster, and many of their parents still lived there. Siblings, like themselves, were scattered over south Bristol. Frequently they had lived in more than one of these areas, usually moving in pursuit of housing.

The TWU stewards were noticeably more concentrated in the traditional, inner areas. Four of them lived in Bedminster and Knowle. This was partly accounted for by the greater average age of the TWU stewards, which often meant that they had achieved the common ambition to live in these inner districts. The significance of where the TWU stewards and their families lived will become apparent when we examine their special position at Hampers.

On its inner edge the south of the city contained some of the oldest working-class residential areas – Bedminster, Windmill Hill, Ashton Gate and Totterdown. Even here the houses were not especially old (mid-nineteenth century), but they were characteristic 'artisan dwellings', small, soundly built, terraced two-storey houses, tightly packed in clearly defined rows on the steep hills rising from the river.[4] They were built of a uniform red brick which, combined with the diffused, misty light, gave the area a visual homogeneity. This visual integrity was reinforced by the clear northern boundary of the river, the floating harbour and the docks that separated it from the town centre.

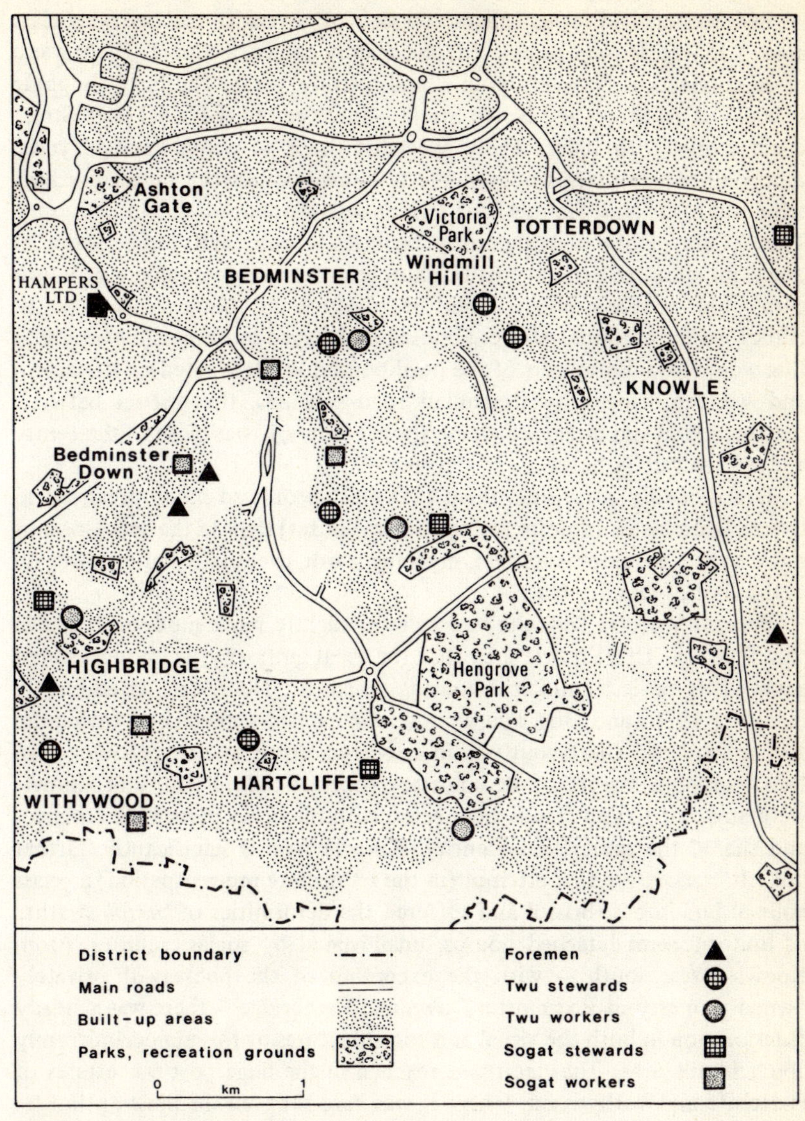

South Provincial showing Hampers Ltd and residence of 23 couples

Bedminster had other characteristics of a 'traditional working-class area'.[5] It was densely populated, and mainly owner-occupied. There was a close connection between 'public' and 'private' areas. The busy shopping streets — East Street and North Street — interspersed the usual High Street chain stores with older family specialist shops — second-hand bicycles, motor-bike spare parts, wool and old-fashioned underwear, butchers selling tripe and lights and Wixon's Kink (which sells more up-to-date underwear). There were plenty of community facilities — pubs and corner shops at every junction, community halls, churches of every denomination, youth clubs, old people's clubs, adventure playgrounds, bingo halls, schools, clinics, police stations. All were housed in decayed but accessible buildings that were recognisably part of the neighbourhood. Decimated on its eastern and western fringes by draconian road schemes, the district between remained vital and intact. As an additional bonus, it was close to the centre and well served by buses.

It was hardly surprising, then, that most people so much preferred to live in Bedminster (despite the age of the houses) than in the succession of more recent developments that, creeping south, eventually halted abruptly at the foot of Dundry Hill.

Beyond Victoria Park the houses were slightly more modern. It was in this Windmill Hill/Knowle area that the local authority had concentrated some of its earliest municipal housing schemes.[6] The houses dated mainly from the 1920s and '30s, and were semi-detached — larger and with quite sizable gardens. The layout was in crescents, drives and ways rather than the roads and streets of Bedminster proper. Windmill Hill and Knowle were adjacent to and closely connected with the other parts of Bedminster and shared the same local identity. Knowle West is significantly 'farther out'. It marked the first attempt (in the immediate pre-war period) at mass council building in Bristol and suffered the deformities of barren swathes of uniform semi-detached houses, unalleviated by social facilities. From Knowle West south — with the exception of the pockets of privately owned property in Bedminster Down and Highbridge — there was a steady deterioration in both the visual and social features of this almost uniformly council-built area. The nadir was reached in the huge post-war estates of Hartcliffe and Withywood, where it was hard for even the most optimistic resident to find redeeming features.[7] Featureless acres of jerry-built houses were punctuated by tower blocks and interspersed with windswept, unkempt open spaces. Social facilities were almost non-existent (one youth club), shops were scarce and expensive (the only chemist was a bus ride away), entertainment was nil (there were about three pubs); schools were barrack-like and the bus service unreliable and expensive. There was little local employment. Just before the study began, a large new factory had been opened expressly to 'catch' the captive women of Hartcliffe. The whole area had been an acknowledged planning disaster; even so, people had to live there and would have to for the foreseeable future.

Thus, although the Hampers workers and their wives lived within a comparatively small area between Bedminster in the north and Hartcliffe in the south — all of which could be designated 'working-class' districts, there were considerable differences socially and culturally, as well as geographically, between the different areas.

Most of the sample lived in council-built property. In fact sixteen out of twenty-one worker couples did, and one in five foremen couples. This did not mean that they were all tenants — half had taken up the chance in the previous two years to buy their house on a council mortgage.[8]

The houses and flats themselves varied from the small but reasonably solid Bedminster houses, with their concomitant damp and lack of modern facilities, to much larger four-bedroomed houses in Hartcliffe where poor-quality building detracted from the apparently greater comfort.

Contact with parents and at least some siblings should have been easy, but even if relatives live only three or four miles away it may not be easy to see much of them if you are hampered by inadequate bus services and the needs of small children. These difficulties were felt most acutely by young wives in Hartcliffe, who expected to be in daily contact with their mothers in Bedminster. Men who worked in Bedminster often found it easier to 'pop in' regularly to see their parents — and it was resented if they did not do so.

The women tended to have, and to rely on, one or two close 'friends' (who might be relatives) living near by. Men less frequently made comparable friendships at work or among neighbours. More often they formed a 'foursome' for social events with other couples bound together either by the *wives*' association or by some previous bond.

Otherwise friends were not important. No one had the 'middle-class' idea of a wide circle of friends sharing common interests. The nearest likely focal point was the firm's skittles club, which a good number of the men frequently. Otherwise even 'entertainment' was limited. Few couples 'went out' more than once a month. Nor did they join clubs, or take part in organised activities. There was one active churchgoer, one active Labour Party member, one Buffalo. The women joined nothing and claimed to have no 'leisure' anyway. Essentially the couples' social life revolved around their own nuclear families. Wider kinship, friendships, interest groups and community organisation were all equally irrelevant to their central concerns.

Twelve families (three of them foremen's) either had a child in a play group or nursery, or had their name down for one. This was quite a high proportion.[9] Because the families lived in a geographically restricted area, and the schools drew from geographical catchment areas, the number of schools attended by the children was also limited — twelve primary and six secondary schools. The primary schools were all local authority junior, mixed and infant schools. The secondary schools were all comprehensives (except one private school attended by a foreman's child and two children at special schools) — but three were single-sex. All the secondary and most of the primary schools were purpose-built. With their large expanses of glass and profusion of labs, art and craft rooms, etc. (not always adequately equipped), they *looked* quite different from the schools the parents had attended themselves.

The workplace: Hampers Ltd

Architecturally Hampers was undistinguished. Unlike many of the buildings of the tobacco industry which were fine statements of Victorian industrial confidence, Hampers' original buildings were conceived in the narrower manner of the twentieth century. The older parts were nondescript red brick that harmonised with the adjacent residential areas. Since then the buildings had been modified and extended piecemeal over a three-acre site, and the resulting hotchpotch had neither aesthetic nor practical logic.

Inside, the factory was equally unremarkable, having all the characteristics of any medium-size light industry. It certainly had none of the striking features associated with a steelworks or a car plant, for instance. Size, noise, danger and level of technology were all within the normal bounds. There was nothing to excite the visitor or potential worker.

Cardboard was everywhere — in rolls 6 ft in diameter, stretched out as an endless carpet on machines, lying around in discarded scraps, being printed, stapled, cut, bent, slotted, folded, stitched and subject to all possible indignities before it emerged as the disposable wrapping round another product. It also hung in the air. A tangy dryness distinguished the atmosphere from that of other industrial processes. You could smell the dryness and the dust along with the cloying, almost school-like, odour of fresh cardboard. It was the dryness and associated dust that constituted the greatest physical disadvantage of working at Hampers. Men frequently complained of coughs and chest or throat irritations, and some had trouble with skin infections such as dermatitis, caused by handling the fibreboard.

The briefest visit to the factory would prompt the mundane observation that making cardboard boxes was a dull business. There were machines of varying size and complexity, with ancillary operations such as form-making or driving fork-lift trucks. Few of the jobs were as lowly as humping bags on to a lorry, but none would count as more than semi-skilled — pulling levers, feeding in card, removing stacks of card, watching machines for snarl-ups, manhandling rolls of paper. There wasn't a job on the factory floor that would take more than a fortnight to learn.[10] After that it became monotonous but tiring work in an atmosphere that was unpleasantly hot and dusty.

The machines varied in size and sophistication. The simplest were the hand stitchers and strappers, usually operated by boys or women. At the other end of the scale was the corrugator, operated by seven men and over a hundred yards long. Bonus, under the scheme that operated at the time of the study, was awarded by machine, so the basic working unit was the machine crew. Men who did not work on machines might drive conveyor trucks, make 'forms' for the stamps or work on dispatch. Then there were the skilled jobs of maintenance and printing. The printers worked alongside production workers on the machines, and often appeared to do very similar work, for which they were paid substantially more.

Although the work was not especially dangerous, there were accidents: usually strains or other back injuries, from lifting heavy weights; falls, or fingers and hand injured in machinery. During the twelve months of 1973 there were fifty-six reportable accidents (i.e. employees off work for three or more days), of which 50 per cent were falls or sprains.

There were 540 people on the weekly-paid payroll in 1974. There were also 110 monthly-paid staff, which included the head office staff. There were 450 production workers, a figure which included about thirty women and thirty boys (under the age of eighteen) who worked days. Only about forty male production workers days at the plant, mainly older men or ones with special problems. About 150 men worked three shifts, including nights, and the rest — about 200 — worked two shifts. Bristol people were much more reluctant to work nights than the company's employees at its two plants in other parts of the country, where all the men worked three shifts.

Hampers Ltd had gone through three distinct phases of development since it began as a packing-case factory in 1909. The period 1947–61 had seen its growth as an independent fibreboard-making company. The period 1961 onwards had seen its gradual incorporation into the same giant tobacco combine that it originated from. This period had also seen the disappearance of the old 'family firm' structure in favour of an increasingly 'rationalised' management.

The pay rates for all production workers were subject to the Fibreboard

Packing Agreement of 1962 (which was up for renewal at the time of the study) but were modified by local agreements with the unions concerned. The accumulation of these over the years had led to a complicated system full of anomalies and inconsistencies.

All production workers were graded according to the job they did, from grade 1 to grade 5. The vast majority were on grade 3. In July 1974 the basic rate for a grade 3 job done by a man[11] was £26·19. In addition, the average bonus was £8·50 and the shift allowance for all shift workers was £1·10, making a gross of £35·89.[12] Three-shift workers got the night rate of £30·57 basic plus bonus, but only for the weeks when they actually worked nights. There might also be an extra allowance for particular machines, and some machines earned more bonus than others. In fact on some machines, especially the largest, the attainment of top bonus each week had become so customary that it was taken for granted. Because they were variable and negotiable, bonus rates were the subject of continual disputes. A man working on a grade 1 job on the highest-rated machine could, in theory, gross £59 per week. In practice that was exceptional. Most men reckoned to take home between £24 and £27.

The unions: TWU and SOGAT

Three groups of unions represented the workers. The maintenance men had their own 'trade' unions — the AEU, ETU, etc. The numbers were small and the unions were not particularly active. The thirty or so printers were all members of the National Graphical Association, which was very effective at national level in assuring high pay rates. Again, the union was not noticeably active in the factory.

The production workers all belonged either to the Tobacco Workers' Union or to the Society of Graphical and Allied Trades. The men were evenly divided between them, with about 220 in each union.

Traditionally the TWU had always represented workers at Hampers, because of its origins in, and connection with, the tobacco industry. Nobody at Hampers, of course, actually made cigarettes, and since 1947 by no means all the firm's output had gone to the tobacco industry. SOGAT was basically a printing and paper makers' union. Which union should represent Hampers workers depended, at least partly, on whether the firm was still seen as part of the tobacco industry or as part of the fibreboard industry. There were many, both among management and among the SOGAT membership, who felt that the TWU was an historical anomaly and that its claim to represent the workers was no longer valid.

SOGAT came into the factory in 1967; surreptitiously because of the

Bridlington Agreement.[13] Its advent aroused strong feelings, many of which were still evident at the time of the study. In 1967 the TWU organisation in the factory was moribund. Not even the union dues were collected. All the same, the TWU leadership strongly objected to SOGAT's intrusion and resisted it as long as they could. SOGAT's official defence was that it was the proper union to represent people working in the fibreboard industry. This was substantiated by the fact that it was SOGAT, and not the TWU, that was represented on the Fibreboard Packing Agreement Board. Management had welcomed SOGAT, partly because they felt it was to their advantage to have two unions competing with each other. SOGAT and TWU leadership existed in a state of guarded co-operation. Most stewards claimed that it made no difference having two unions on the same ground, and that sometimes it was positively advantageous. The TWU admitted that it was in poor shape in 1967. Indeed, the arrival of SOGAT seemed to have given it the jolt it needed to reorganise and build up the strong presence it had by 1974. SOGAT members were often men who had been disillusioned with the state the TWU was in, and so had jumped at the chance to form a more active union branch.

SOGAT, which was a much bigger union nationally, had a Bristol branch, and a chapel within the factory. In the TWU the factory organisation was the branch, although it also had a district organisation in Bristol. SOGAT had ten stewards and a bonus representative in Hampers, including two elected chapel officials. TWU had fifteen stewards (including the chairman and secretary of the branch) and a bonus representative.

Further tension between the unions was created by two strikes (in 1972 and 1973) called by the TWU. Both disputes were over wage increases which went against the national agreement, to which TWU was not a party. The unilateral action that it took was therefore over the acceptance of an agreement to which it had not been a party, as well as about the actual increase. The TWU was divided about whether it should be represented on the board or should resist the board's right to decide Hampers' pay rates at all; but united in feeling that it was not bound by the national agreement so long as it was not a party to it.

We will now take the strike of 1973 and examine it in some detail. As an event it was apparently both relatively insignificant and specific to the *men's* work experience. But, as we shall see, the ideological significance and consequences were much greater than the bare facts would lead us to suppose.

Notes

1 In 1975 47·9 per cent of all married women were economically active (table 5.3, Government Statistical Service, *Social Trends*, No. 8, HMSO, 1977).
2 It should also be borne in mind that some of the women (notably the TWU stewards' wives) had made a deliberate choice *not* to return to full-time paid employment.
3 One couple, the Griffithses, broke up during the course of the study.
4 They were *very* small. Many lacked indoor sanitation, central heating and other amenities. Some were damp.
5 As portrayed by R. Hoggart (1957) and M. Young and P. Wilmott (1957) in their studies of Hunslett (Leeds) and Bethnal Green (London) respectively.
6 For a general coverage of this topic see J. B. Cullingworth (1966) and Hall *et al.* (1975). For a detailed description of one Bristol estate see R. Wilson (1963).
7 Most of them mentioned the 'fresh air', of which there was indeed plenty, as the wind, funnelled between the tower blocks, had been sufficiently strong to lift the roof off a primary school, killing one child and injuring another.
8 A possibility opened up by the Housing Finance Act (1972). For the government propaganda on council mortgages see HMSO (1973).
9 A surprisingly large number of families had managed to avail themselves of what facilities there were. The figures for the County of Avon on 31 March 1976, when the total population of children under five was 58,600, were as follows: places in local authority day nurseries, 550 (9·4 per thousand); places in private day nurseries, 347 (5·9 per thousand); registered child-minders, 812 minding (13·9 per thousand); part-time playgroup places, 8,311 (141·8 per thousand); places in nursery school and classes (excluding rising fives): full-time, 1,407 (24·0 per thousand), part-time, 1,005 (17·2 per thousand). Figures taken from Central Policy Review Staff, *Services for Young Children and Working Mothers* (HMSO, 1978).
10 There were two grade 1 jobs, but they were the chargehands on the biggest machine. They owed their position to experience, that is, to seniority, rather than skill.
11 Women got 90 per cent of the male rate. No women were on jobs graded higher than grade 3. Boys got the basic rate of £14·70.
12 This was still below the national average. In 1975 the *gross* weekly earnings for a male manual worker were £54·7 (*New Earnings Survey*, Department of Employment, 1976).
13 The Bridlington Agreement — the outcome of a lawsuit between two rival unions — lays down the terms under which one union can move into the territory, or recruit members, of another union.

TWO

THE STRIKE: A PROBLEM IN EXPERIENCE

The dispute at Hampers in the summer of 1973, like many other disputes,[1] did not make the headlines of even the local press. It was small-ccale, complex and ambiguous. There had been some action in the previous two years — working to rule and overtime bans, but nothing on the scale of the action in 1973. The dispute centred round a wage demand, but it was essentially about recognition. SOGAT had come into the factory in 1967 and almost immediately had become a 'recognised' union by virtue of the fact that at the national level SOGAT was represented on the Fibreboard Packing Agreement Board, which decided wage rates throughout the industry. Because its presence at Hampers was simply the result of an historical accident the TWU was not represented on the Board. Of course, at the factory level this made no difference, and both unions negotiated with management about issues outside the FPAB's purview. As a branch officer said, 'We do our own negotiations on everything bar the thing which matters the most, which is the rates.' The *local* SOGAT branch had no say in the national negotiations either, except via its national leadership. It was thus *effectively* in the same position as the TWU within the factory. By 1973 *all* wage negotiations had been removed from plant level and put into the hands of the FPAB. The consequences were felt all the more because of the constraints imposed by the government pay freeze at the time.

In March 1973 the FPAB agreed a £1 + 4 per cent pay rise to take effect from 30 September — the date adopted by the Board as the one from which annual wage negotiations would run. At the factory level SOGAT accepted this, but the TWU claimed that the rise should run from 1 July, i.e. three months earlier, because this had been the date from which *it* had negotiated its annual wage increases before they were taken out of its hands. The sum of money at issue was, therefore, no more than £50 per worker. The men stood to lose more than that in even a short strike — or indeed in a go-slow, work-to-rule or other action short of a strike.

Negotiations began in June and dragged on until mid-August, when TWU officials felt they had exhausted negotiating possibilities and had to take action. For tactical reasons they decided against an all-out strike and instead began six weeks of 'non-co-operation', using a variety of go-slow, work-to-rule and overtime-banning techniques. The tactics were so effective that within a few weeks production was at a standstill.[2] Finally, on Thursday 30 September management locked the TWU men out. At a mass meeting 'on the Marsh' that afternoon they decided to demand their jobs back, and a meeting of union officials with management on Friday produced an 'ex gratia' payment of £30 per head and a return to work on Monday. Although the outcome was generally seen as a complete victory for the TWU, the issue of the TWU's negotiating rights was unresolved and even by the summer of 1974 still not settled.[3]

If the dispute is seen as being 'about' money, then it was not particularly 'rational' and was designated by management and by SOGAT officials as irrational — or just 'stupid'. But it was *not* primarily about money: it was about negotiating rights. It was about the right of any union which represents a body of men to negotiate over pay on their behalf, and it was about the right of each group of men to negotiate direct with their own immediate management without being bound by a higher-level agreement. Both rights embody tactical advantages for the workers and issues of principle. The dispute was also an attempt by the TWU to reassert the rights of what it saw as the 'proper' union, and to recreate the legendary 'strong union' of the past against the claims of the upstart usurper. To this extent it was a dispute about union demarcation, but behind the pettiness that that phrase invokes there is an important if inexplicit ideal of what effective union representation should mean.

Here we have, then, a small-scale industrial dispute. It was not 'typical', but nor was it 'untypical'. That is not the point. It was important because it enables us to examine in some detail one small experience in the lives of the people concerned, how they interpreted it, how they mediated their interpretation to others and how they integrated it into their existing ideology. It enables us to pay particular attention to the responses of the wives to an event situated in the industrial context of their husband's work.

Levels of experience

As the heart of the dispute were the TWU stewards, led by the two branch officers, Max Fennel and Keith Thomas (who were helped by the District

Organiser, Garry Roberts). Behind them were the TWU rank-and-file members. They confronted Hampers' management, backed (or undermined) by the vast industrial and financial remifications of the parent group. These were the protagonists; no one else can be said to have been *directly* involved, although many others were affected and concerned in various direct and indirect ways. Indeed, on the workers' side, only the TWU stewards had first-hand knowledge of the long-drawn-out and complicated negotiations.

Other people who were directly *concerned* with the strike were men and women working at Hampers who were not TWU members — represented in our sample by all the SOGAT members — stewards and rank and file — and by the foremen. In addition there were people who were indirectly concerned — notably the wives of men working at Hampers. This introduces a different *kind* of connection. A worker who was a member of SOGAT, and the wife of a TWU steward both had connections with the strike, but of a very different character. The wife of a foreman was removed from the strike in two *different* ways.

The different groups not only had varying connections (of kind and degree) with the dispute, but they also got their information about it in different ways. A rank-and-file member of SOGAT got his information from his steward, who got it from management, who, in a sense, got it from the TWU stewards — a three-step process, but all within the factory. The wife of a TWU steward heard it direct from her husband, but she was outside the factory. This is illustrated in Fig. 2. All these differences are important in an account of the impact of experience upon consciousness. A study of the direct experience of the dispute would be limited to TWU stewards (and possibly their members). But that would be to miss the fact

Fig. 2   Main lines of information

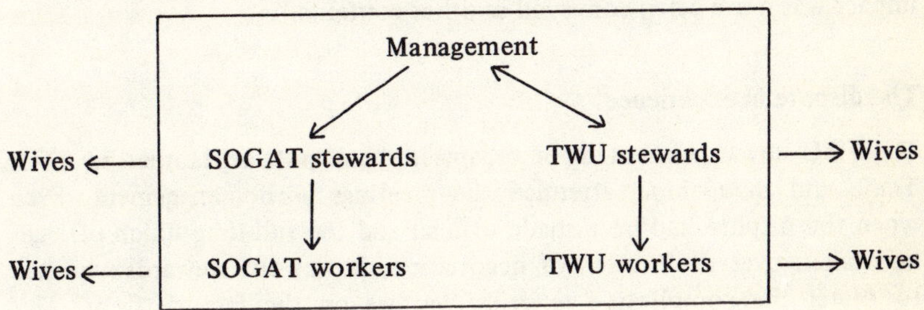

that, in order to generate consciousness, experience need not necessarily be direct. In fact most 'experience' is removed in an infinite variety of ways and degrees. This is an example of just that kind of complex situation, and of the difficulties of unravelling it without resorting to a more or less mechanical 'reading off' of apparently correlated events.

It also raises problems about deriving *general* conclusions about people's understanding from their attitudes to any *specific* events or areas of experience. They may be on quite different levels of importance for different people: what is a peripheral incident for one may be critical for another. In other words, an 'experience' may be located in a different structural position in their ideology, connected with the individual's position in the social structure and reflecting back to their understanding of the situation. So that it would be unlikely that the strike would have as much consequence for a foreman's wife as for a TWU member. This means that generalisations from a particular experience are likely to be slanted towards the people most involved. While being illuminating about those people, it may well be misleading if applied to people who, for any reason, are less involved. Research into industry focuses, naturally enough, on industrial events like strikes, and often conclusions are drawn about the 'radical'[4] potential of the participants. This is valuable as far as the active participants are concerned, but it is not then valid to assume that other people — for whom that event is not significant — therefore share, or lack, similar potential. Certainly, particular kinds of radical expression may have more potential in terms of overall political importance, but that argument can only begin when experience is accurately located in the structure of ideology.

In this case there is a simple quantitative difference between how much TWU stewards talked about the strike and how much everyone else did — and particularly so for the women. For most of the women the strike was a total non-event, and they often did not say much about it directly. Its impact was more often conveyed in other contexts.

The dispute in experience

The TWU stewards initiated and organised the dispute at Hampers in 1973. They, and they alone, attended the meetings with management. Even when the dispute had been made official and the full-time union officials had taken over the burden of negotiation, it was the stewards who had to direct the complicated guerrilla warfare on the factory floor. This experience as the organising group meant that their account of the dispute was collectively produced, coherent and vivid. For all the stewards it was time-consuming and exhausting but also new and interesting. As the dispute went on they discussed tactics, assessed progress and pondered management's response among themselves. In fact it was 'a military school'.

Rank-and-file members of the TWU were also directly involved, although information came to them second-hand from their stewards. And, despite the efforts of the stewards, communication was sometimes lacking or inaccurate. In particular they never saw or heard for themselves what management was doing. They could, however, see what was going on on the shop floor, and feel an active part of it. They 'sat down doing nothing', refused to operate certain machines, got locked out, heard speeches 'on the Marsh' and then went back to work and got £30 in their pay packets. They also lost money—bonus and overtime (an important part of their usual take-home pay), two complete days' pay, and many individuals also lost a day's pay when they were 'sent home' at various times. Altogether it was an expensive episode and cost them a number of 'luxuries' such as holidays, school trips for the children and new furniture that they had planned.

The TWU stewards' wives were affected by their husbands being busy, involved and sometimes worried while the strike was on. Their husbands were phoned up at home and spent long additional hours in meetings and down at the factory. Men whose main focus of life was usually their home were suddenly caught up in something that excluded their wives. And the wives, who in some sense regarded the wage packet as 'theirs', were made acutely aware of how distant they were from the source of the wage packet and how little control they had over it. Loss of money was obviously important for all the wives of TWU members, although the impact varied according to whether the families were living up to the limit of their usual pay packet. In addition, they all had to adjust to the fact that their husbands were 'strikers' and to reconcile it with their usual hostility to strikes.

The amount of factual information they got about the strike varied widely according to the attitude of the husband. Some refused to discuss it with their wives: 'I would say I try not to talk to her ... they're outsiders to the problems that exist in the factory' (*Keith Thomas*). Some were eager to discuss it, but their wives wouldn't listen. 'He doesn't tell me much because I get so mad about the unions' (*Ann Davies*). Others would have liked to tell their wives more but they didn't know much themselves: 'But then it's only rumours he gets' (*Cath Grimshaw*). In any event, the wives lacked their husbands' direct experience. Information was now third-hand (see Fig. 2). They were physically distant from the factory, and what they knew was not only funnelled through each individual husband but received in isolation by each individual wife.

As for SOGAT members, they were affected directly by the chaos in the factory. Their money — bonus and overtime — was also increasingly affected as the work-to-rule took effect, until finally they too were on the bare basic wage. They suffered more than the TWU members from the lack of information. For the most part their stewards learnt of the progress of negotiations from management. The stewards then met, agreed a union policy over the dispute and handed it out to the rank and file. They agreed that they would neither join the dispute nor obstruct it. The tension between the two unions — such that both sets of stewards instructed their members not to discuss the dispute with men from the other union — meant that a wall of silence cut SOGAT members off from the positive experience of the TWU members. They merely suffered inconvenience.

SOGAT wives — of stewards and of the rank and file alike — were similarly affected. All felt the loss of money, and although they did not lose as much as the TWU wives they resented it more, because there seemed no reason for it. Their own husbands were not in dispute. Apart from the money, there seems to have been little that the SOGAT men felt worth discussing at home. Individual differences in communication mattered less than in the TWU, because the whole affair was regarded as of no great consequence. In any event, for all the wives — TWU and SOGAT — industrial affairs at both local and national level seemed less relevant to their day-to-day existence than prices, schools or welfare services.

Thus there were certain general and objective differences between the experience of TWU and SOGAT men and their wives. What follows will attempt to explore further these different experiences of one dispute at work and the effect it had on the different groups.

The dispute in ideology

Perceptions of the strike have to be located within people's existing ideology. It therefore seemed useful, if arbitrary, to set the perceptions and evaluations of this particular strike against the perceptions and evaluations these people held of unions and strikes in general — or at least in the UK as a whole. For the dispute was part of a pattern of political and industrial events in the UK in 1974, and they can be viewed as a series of concentric circles round this very specific instance.

In the period January—August 1974 three disputes in particular hit the headlines. The National Union of Mineworkers precipitated the general election of February 1974: the AUEW called a one-day strike in protest against a fine imposed on it under the Industrial Relations Act; and, on a quite different level but given just as much prominence by the popular press, on 23 April the wives of the workers at Cowley motor works demonstrated against their husbands, who had struck in support of a sacked shop steward. It was also a period of high and rising inflation, immediately after the first big increases in oil prices.

It is all too easy to assume that an individual's attitude to, say, the miners' strike will have some predictive value for his attitude to a dispute in his own factory, an assumption that often turns out to be wrong. A firm adherent of the Hampers strike might violently oppose the miners' action; someone who said the unions had too much power and ought to be restrained castigated SOGAT because it weakened the position of the unions at Hampers. Faced with these 'contradictions', a number of explanations can be offered: that the individual is wrong about one or the other because he is working on false information; that he practises total separation of his ideas and does not expect the whole to add up sensibly; that particular events change responses to that situation, but general ideas on the same kind of event take longer to change – a kind of ideological 'lag'. However, the 'contradictory' ideas on 'related' topics may not be so connected in the mind of the individual. They may have a different ideological 'weighting' – one is more important, more interesting, more thought-out and discussed, especially if there is more information available. The other may only get a passing comment, a snap judgement lifted straight from another source. To make any predictions about other views, or even to analyse the ones available, this 'weighting' has to be established. In this case one of the objective factors we would assume was relevant was the individual's relationship to the union structure. It clearly was important, but it was cross-cut – reinforced or contradicted by other factors. Like sheep tracks across a hillside, splintered and fragmented with junctions, detours and dead-ends, there is a confusing multiplicity of options any of which appear perfectly valid in the light of the cross-cutting factors.

This was all doubly true for the wives, partly because they did not share the relatively strong ideological framework of the unions like their husbands, and partly because the whole area was relatively less important to them. Both these factors reduce the strength of such pull to consistency as is imposed by the union structure and increase the power of cross-cutting factors. The factors that did affect their ideas on these issues included, firstly, where they lived. There was a clustering of TWU stewards in Bedminster (all except one). The other couples were dispersed mainly in Withywood and Hartcliffe, while the foremen were scattered in little pockets of private housing in the more salubrious areas. Thus only one group of wives – the TWU stewards' – had any opportunity to know one another in the community, other than at work-based social events, and only they were open to the influences of an established working-class area. Secondly, a number of wives had had fathers whose strong views had impressed themselves on them, and because this was regarded as 'male' subject they were more inclined to remember influence from that quarter. Alternatively their own experience of unions may have been contrary to that of their husbands, especially when the union did very little for them (as was often the case).

Lastly, a significant variation lay in their husband's attitude to their views on the subject. Without his co-operation they could know little about the particular situation at Hampers. Even with it, it was hard to know much, but if a man actually refused to discuss what was going on, and made it clear that he regarded it as none of her business, then at the very least his wife was going to find it hard to share his identification with the unions. She might respond as he expected, with total indifference, but more commonly she responded with varieties of inchoate 'feminism' which, on such subjects, tended to be negative – 'It's men's business, and a fine mess they make of it.' Occasionally this attitude enabled them to cut through the pretentious claims and make cogent criticisms, but usually it had the effect of making the whole area seem irrelevant, and thus of removing it as an active ingredient in their ideology.

Ideology and experience: the case of the TWU

TWU stewards

The key group in the dispute were the TWU stewards. Not only were they the most closely involved, but they were forced to develop a coherent and cohesive defence of what they were doing. They did so as a group that worked and talked together throughout the period. This experience of a socially constructed perspective was arguably the most important result of the strike for them. Certainly it was in marked contrast to the fragmented and individual experiences of the other groups.

All six TWU stewards that I talked to were devoted to their union and prepared to work hard and enthusiastically on its account. All of them could detail the complicated series of events that led to the action, and describe how it was organised. And the accounts were remarkably consistent with one another. They were all prepared to defend both the principle behind the strike and its organisation. Jim Smith said:

There was marvellous support. I thought the majority would be against it, but they weren't. We had one hundred per cent backing. You'd expect about eighty per cent but everybody backed us right up.

All were grateful and impressed — and surprised — by the rank-and-file support they got, and by the support and help of the paid union officials — notably Garry Roberts. They were aware of opposition or disapproval from SOGAT, management and, at least potentially, their wives.

She reads so much in the paper about strikes. For what we get out of it she doesn't think it's worth it ... if you've got your wife against you, you've got no interest in striking. You want to get back to work.

Hugh Davies

One effect of the strike was simply the heady knowledge that they had fought the management — and won.

We kept it up for fifty-four days, which was brilliant. I know now that if I said to Tom Dyer, our manager, I was going to do something with out branch, he'd know full well that I *would* do it.   *Keith Thomas*

I think as how it got a little bit out of hand, because within a week we stopped the factory. They didn't realise we could, and I don't think *we* realised we could, because it was quite a surprise, really.

Tommy Turner

They all recognised that there was conflict between them and management, and all thought they had a good case. Jim Smith blamed changes in management personnel for worsening relations.

You get verbal promises from one and next time you get somebody different, and the trust starts to go.

Keith Thomas just despised their weakness.

Well, I felt they were the biggest load of soft-hearted ninnies and frightened load of babbies I ever met in my life.

None of them was an active unionist before becoming a steward for the TWU. Most just drifted in and then gradually got involved. 'I just took an interest and got voted in. And I've never been voted out.' They tended to stress the advantages of a small union — which also helped them to dissociate it from the giant unions that made the headlines.

They all had grave reservations about unions at the national level, which were usually couched in terms of size and remoteness. They had an especial concern with their failure to be accountable to rank-and-file members, which was in strong contrast to 'our union'.

In big unions only a few attend branch meetings and it lets the unions get out of control. The attendance at TWU meetings is seventy-five per cent. It's very good, and there's a pleasant atmosphere ...   *Hugh Davies*

The cohesive and positive evaluation of their union and their dispute contrasted with the diversity and caution of their views on all other subjects, including the (apparently) related issues of unions and strikes at national level. The ideology of most of these men was informed by a 'trade union consciousness' — but of the most limited and conservative kind. All of them condemned strikes in general, and in 1974 all but one of them even condemned the miners' strike. Thus they had some difficulty in accounting for their own militancy. They did it by using a series of special-case arguments based either on an individualist morality (car workers were 'greedy', nurses 'deserved' more) or on a feeling that the union movement and industrial disputes were acceptable only as long as they were not *too* effective and thus a threat to the 'balance' of society.

There is a real problem — which was not confined to these stewards — of working out on what grounds a strike can be 'justified'. With few exceptions they accepted the received wisdom that strikes were a bad thing — for the kind of reasons outlined by R. Hyman (1972). They also simply did not like them; they were untidy, uncontrolled, threatening and, moreover, implied that conflict was natural in a way that was anathema to these adherents of the consensual society. In spite of this, they did uphold a man's freedom to withdraw his labour. It is an *individual* freedom, yet they were forced to acknowledge that they could see no alternative means of achieving their end in the last resort. However much they deplored them, very few could contemplate having strikes outlawed. The nurses (whose industrial action had so far stopped short of a strike) were one group whose cause was generally acknowledged to be 'justified'. Of course, the nurses were no threat. No prices would go up as a direct result of their claim, so people could, in a sense, afford to support them. More positively the nurses exemplified a *moral* right to more money because (a) 'it is a "necessary" job'; (b) 'it is a hard job', and (c) 'the money is poor'. All these reasons were, of course, relative. Despite the strong moral content of the arguments — which might indicate that conditions, not pay, are what you should strike over — that was not the usual response. You fought bad conditions by demanding more money to compensate. Indeed, some people (like Max Fennel) held that *only* strikes about money could be legitimate. As Gouldner pointed out long ago, 'a wage demand is always legitimate'[5] and so other non-wage demands have to be translated into money terms before they can become acceptable. This weakens the conventional distinction between strikes about conditions and strikes about pay. Neither can be divorced from the other. Given that the capitalist process reduces all relations to the cash nexus, it is not surprising that workers translate grievances about conditions into the only language that management appears to understand. And, possibly, the only language their *wives* may accept.

Another device commonly used to justify particular strikes was to shift the blame on to the management (or, in the case of the miners, the government).

> The miners should have a rise, but it's wrong to cripple the country.
> (Who is to blame?)
> Well, the government is, for not giving them the rise.   *Max Fennell*

This argument was also used about the dispute at Hampers.

> I think the management was a lot to blame for this because I don't think there was any need to go that far ... I don't say we made a mistake, but I think management did in letting it go too far.
> *Tommy Turner*

The first thing to notice about these arguments in favour of particular strikes is that because they made each supported strike a 'special case' they did not disturb the general thesis that all strikes were wrong. They also mean that the debate did not take place in a tactical or even economic framework but in a moral one, making use of general entities such as 'the national interest', 'public concern'.[6]

The TWU stewards, in particular, were more obviously motivated by moral ideology rather than by political ideology.

> It's a rotten job, but I can't see why they [the miners] should be favouritised.
> *Hugh Davies*

> I think this is how it really starts — people being greedy. Instead of making do with a couple of quid they want the lot.   *Tommy Turner*

Strikes, then, acted as a kind of fuse, a balance in the system, an allowable escape that could not, and should not, be allowed to open up a real challenge to Capital itself. Strikes could be accepted reluctantly, as a necessary evil, provided that, in some fundamental way, they didn't work. The same held for trade unions. They must not be too big, too powerful or too effective, even within their own brief. Both strikes and unions were 'necessary' — in terms that showed a clear recognition of basic conflict: 'We'd be trampled on,' 'It would be back a hundred years,' 'Management would have it all their own way' — but this was held in check by the recognition, endorsed by Lenin, that they are only *defensive* institutions, operating within capital's terms.

Perhaps the most crucial effect of the strike was to force the stewards to face and question their conservative ideology, sometimes with dramatic results; like Tommy Turner, who paused in a flow of conventional statements about over-powerful unions to think who made the big national decision. 'Well, I wonder sometimes. Now I think mostly it's people with money, big money, like big firms, like ICI.' Their ideas were not static: the strike showed that. They were capable of thinking sensibly about their position, and, if necessary, of changing their minds. The gaps and discontinuities in their ideas, especially between the particular experience of the strike and general industrial issues, left room for quite new orientations. Furthermore, once they had decided on the rightness of their cause they could act to achieve it — and with the experience of the strike behind them they had confidence in themselves and in the men they represented. These hesitant steps towards extending the limits of their 'trade union consciousness' should not be overstated. There are strict limits to the effects this kind of experience can have, and these men were a long way from even those limits.

TWU stewards' wives

How did the stewards' wives reflect their husbands' changed perceptions? The most remarkable characteristic of the women was their conservatism. All were firm, definite characters with articulate and unambiguous views. They disapproved of the union and their husbands' part in it and were openly hostile to the dispute. They did not mince words.

> My husband was on strike ... and I kept on at him then to get back to work properly.
>
> *Ann Davies*

> I don't believe in strikes at all.
>
> *Jane Smith*

> He doesn't tell me much because I get so mad about the unions.
>
> *Ann Davies*

> I'm not very much for unions myself, that we do differ on. If he'd asked me I would have had to have said, 'You can't go on strike.' As I said, I don't agree with strikes.
>
> *Betty Turner*

What marked them out from other wives was that they knew more and cared more. Other wives who were hostile tended to cloak it with indifference. But the impact of the dispute was such that these wives could not, or any rate did not, ignore it:

'I've got a meeting,' 'What time will you be home?' 'I don't know.' —
So you're stuck then, and you don't know whether to clear the table or
leave it, and sometimes he'll come home at seven o'clock and not want
anything. That's when you feel like picking up the table and throwing it
at them.   *Sharon Thomas*

Nor did the wives see the dispute as having any material benefits for
them. The strike cost them money without gaining any significant pay
increase, and that confirmed their scepticism. Although they had quite a
clear understanding of a mechanism connecting wages and prices, this
only made them dismiss wage increases as spurious, because 'the prices will
only go up to match them'. They saw no way of breaking the spiral, so
strikes lacked even a tactical justification. And as their husbands, with a
much more developed 'trade union consciousness', made few connections
between local action and national industrial disputes, and certainly did not
see them in terms of concepts such as 'working-class struggle', it is not
surprising that this wider significance totally escaped their wives.

In any case the TWU stewards' wives regarded all union involvement as
a distraction from real life. What the men should be concentrating on was
bringing home a steady wage so that the important business of running the
home could go forward. These women, in particular, gave the home — and
their role as home-makers — a high priority. They saw it as a haven where
personal values could be expressed — in contrast to the harsh and impersonal world outside. They railed against the bureaucrady of the Welfare
State; they preferred to take their part-time jobs in positions that involved
personal contact with their employer, such as small shops. But essentially
they felt powerless against the world outside. Inside their own homes they
could control what happened and create there what they would have liked
to see outside. In this aim they were usually supported by their husbands.
And some of their virulence about the dispute may have sprung from a
sense of betrayal. They felt that, suddenly, their husbands had taken leave
of their senses and rejected the home in favour of the alien outside world.
Given opposition on these grounds, it is all the more remarkable that the
men were and remained so committed to the strike.

Part of the wives' dislike of unions was due to their size. Any organisation that big, whatever its politics, would seem frightening because it
was so clearly beyond their control:

In the beginning they were ideal, but now they've gone a bit beyond
what they set out to do. I think they're getting too big.   *Betty Turner*

The unions also did things that the women regarded as morally wrong:

You've got to think of the old people who rely on coal. They didn't seem to give the old people enough consideration. *Ann Davies*

Well, they just go on and on, getting greedier and greedier. Its just greed with lots of them. *Sharon Thomas*

They used to be for workers right but now it seems all they're after is more money and strikes and that kind of thing. *Betty Turner*

As a group, then, the TWU stewards' wives had a homogeneity equal to that of their husbands bot not apparently connected with it. The experience that had opened up new horizons for their husbands had engendered deep hostility in them. It reinforced their conservatism, and shut off ways in which they could either have shared their husbands' experience or made new connections with other parts of their own experience. This negative result of the union activity of Hampers merits at least as serious consideration as the more positive results it produced among the husbands. A key point here is that there was no necessary or automatic direct correspondence between the consciousness of the wives and the fact that their husbands were on strike. There is no simple way that their consciousness can be 'read off' from their husbands' apparent militancy. Indeed, an underlying theme of this book is that without close inquiry into the *particular* ways work experience is mediated to the wives of workers, taking account of the different experience of groups of workers, and of the prior consciousness of both the men and their wives, it is dangerous to generalise. Indeed, it is just this complexity that bedevils attempts to apply the grand theories of consciousness and ideology to 'real-life situations' and yet makes it all the more necessary to do so if the two areas are not to remain inevitably divorced from one another.

TWU rank and file
The rank-and-file members of the TWU were neither so active nor so united as the stewards during the dispute. Indeed, most of them were critical of both the union and the handling of the strike. The strike was too long-drawn-out; they lost too much money. They were even doubtful about their success:

There's no point in crippling the firm. *Don Grimshaw*

I don't agree with the unions domineering the firm ... the boss is the boss, but the boss should keep with the unions so everyone's happy. *Dick Griffiths*

In any event, the strike was nothing like so dramatically significant for them as it was for the stewards. They were not so deeply involved in running it or in the decisions that were made; but, more important, they were not forced to talk about the strike among themselves as it was happening and thus forge a unity.

All this meant that they did not feel the same pressure to justify the TWU's action, or to locate it *vis-à-vis* other strikes — either as similar or as different; in fact the pressure to integrate it into a coherent ideology. Thus the kinds of fractures that the stewards struggled to paper over tended to show up more clearly among these workers. For them the strike was simply about money. While the stewards talked about negotiating rights, they complained about the loss of wages, and the unfairness of SOGAT workers' getting the rise as well:

> We lost money while the blokes inside [in SOGAT] were getting it. They'll get the benefit of the rise as well as us. *Don Grimshaw*

It was natural to get impatient, and it must have been particularly difficult for the stewards to convey the effectiveness of their tactics to workers who could only see their own small corner of the shop floor. However, they were not unprincipled men. John Pollard, for example, was impressed by the real development that had taken place in the union since the strike.

> It changed after the dispute. In a way it is a union now, because before you always used to have these little arguments in one corner ... but now it is a union. There's strength in the union now. That dispute, management came off worst, because the union is twice as strong now as it ever was ... every bloke likes to think he's is a strong union, but you never find out till that sort of thing happens. Now everyone knows.

But the principle that counted most was the primacy of the family:

> My family and babies come first. If there's a choice between them and the union, the family comes first. *John Pollard*

> I wouldn't back the union one hundred per cent if it meant the wife and children had to suffer. *Don Grimshaw*

Thus the workers saw concern for their families as being in direct contradiction to their union loyalties. (Interestingly, this conflict between 'home' and 'work' is more conventionally associated with *women* workers.)

The TWU rank and file's experience and interpretation of the strike was thus in marked contrast to that of their stewards. This is all the more interesting when we find that their attitude to disputes and industrial matters was more radical than that of the stewards. Only one was less than totally in support of the miners — and even he declared, 'If it wasn't for the union you'd get knocked to hell' (*Paul Dixon*). Virtually all other disputes got their support. Even the car workers were excused their action because 'they get so bored'. And anyway, 'sometimes you have to strike — like ours here' (*Paul Dixon*). They were scandalised that the nurses had not won their claim despite the clear justice of their case. To make their case, they used the same kind of essentially moral criteria as the stewards did, but this time to support the actions of *strikers*. They were quick to lay 'the blame' on management — or the government. In fact they were a good deal more sceptical about the good faith of both businessmen and government. But such criticism was isolated and sporadic and sprang from the collective failures of the ruling ideology rather than from any alternative analysis. It is arguable that they were less likely to be 'radicalised' on the basis of these unspecific suspicions than their stewards, whose objections were rooted in their own direct experience.

TWU rank-and-file wives
The rank-and-file wives knew very little about either the TWU or about the dispute — except that it had happened. Some of them expressed frustration that they had so little information:

> It would be good to know more, you worry about it.   *Sue Pollard*

> Women can't get enough information — it's all second-hand.
>
> *June Hannam*

They didn't like the strike. A few felt they had a duty to support their husbands, and the rest were either mildly opposed or apathetic. One view they did express was that 'the union aren't doing much for him'. But even that had to do with their husbands: there was no suggestion that there was anything in it for them.

In a sense they were right. The dispute was not about money, and in fact they lost money by it, overall. Generally, their response was low-key, perhaps surprisingly so considering that they were affected — albeit not as closely as the stewards' wives. But as their husbands did not identify strongly with it, nor did they. Nor did they feel they had to disown the label 'strikers' wives' as much as the stewards' wives felt they had to. The principles involved in the strike were not important to them and it did not raise issues in such a way that they or their husbands had to think much about them.

The situation of the TWU workers and their wives had the effect, therefore, of stifling interaction between husbands and wives. The channels of communication were blocked. One context in which the process of absorbing information, analysing and expressing it — the making real of experience in language — was removed. As a result the whole area of union activity was simply a vacuum for both men and women, and they became prey to the media representation of those issues.

Perhaps surprisingly, then, these women turned out to be marginally more sympathetic to the trade union cause in general than their husbands. This meant that they were perceptibly more inclined to a radical interpretation than the TWU stewards, and a great deal more so than the stewards' wives. They had the usual reservations about 'holding the country to ransom' and the 'greediness' of the car workers. But, apart from that, they were inclined to treat all strikes with the same detached sympathy:

> It's the only thing they can do, really.   *Cath Grimshaw*

Similarly, they accepted the unions:

> Workers have to have someone to help them.   *Sue Pollard*

In their views unions had an essentially negative role, as a last-ditch defence, but they were necessary, for all that. Their main criticism, as it was of the TWU, was that they were not effective. This appeared as an 'instrumental' view, but, whatever importance it had, it led them to a position which was much more oppositional than that of the stewards' wives. Even when it wasn't, it had a kind of committed fatalism about it:

> They're necessary in a way, but they get you into a hell of a lot of trouble.   *Diane Dixon*

Fig. 3 serves to summarise the views of the groups of people we have

Fig. 3   Views on disputes

TWU

(Left)   *Stewards   Workers   Workers' wives   Stewards' wives*   (Right)
Views on the unions at Hampers and the dispute

SOGAT

(Left)   *Workers and wives   Stewards   Stewards' wives*   (Right)
Views on national industrial disputes and general trade union issues

discussed and to point up some of the contrasts. As S. Finer (*New Society*, 10 June 1976) has pointed out, the one-dimensional right—left spectrum is used by intellectuals both frequently and loosely. As an organising principle it is useful if we treat it with caution, bearing in mind that 'ordinary people' do *not* use it to locate their attitudes. From this it can be seen that only the stewards' wives, and to a lesser extent the production workers, held a 'consistent' line across the two related areas of discussion, i.e. the particular industrial situation and general industrial issues. But, as we have said, consistency of itself need be neither interesting nor important, and fractures and difficulties are often more revealing.

Of the two unions, the TWU was certainly the more militant. As we have seen, the dispute had only a limited effect, and that only on the people most directly involved. The evidence does not seem to indicate that there were significant differences between either the behaviour or the attitudes of men with supporting wives and those without. But men had an alternative ideology and social group — the union — to fall back on. Their wives did not have this relative autonomy. A husband anxious to involve his wife did not necessarily get her sympathy, but an uncommunicative husband left his wife few alternatives to rejection or apathy, because she was cut off from the union as the only other source of information.

There were no direct contacts between the wives and the factory, nor was there any direct contact between the wives themselves. There were no institutional means whereby they could have had a direct effect on what heppened in the factory, and many of them felt that such influence as they could have on their husbands would not, in any case, be legitimate. Yet the wives' response to the dispute was not without effect. Open opposition, as voiced by the stewards' wives, or indifference, as shown by the rank-and-file wives, can both have an adverse effect on the strength of union action. Many of the men, especially the stewards, were aware of the danger and dwelt on the difficulty of prolonging a dispute without support from home. Yet they themselves had managed. They did so because the experience of the strike had forced them to develop a positive response to at least their own dispute — and they carried their rank and file with them, albeit reluctantly. But it was at the cost of deepening the ideological chasm between 'home' and 'work'. The wives' attitudes to the dispute had inhibited any positive effects it might have had on them, and that in turn reacted on the husbands' making it difficult for them to develop their new perception: a kind of negative dialectical process.

Both men and women were aware of the separation of home and work, and many of the men felt divided loyalties. Men who made their home the focus of their lives did not want to be torn in this way. So they limited not just their working lives but also their ideological identification with the union. It was corralled, regulated to manageable proportions, like an evening's skittles. The wives reinforced this by their attitudes, which were in part the result of their exclusion from their husbands' world of work. Thus both men and their wives, with the partial exception of the stewards, remained locked in a syndrome of seeming indifference, if not hostility.

Ideology and 'non-experience' — the case of SOGAT

SOGAT stewards and rank and file

Turning to the other union at Hampers, SOGAT, we came to a group of men with a different kind of experience of the strike. It was not simply that their distance from it was greater, but that they were significantly *not* part of it. In fact, despite their *sotto voce* mutterings of support, they were really ranged with the foremen and management against the striking union. The stewards' neutral line did little to disguise the fact that SOGAT officially opposed it. For SOGAT members, then, to support the TWU's action would have been to go against their own union. SOGAT had been introduced into the factory by 'radically' minded men impatient with the (then) moribund TWU, and it had subsequently attracted the more militant members of the TWU. A process of natural selection had therefore placed men with 'radical' views on industrial issues in SOGAT. A number of them were disappointed by the decision (which had been taken, effectively, at national level).

> If you listen to the so-called officials, some of them talk all day implying you should do such a thing. You must be prepared to fight. As far as I'm concerned you must be prepared to strike for it — but if you are prepared to fight, they turn round and say, 'You can't do that', so you're left holding the baby.   *Fred Fletcher*

Indeed, in a way, it was the 'wrong' union that took action, for it meant that men whose other ideas would have lead one to expect them to support the dispute did not. Nick Skinner, for example, was bitterly disappointed:

> I was disappointed SOGAT didn't go along — our agreement wasn't legally binding, and we were quite entitled to. The strike would have been stronger with both unions.

And even the most cautious confessed,

> It did cross my mind that if we'd gone in with them we could have got it earlier like.   *Steve Gray*

Like the stewards in the TWU, these men found it difficult to explain why they took the line they did. In their case the difficulty was to justify not supporting the TWU in its action. Most of them did so either by denying that the TWU had any right to represent workers in the factory at all or by claiming that the dispute was 'silly', because it was lost money and the settlement had already been agreed to by the national negotiating body.

The SOGAT members' experience of being close to, but only marginally affected by, industrial action is a lot more common than actually being involved in a dispute. For every few hundred men who go on strike in the car industry, for example, thousands are laid off in the peripheral firms. And it is not just in the car industry that stoppages, sometimes by only a few key workers, can have a 'ripple' effect on many more.

For this reason it is as important to notice what happened to the SOGAT men and their wives as to the TWU couples. If we are to take experience seriously as a positive influence on the formation of consciousness, we must also take seriously the consequences of non-experience — in this case, of being marginally and passively involved in another union's dispute. These men had a previous disposition towards militant action, but it was denied by the dispute. Experience — or rather, coping with the non-experience of standing by — vitiated their potential consciousness.

Evidence for this can be drawn from their views on general industrial issues. In contrast to the TWU men they expressed strong support for unions and sympathy for many other strikes — even for the much maligned car workers.

> The miners' is a necessary strike. They'll win it — they can't afford to lose it. Both sides will dig their heels in and it will go on a long time. The government will squeeze out of it somehow. Most working people don't understand what it's about. They won't back them while the NCB is putting advertisements in the paper and Heath is blaming the communists. But if the public knew the true facts they would.
>
> *Nick Skinner*

> Take the miners. If there wasn't a union in there, God knows what would happen. If it was left to the management they'd be paying them in lumps of coal.
> *Simon Steele*

> ... all the other big unions will put in for an increase [after the miners] and it's right that they should do so. The miners' victory will help others — at least, I'd like to think it would.
> *Steve Gray*

There was no mention of 'the country being held to ransom' or of workers being 'greedy'. There is a startling gap between this active 'trade union consciousness' and the men's impoverished view of trade union activity in their own work place.

SOGAT wives

The wives of SOGAT men, stewards and rank and file, had very little connection with a dispute by another union at their husbands' factory. In fact they were more directly affected by, and had more information about, the miners' strike. Unless they or their husbands were particularly interested in discussing it there was no reason why they should do so.

Positive and voluble on any other subject, this one failed to interest them. Six months later one woman only dimly remembered there had been a strike, 'because Ernie had to go to a meeting about it'. Some were glad their husbands were not involved; 'no one likes their husband on strike' (*Felicity Skinner*), and several felt a duty to support their husbands anyway, whether they agreed or not. Aw with the TWU wives, it was a duty that appeared to have more to do with their marriage vows than working-class solidarity. One, commenting on how little part women played in union affairs, said sagely, 'It's just as well, or you get arguments with your husband' (*Jo Lee*). But on general industrial issues — and indeed on other political issues — the SOGAT wives had the most consistently radical views of any of the groups we have looked at. They were noticeably more radical than their husbands — who were, in turn, more radical than the TWU men. Just as it was possible to see a connection between the views of husbands and wives in the TWU, so the views of the SOGAT men and women at least suggest that the dispute had a restraining and negative effect on the men but left their wives free to retain and develop their views.

Let us look a little more closely at the views these women did hold. They were strongly in favour of the unions in principle:

> They were the fighters, really. If it wasn't for the unions I don't know where we'd be. There wouldn't be a chance for workers without them. They'd be forced back by troops.
> *Mavis Gray*

The women offered loyal support for national strikes even when they themselves would be affected:

> If it happens, it does. We'll have to take what comes with it. Yes, they ought to get it: they're right to strike.
> *Molly Rees*

This kind of support was extended to any group they considered worthy — including seamen, nurses and students — although most of them drew the line at car workers. (It looks as if the car workers were the token scapegoats that allowed them to support all other strikers, as they gave no good reason why the line should be drawn there so firmly.) None of these women argued that 'the unions were too powerful' or accused them of 'holding the country to ransom' as the TWU wives did.

Yet their own personal experience of unions, like that of the TWU wives, was unsatisfactory. Those who did have jobs were in non-unionised sectors such as small shops and domestic cleaning. Although most of them were 'hot on my wages', they expected to have to do their own bargaining or even to have to oppose a male trade union leader. And they regarded their husbands' experience as irrelevant or worse. Jo Lee, for example, exasperated by the apparent pettiness of job demarcation, said:

> I didn't really approve; Mike's a real union man. He comes home and says, 'They said to fill the ink pots up, and I said, "No, that's not my job".' To me that's just silly talk. If the pot needs filling, I'd fill it.

The wives found it easier to see the structure of the relations of production at the point of consumption. Here is Jo again, on the miners' strike:

> It all comes back to the working man. Now they'll say, 'We've given the miners their rise,' but in the end the coal will go up a hell of a price, and the people will pay for it.

At the point of production the wives also saw a basic conflict between capital and labour, but less in terms of structure than in terms of moral corruption. Management, certainly at Hampers, but also more generally, was unscrupulous and untrustworthy. 'They get their profit by robbing the men' (*Gladys Hutchings*). In their hands morality – the same morality that the TWU stewards' wives used to support the *status quo*, had boomeranged against capital, which stood condemned by its own ideology.

If information about Hampers was mediated to these women in an inadequate and privatised way, 'news' about national disputes was readily available and publicly discussed 'down the shop'. This is not to say that they uncritically accepted what they saw and heard on television. In fact an aspect of industrial struggle that had impressed some women was the way the media falsified the situation against the interests of the workers. 'I really get annoyed with the TV when they are saying about it. They just didn't know ... it's disgusting' (*Jean Martin*). In this situation the unions were seen as the only institution strong enough to confront the media with the workers' case. As the unions have no way of making their voice heard outside the capitalist media, this seems unlikely, but it was some indication of the trust the women had in the unions as a last bulwark. It also indicated that they could think of no other organisation which could represent working-class interests.

Thus these women represented a reservoir of untapped trade union support, even though their husbands had been disillusioned by their contact with the dispute and had consequently adopted a negative response to their own union. Althouth they could not prevent their husbands developing a negative response, they themselves appeared to have escaped its baleful influence. Yet it should also be noted that these wives were also thwarted, prevented by loyalty from criticising their husbands, and unable to play an active part themselves. They were limited to having arguments 'down the shop'.

The initial source of the women's more favourable disposition to trade union action lies elsewhere in their experience, and it could certainly not be 'read off' from the attitudes and actions of their husbands.

Between capital and labour

The foremen

Foremen are on, but not of, the shop floor. While not involved in the dispute, they were responsible for 'policing' it. Yet the strike had brought home to them a greater awareness of their structural position than it had for most of the workers.

All of them condemned the dispute. Some blamed individuals, some the unions, some the management; some attributed it to an inevitable aggrandisement on the part of union leaders.

> I don't think they represent the men. Well, fair enough, they're sort of elected, but when they get this job and know the power they've got, it goes to their heads a bit.
> *Norman Sykes*

All were prepared to accept management's view of the strike, but the virulence of their opposition derived from the effect the strike had on their *own* position.

> ... management swore blind they weren't going to give in — and then they did. We felt very bad about that one — not that they gave in, but that the wool was pulled over our eyes ... foremen took a lot of ridicule in this one. That's what started the rot. We really haven't got over it.
> *Martin Neale*

As a result they were thinking seriously about the need for a union of their own, and this despite their predisposition against unions. Their ambivalence stemmed from the ambiguity of their position. In their role

as management's outriders they had learned that unions should *not* be
necessary for them. Yet their memory of working-class roots, and their
own experience, told them that they were. In particular the strike had
created an increasing realisation of their objective position in the capitalist
relations of production, *and* their inability to cope with it. Here is Norman
Sykes — virulently anti-union, and especially anti-SOGAT and TWU —
when I asked him direct, 'Do you think unions are still necessary?'

> Well, it might sound funny. I mean, I'm more or less a member of the
> management. I think if they can get away with something they will. I
> find this in my own case, because I'm not a member of a strong union.
> If someone makes a contract with me I expect them to honour it,
> especially on management' side. But unless it's in black and white you
> can't prove it.

They showed a surprisingly high degree of support for the miners. There
was a combination of giving them credit for a dangerous, underpaid job
and a grudging admiration for the effectiveness of their tactics.

> You got to bang the table. If you've got enough people behind you it's
> all right. It's a case of the bigger the stick, the more you get. It's like
> the miners.
> *Norman Sykes*

Indeed, the foremen showed a very explicit understanding of the powers
ranged against the workers, and a deep cynicism that management would
be anything less than ruthless in trying to get what they wanted.

For these men one source of ideological confusion had been laid on
another. They were working men who had become 'incorporated' as a
result of their promotion into the ranks of 'management'. Then, because
of the strike, they began to see the limits of their incorporation. They had
therefore re-evaluated their position in the world of industry and started,
hesitantly, back along the track to the only source of resistance they
knew, in the working-class culture they thought they had left behind. It
was one more response to the experience of the strike, from a different
structural position and ideological perspective.

Foremen's wives

Their wives can also be regarded as a kind of ideological 'bench mark' from
which their husbands may have moved. The foremen were not especially
conservative on general industrial issues, and their hostility to the strike
was explicable in terms of their own position. But the foremen's wives
were both distinctively conservative and very hostile to all aspects of
industrial struggle.

They were totally removed from experience of the strike. Their husbands were not directly affected, nor was their money. It meant more work for their husbands, but no longer hours. Consequently they were not well informed about Hampers events, and expressed this in indifference to them. Few of them even mentioned the strike. However, when they talked about industrial issues there was a curious conjunction between them and the TWU stewards' wives. They hated strikes and were deeply suspicious of unions, and the arguments they used had the same moral base as those of the stewards' wives. Like them they felt that the unions were too big and powerful, that workers were 'greedy'; and that troublemakers led the rank and file astray. They even condemned the government for weakening.

> The power frightens me — that they could just drop everything because there are so many of them and we needed them, but the government's attitude was very hypocritical, because they were paid far in excess.
>
> *Anna Roberts*

Like the TWU stewards' wives they stressed the importance of 'the individual'. One of the reasons for their dislike of the power of the big unions was their fear for individuality in such vast concerns. In their case this was attached to the middle-class concern for individualism and privacy, well supported by their own life style. Their houses, privately owned and in select suburbs, were a testimony to *individual* advancement.

Their views reflected a stratum that was trying to dissociate itself from its working-class origins. Industrial struggle was part of the world they felt they had left. That they had not left it was clear from their husbands' predicament. But they themselves were insulted from that experience, and from its consequences.

The difference between the husbands — wavering between two opposed ideologies and their more certain (if misguided) wives — can be attributed, at least partly, to the immunity conferred by industrial non-experience.

Ideology and potential consciousness

In this chapter I have taken one event in people's lives and tried to describe their reactions to it, their interpretation of it, and the effect it had had on their ideology.

Industrial disputes, for theoretical and political reasons, have a special interest in the study of working-class ideology and consciousness. Yet in the literature there are few detailed descriptions of industrial action, fewer that concentrate on the ideological dimensions, and none that has described the effect on the *wives* of male industrial workers. In fact, as I have pointed out, the situation was more complicated than that, and each of the groups I have distinguished — TWU stewards and their wives; TWU workers and their wives; SOGAT stewards and workers and their wives; foremen and their wives — had a different experience of the dispute. Only two of them — TWU stewards and workers — could be said to have been directly involved. Yet, as we have seen, it was also significant in various ways for the much larger number of people who were *not* involved. The analysis has meant treating 'non-experience' as a category of comparable importance to 'experience' in the formation of consciousness.

Of course, militancy cannot be conflated with radicalism *tout court*, and involvement in an industrial dispute is no indication of political involvement. We are talking here about a small group of union members who wanted a small amount of money and a slightly larger amount of recognition, and the effects their action had on them and on others near by. This is a long way from the development of full working-class consciousness, and it not even near the limits of the trade union consciousness described by Lenin.

But, limited as they are, both economically and ideologically, the unions are the only institution that stands between the working class and capital. What I have been concerned to do in this chapter has been to draw attention to the groups marginal to the dispute and outside the trade union sphere of influence; that is, to the wives.

The TWU women showed all the 'conventional' hostility to unions, and their hostility helped to minimise the positive effects of the dispute on their husbands. But the SOGAT women — those furthest removed from the dispute — showed exclusion from the union and the 'men's world' of work operating in a different way. Indeed, it raises questions about the assumptions, firstly, that 'radical' ideology is created by union experience, and, secondly, that, in its absence, there remain only hostile media interpretations of industrial issues. For it is arguable that the particular union experience of the SOGAT stewards resulted in a kind of blocked radicalism: the greater radicalism of their wives deriving from the absence of that negative union experience and resulting in a consciousness that was 'imprisoned'. For, while these women demonstrated their vigorous and intense opposition to the structure of society, it is clear that they lacked any ideological organising principle. Isolated and angry, each woman reacted with private frustration. They were effectively cut off from the trade union movement, both in practice and in terms of ideological leadership, and there was no effective alternative.

Richard Hyman, discussing sectionalism within the work force, has said:

The immediate context of the world of work is necessarily sectional: it is in fragmented contexts that men and women share their hopes and fears... Class consciousness is not an abstraction which replaces localized sympathies and face to face collaboration: it must be built on, and grow out of these, through the imaginative extension of what is directly experienced.[7]

In this chapter I have tried to draw attention to a sectionalism in the working class as a whole: between those, like the husbands, who have direct experience of the reality of capitalist industrial production and, in this case, of overt industrial conflict, and their wives, who lack direct experience and who have to try to make sense of it in other ways.

Discussion of the dispute at Hampers demonstrates, above all, the complexity of the relationship between experience and consciousness. There was no simple one-to-one correspondence between the men's experience of the dispute and their wives' consciousness of it. This has a particular relevance, for the failure of working-class organisations to activate large sections of the working class in *non*-work-based struggles has had a crucially inhibiting effect on working-class resistance. Traditionally certain issues — namely, industrial issues — have been considered crucial to the formation of active working-class consciousness. We have already seen that the women in this study had their own independent approaches to their husband's experiences.

Later I shall explore the idea that the sexual division of labour in capitalist society creates a specific 'sectional' consciousness among women. The strike at Hampers was a particular event, or non-event, in these people's lives that had complex effects on the formation of their ideas and class consciousness. Later I shall argue that the particular experience of being a woman is another 'case study', and requires a similar close inquiry, for women develop their own strategies for understanding and coping with their experience and with other experience as it is mediated to them.

Notes

1 See R. Hyman (1977), chapter 2, for a discussion of the difficulties of interpreting official strike statistics. He concludes that the majority of strikes are short-lived, and adds that many disputes are so borderline that they escape the statistics altogether. In this instance the dispute lasted for six weeks — but only for the last three days were the men officially 'on strike'.

2 Here Keith Thomas, TWU branch secretary, gives a description of their tactics: 'We got a paper lorry down there, which is the key to

this factory — and dispatch. So what we did is say no outside lorries would be loaded by us, so we'd only load our own drivers, i.e. about 35 per cent who were our own drivers on dispatch. That quickly increased to 45 per cent, which was as much as they could absorb — so we were all right there. Then we'd say, "Can't load that lorry — it's black." We'd black a job. A steward would put a mark on label. In fact we made our own rules as we went along. With this paper lorry: we used to have collectors round the factory once a week, and one of the paper men would go home every day, and we'd say, "Sorry, we can't work there because the gang's not full," and they'd say, "Fair enough, we'll get a man from somewhere else," and they'd do that, and the man would say, "Sorry, I can't work there — it's not my job" — so gradually we choked off the paper supply in twelve days, and we blocked it up the dispatch end. And then we'd watch — I remember an example of one of the fork drivers. They suddenly decided to make a lot of [a sister company's] cases — we'd been choking [them] up by this time, because if you hit [them] you're hitting [the parent combine] and the bosses are beginning to ask, "What's up at Hampers?" So as soon as the machines started on [their] cases they'd say to the fork driver, "You're on strike," and he'd come straight off and leave the machine choked up, and it couldn't be used or put on to anything else, and we could do it the other way round.'

3 In fact another dispute over the same basic problem did break out a few months after the completion of the fieldwork.

4 The dictionary definition of this word has allowed it a broad usage: 'pertaining to, constituting, proceeding from or going to the root; fundamental; original' and so on. *Chambers's Twentieth Century Dictionary* lays down broad parameters. One such is indicated by J. M. Westergaard in the course of his debate with D. Lockwood in M. Bulmer (ed.) (1975), p. 252, when he defines a 'radical class consciousness' as involving identification with, a recognition of common interests with, workers in other situations, outside the immediate locality, outside the particular conditions of an occupational community ... it involves at least a tentative vision of an 'alternative society', and D. Lockwood responds (p. 258) with: 'It is then the combination of class-wide solidarities and an oppositional consciousness that characterises the radical worker'. It is within this (still very broad) image that I employ the word 'radical'. I lay most stress on the ingredients of 'oppositional consciousness' and 'tentative vision of an "alternative society"' which, more succinctly, mean that I use it to point to expressions of resistance, anger and refusal to surrender to hegemonic interpretations of capitalist society which seem to have the potential of 'radical class consciousness'.

5 A. Gouldner (1955), p. 127. T. Lane and K. Roberts (1971) found a similar process at work in the dispute at Pilkington's.

6 P. Toynbee (1967), p. 97. 'The British, in particular, are a moralizing nation, and it is by scarcely disguised moral arguments that we are constantly urged to accept the present structure of our society.'

7 R. Hyman (1971), pp. 41–2, 51.

THREE

WOMEN, MEN AND EXPERIENCE: FOUR COUPLES

I want to look now at a different kind of experience, the personal experience of four married couples, and at the ways in which the husbands' and wives' ideas are related to their different experience of the world, and to their common experience of marriage, home and the family. I have chosen to concentrate on these particular couples because, in their different ways, they illustrate a variety of experiences and responses to them. Their unique biographies serve, once again, to warn against premature generalisation. It is only by looking carefully and sympathetically at the specificity of their experience that we can understand some of the processes by which ideology is constructed, and the role that gender plays in that process.

The Turners and the Davieses appeared on the surface, to be very similar. Tommy and Hugh were both active TWU stewards. Both wives had 'little jobs' in catering. All were much the same age and lived in similar homes in the same area. Conventional studies could well 'categorise' them as almost identical. Yet they were not, and we are concerned to illustrate the significance of the differences. The predominant split in attitudes and views was not between couples but between men and women, based upon their very different gender-related experience of the world.

With the Hutchinges we move to a different part of Bristol and to the other union — SOGAT. Both the home and the work situation were in contrast to the Turners' and the Davieses'. The effects were compounded by the Hutchings's problems with the welfare services. Tommy Turner's and Hugh Davies's experience of managing the dispute at Hampers had had a positive effect on them, which was inhibited by Betty's and Ann's disapproval. In the case of the hutchingses, Gladys's experience of the welfare services caused her to challenge the conventional explanations — but this effect was inhibited by her husband Alan's detachment, and by the lack of any organisational means through which she could express it.

Finally, with the Grays we come to a more evenly balanced couple, both in terms of their experience and in terms of their careful, thoughtful interpretations and radical inclinations. Like Alan Hutchings, Steve was a SOGAT steward and thus had had the negative experience of *not* being involved in the dispute. But Steve had a well grounded adherence to the principles of trade unionism. What he could not do was extend his ideas to other arenas. Gladys *did* see the connections between the experience of work and the problems, especially prices, that confronted her at home. In this case both husband and wife had a partial understanding of their experience. What inhibited its development was the total separation of the 'men's world' from the 'women's world'.

The Turners and the Davieses: reluctant militants and moral guardians

The Turners and the Davieses lived within a few streets of each other in identical pre-war council-built homes in Bedminster. Both were three-bedroomed, red-brick and semi-detached, with small gardens at the back and apolegetic scraps at the front. Inside, the Turners' was comfortably furnished, with thick pile carpets, a warm three-piece suite, a large colour TV and numbers of ornaments. While not so lavish, the Davies's home was comfortable enough, with the same welcoming, friendly atmosphere. The Davieses were slightly older than the Turners (forty-six and fifty as against forty and forty-four). Both couples had children ranging from primary school age to adult wage-earners, so that they were at much the same stage in family life. But whereas the Turners had brought up three children the Davieses had brought up eight (two of their own and six adopted or fostered) in similar housing conditions and on similar money. It was only to be expected, therefore, that the Davieses would feel the financial pinch more acutely, and that this would influence their ideas. Indeed, it was the only subject on which opinion divided according to family rather than according to sex.

All four had left school at fourteen. Tommy Turner had worked in two other firms before he went to Hampers ten years before, but Hugh Davies went straight to Hampers from school and, apart from a short break for National Service, had been there ever since. He therefore had no other direct work experience with which to compare Hampers. Moreover, both men regarded themselves as permanently employed there, so that they had to look for solutions to problems either by altering conditions within the firm, or by just 'putting up with it'. They did not feel they had the option of changing jobs any more.

Both Betty and Ann had part-time jobs: both for four hours a day, and both in catering — Betty at the university union, and Ann in a chain-store café. The difference here was that while Betty had always worked in service occupations, Ann had once worked at Hampers herself and so had first-hand experience of Hugh's workplace (not that it made her sympathetic to his position). Neither took her paid work very seriously. It was pleasant, it was a break, and the money was certainly useful (especially to Ann) — but it was only an interlude in their 'real' work — at home.

For both couples their family took priority over all other concerns, including the union.

> The way I feel, I'm a very lucky man. I got the house, the family ... free time. I'm what you call a proper family man. I'd rather be home. Doing all sorts. The wife does cakes, I help her. In summer it's the garden.
>
> *Tommy*

This affected the relationship between husband and wife and created similar connections in both families. Both husbands were kind and considerate, anxious to avoid conflict if they could, and devoted to their wives: both the women were energetic, vivacious and independent-minded; Ann, at least, revelled in a scrap.

Hugh and Tommy were typical Hampers workers, and Betty and Ann were typical of the women who lived in Bedminster and whose husbands worked at Hampers. But Tommy and Hugh had a more specific shared situation. They were both stewards in the TWU. What we must ask is how these special experiences affected their lives outside work, and especially how they mediated them to their wives, and what their response was.

Generally speaking, the women knew very little about their husband's job — and cared less. They did not talk to their husband about his work. It was seen as his affair. 'He's never come home and said, "I'm fed up, I'll look for another job," so he must be quite satisfied' (*Betty*). This was re-inforced by the men's desire to forget work when they were at home, and it did not help that the women disapproved so openly of union affairs. As Ann said, 'He doesn't tell me much because I gets so mad about the unions.' When they did talk, the men found it difficult to convey what was really happening to wives who had already received a blueprint from 'the papers'.

> She reads so much in the paper about strikes. For what we got out of it she doesn't think it's worth it. The miners got £10. She wants to know why the cost of living hasn't gone up for them as for us. She's quite right.
>
> *Hugh*

Both women roundly disapproved of their husbands' union commitments, and condemned all industrial action — including their husbands'.

I agreed with industrial action, but not to a strike. A go-slow would
have been enough.   *Ann*

That I did disagree with him about.   *Betty*

All strikes, in their view, were wrong, and they saw no reason to make an
exception for the one at Hampers.

In the beginning they [the unions] were ideal, but now they've gone a
bit beyond what they set out to do. I think they're getting too big.
They used to be for workers' rights, but now it seems all they're after is
more money, strikes, that kind of thing.   *Betty*

Well, he's always been interested. I'm not very much one for unions
myself, that we do differ on, but I don't mind. I don't like strikes. I
mean, it's no good my saying, "You can't go on strike" — I would have
loved to have said that. Y'know, as I said, I don't agree with strikes. I
don't *like* strikes. I mean, you can't oppose him. It's nothing to do with
me. I know it affects our weekly wage, but then you can't ... it wasn't
my place of work, it wasn't my union, so it wasn't up to me.   *Ann*

As they saw no reason to change their views, it was the men who had to
moderate theirs, and this made obvious difficulties for them, especially
after their active involvement in the 1973 dispute.

Ironically, the men felt that their wives' support, especially their
support during a strike, was vital. With some feeling they said that 'if a
wife was against a man he'd worry' (*Tommy*).

If you've got your wife against you you've got no interest in striking.
You want to get back to work. If the dispute goes well *they* get a rise.
                                                                    Hugh

When they discussed promotion the difference between the men and women
was very clear. Neither of the men wanted it. Tommy said he'd be 'miserable,
because you got so much to worry about'. Hugh very explicitly saw it as a
step on to 'the other side' — a kind of betrayal of his principles.

I'm not interested in promotion. I didn't like the foreman and chargehand, and I didn't want to be one of them. You've got to change,
haven't you? Got to give the union up. You're one of the other side.
You've got to make a go of it. If you come back the blokes won't like
you.   *Hugh*

But Ann was unaware of all this:

I can't understand it — he's been there all these years and he's still there, and the young ones have come in and gone up. I'd have liked it.

Both men had been stewards for a long time, Hugh for nearly thirty years. They took their duties seriously. They did not regard themselves as leaders in battle but as reliable, honest and sober men, sensitive to the needs and wishes of their members. Neither came near to challenging management's 'right to manage', although both had criticisms of their own managers. But over certain issues (safety, for Tommy; redundancy, for Hugh) they appealed to a level of morality that transcended management's rights.

He shouldn't just be cast outside the door because the firm doesn't want him.   *Hugh*

At times, too, their desire for consensus was shot through with bitter realism.

Management would get rid of unions if they could. Oh yes — and then you'd have chaps waiting outside, like years ago.   *Hugh*

Both men had entirely supported the TWU action and both were surprised by the extent and enthusiasm of the men's support for the strike. 'There was marvellous support. I thought the majority would be against it, but they weren't' (*Hugh*).

Tommy's account (given to me some six months later) raises some important points that were generally true for the TWU stewards.

Well, that goes back — not to this one, the one before. They turned round and said that TWU didn't have the rights to negotiate for wages. Of course, we didn't like that — well, the men didn't like it — and we went out. Anyway, they got us back in, saying that they made an agreement, that we have got the right to negotiate.
(Why did SOGAT have negotiating rights and not TWU?)
I think probably it was because they tried to get us out. We got a little bit too strong, and they thought there was an opportunity there to get the TWU out, and as I said, they tried it. Well, we went to negotiate last year, in June. They wouldn't listen. One thing built up to another, and we went on this non-co-operation where we'd take certain men off and slow the job down. I think as how it got a little bit out of hand, because within a week we stopped the factory. They didn't realise we could, and I don't think *we* realised we could, 'cos it was quite a surprise, really, to find we had such, y'know, one hundred per cent backing on this. Everybody was ... everybody backed us right up, and instead of

just slowing the factory down it came to a complete standstill.
(How did you feel about that?)
Well, pleased in a way, and, y'know, it went on quite a long time. It
didn't seem possible that people could sit down for weeks at a time
doing nothing and still getting paid your money. Then I think the
management was a lot to blame for this, because I don't think there
was any need to go that far, because what upset the men so much was
they were giving SOGAT men work *and* overtime when we first started
non-co-operation, and they weren't giving it to the TWU men, and of
course that upset the men, and they started putting pressure on *us* to
put pressure on them, and I think it got out of hand, really. Y'know,
there was no need of it. I don't say we made a mistake, but I think
management did in letting it go too far. I think the information they
were getting back was false. They were under the impression we never
had that — the pull back in — so it was a shock to them as well, and it
was a shock to us. As I said, within a week that was it.
(Was it necessary?)
Yes, because I don't think we'd have got anywhere without putting
some pressure on. I mean, as a last resort we wanted — well, we *didn't*
go on strike — we went on non-co-operation, and then some people
were losing quite a lot of money [in overtime]. Then they had everybody in, and they give them notice and a lock-out notice. We were out,
and we got everybody out there, and we agreed and the men agreed
that we come back here and demanded our jobs back, and we talked
and talked and finally they said, 'Yes.' This was on Friday, and they
said, 'Are you going to start this afternoon?' and we said, 'No, Monday.'
But, y'know, I think if it went on it could have tied the other factories
up as well. I mean, we had backing from *everywhere* in the tobacco
industry. I don't think it could ever happen again. I don't think they'd
go that far. Probably it was a good thing in a way. I know we lost
money, but it showed the management that you could only push so
far.
(Did it do a lot for the men, realising they could?)
Yes, I think it brought them together. What I think *they* liked about it
was that they could prove to this other union that this place can't run
without us.

The first point about this account was that Tommy saw the impetus for
action as coming from the rank and file, 'pressure from the lads'. The
stewards and union officials acted only in response to demands from below.
He was consequently sensitive to the need to keep everyone involved,

'negotiating pickets, making sure everyone had the right information. Y'know. Mostly hanging about, really.' Secondly, he saw the dispute as unequivocally management's fault, and he was clearly shocked by their behaviour. Thirdly, for the first time he had experienced the solidarity of working men, both from the men he helped to lead and from the union organisers.

> Then we had the London people coming down and fighting this. Terry Marsden, she was good. *They* didn't like her. She told them straight that if it got to where they did sack us and wouldn't have us back she'd stop [the parent plant] as well — sort of point-blank!

Perhaps even more interesting are the lessons that Tommy saw himself learning from the experience. He saw his role as steward as a key position in a hard fight against a cunning and well armed enemy. To win against management the unions must prepare and train.

> In the future I think the unionist will have to be a well educated man, college education, because I think eventually that's how it will have to be done. They'll employ people from college and unions will have to do the same, because once you get up with these men up there who start using these words you never heard of before and you haven't got a clue what they're talking about — so you got to have men who can think the same as what they are.

> It was with Savage, one of our chaps took a dictionary with him, and every time he came up with a big word he'd say, 'Hang on', and he'd look it up, and come the finish he weren't using them — he can say, 'We'll call it so and so,' and you don't know what he's on about — I mean, they're just trying to put it that they're better than you in education. Probably they are. That's why I say in the future men will have to be trained properly, well, the top people like Secretary and Chairman. They'll have to be; even the normal shop steward will have to have courses on how to deal with these people.

Though it wasn't all book learning he wanted:

> By going in there and you haven't been in before you could make a lot of mistakes. They can shout and bawl at you and you can be so frightened you could cow down, which if you been used to it you wouldn't. It frightens me how the men aren't getting the experience. It doesn't matter how many courses you go on or you get taught, you should be able to sit down there and *listen* how they talk to the

management and how management talks back, so you can remember. 'You be as good as what they are' or 'Never say that' — y'know.

And if the unions failed, management wouldn't hesitate to get rid of them altogether.

Well, it's only human, that. Well, they could do what they liked then. They could come along to you and say 'Right, you're on nights each week. The week after, you're on days.' As it is we got an agreement that you volunteer for three-shift working, so they can't put you on and you can always come off, if you're on. But I mean, it would be little things like that. They could come along and say, 'I don't like you, you've got the sack,' or 'We want you to work sixteen hours a day and get paid for five.'

But, for all this, neither Tommy nor Hugh extended the understanding they had gained in their own work situation to industrial action by other groups of workers. Here is Tommy discussing inflation.

Well, I think the unions are to blame for this with some of the wage claims they've been putting in. I think this is how it really starts — people being greedy. Instead of making do with a couple of quid they want the lot. I don't think it gets them anywhere, because everything goes up, so they're just as bad off ...

I could understand how the miners felt — but they've gone too far, because I don't think it hurts to have a little bit now and still have a little bit later on. There was nothing to stop them having this bit they offered and banging in for more later on.
(Do you think they're being unreasonable?)
I think so. When it involves ... Now if it only involved — Take it it was here where it was — and it will only involve this firm, nobody outside. I think, fair enough, hang on. But when it involves people's jobs all over the country ... In fact if it went on too long it could *bankrupt* the country. I think it's ridiculous. It's too many men and their jobs involved in this. I think they should think a lot more of this.

And Hugh said:

No. I understand it's a rotten job. But I can't see why they should be favoured. Their wages is adequate. Just because car workers and so on are way out front they want to be up with them. If they do strike it could lead to a general strike if it went on. There's not the sympathy this time as last. You go round the factory and they say, 'We've got to pay the same for bread as they have.'

Both these arguments are defensive. They enable them to justify their own strike while continuing to deplore others. As we have seen in Chapter 2, this is a common device for enabling people to preserve their hostility to strikes in general while justifying their own as exceptional.

In Tommy's and Hugh's case another reason for this rejection of the miners' claim was that both their wives *did* have an explicit and powerful analysis of industrial politics (basically that of 'common sense') which was wholly hostile to the union point of view. The men therefore had to justify their deviation from this norm. They were forced to do so in the particular, but not in the general. Then they could conform. Indeed, they found it a tangible relief when they could join their wives in castigating the car workers and communists. So they were under great pressure *not* to make the connection between their own strike and any others. Nevertheless, there were moments when the paper over the cracks began to tear — especially with Tommy:

I think ordinary people have more say than years ago. I think that's where the unions are getting stronger, they got more power to *say* things. But the unions are too strong, in a way. Well, when they can hold the country to ransom like they're doing now. I don't know how it could be arranged to suit both sides, but they should only be able to go so far. Both sides could go so far, then it must stop. The country *is* being held to ransom. To me it's wrong.

(Who do you think makes the really big decisions in the country?)

Well, I wonder sometimes — I think mostly it's people with money, big money. Y'know, like, well, put it this way, like big firms like ICI. I think they can pull the strings enough to say, like, do this, and do that — but I don't think it's being done underhand. I think they *listen* to what they got to say — the government — put it that way regardless of what government is in — because you got to rely on these people for the money.

Was this conflict the direct result of his new realisations? The hesitancy of his 'Well, I wonder sometimes ...' points to an upheaval going on in his consciousness. The real importance of this lay in the formation of new possibilities for change, which had been opened up and which he was tentatively exploring. Reality was no longer seen as inevitable. He had found real weapons at hand to institute change, although he was still not certain how far he could or should go — and it is clear that Betty's influence would operate against any such movement.

The two couples lived in similar circumstances but their home situation was only *comparable*, it was not *common* to them. The wives, therefore, did not share a work situation in the same way as their husbands did. The women regarded the work they did at home for the family as their defining work role, and both took it seriously, especially Ann.

> It's far easier for these people that go out to work and come back to fitted carpets and only two in the family. They wouldn't stay home all day. They go mad on material things.

> It's a nice job, with the children. The kids make it. The washing's hard but when you sees them going to school all nice it's worth it. When they says, 'The bread pudding's marvellous' — I wouldn't work now if it wasn't for the money. My insurance man has been coming twenty years and he's never caught me out on a Monday morning and I've used the same grocer for twenty-five years.

The part-time work was irrelevant in this respect, because although they shared it with other women it was only secondary.

It is important that in the women's experience of work they were more like each other than they were like their husbands. It is not, therefore, surprising to find that the split in opinion and attitude came more often between men and women than between the two couples. Both Betty and Ann had used the value of what they did in the home to assert its primacy over the outside world.[1] At one level this standpoint was the mirror image of an idea, common among male trade unionists, that anything outside the realm of paid work and direct production is less important, or at least less relevant. The women knew that aspects of their lives such as personal relationships, prices, the care of children, the social services, etc., *were* important, in fact they were the stuff of their existence. They did not separate out the 'economic' as an autonomous category at all: it was merely part of the web of life. This led them to draw a distinction between 'politics' and 'real life'. Contrary to the economistic assertion that only economy is real, they asserted that everything else was, sometimes even to the exclusion of economics. This was illustrated when they were talking about whether men or women knew more about 'politics'.

> I think so. *They* like to think so, let's put it that way. Well, I think, with women, when they're together they gossip, but with men, they talk, y'know, government and football and that kind of thing. Well, with women we're more interested in what's happening next door or across the road. They're more concerned about the old people.
>
> *Betty*

This separation also enabled the women to dismiss their husbands' union activity as something which concerned them alone. It enabled them to accommodate the fact that they did not like it. It did not concern them, and thus conflict between husband and wife was avoided. They were not forced, as the men were, to cope with the contradictions it raised.

The link between home and work was the husband's pay packet. The women were under no illusions that they had as much at stake in the regular arrival of a full pay packet as the men did. They had a direct experience of the pay packet that they did not have of the rest of their husband's work situation. It was intensified because in both cases it was the women who handled the money. Tommy had nothing to do with it at all and Hugh only kept enough for small daily needs. Both men felt strongly that it would have been wrong to keep their wives short, or for them not to know how much they earned. At the same time they expressed a residual disquiet that they did not control the financial affairs of the house. They felt they had to account for the fact that it was the wife who handled the money. In the conventional ideology the sexual division of labour was clear — the man earned money and the woman kept house, but this involved spending the money, and that somehow seemed to diminish the act of earning it. In other words the connection between production and consumption was not clear.

The women's attitude to pay depended less on a comparison with other workers (as Hugh's did), or on what the firm could afford to pay, than on how adequate the wage was for their spending needs. The 'wage' was nearly the same for both of them — but their economic needs were quite different, so where Betty said, 'I think it's pretty good ... we've managed so far,' Ann said, 'It's poor money ... I think he's a fool to stay there all those years for that money ... just more money, how much easier that would be.'

The connection between inflation and prices was made most clearly by Hugh.

> Wages chasing prices. That's where the Labour government fell down. They pegged wages (and we unions agreed) but they haven't frozen prices.

> Going in the EEC was all wrong. If we'd stuck with the Commonwealth we'd be better. Government's not trying to keep prices down. They're trying to keep in line with EEC.

Tommy connected profits with prices, and so did Ann. 'If [Harold] Wilson got back he'd do something about prices by controlling profits.'

Both the women felt strongly about prices and inflation. In Betty's case it was the only thing that ruffled her placid progress, and she expressed real indignation, if not anger.

> Every day it's like a cartoon. Last week currants up 2p, icing sugar up 1p, bananas up 3p. And it's all the time. It's just mad.

She had certainly seen that wages did not go up as fast as prices, and that she was more affected than people like Cabinet Ministers. But there was nothing that any of them could see they could do about it. You could look around for causes, you could see that the explanations given were not good enough, but that was as far as it went. They helplessly accepted what came with such small defensive tactics as 'Well, it's no use worrying.'

Here, then, were four real people making a reasonably good job of living their lives. Whatever the deficiencies of their ideology, it worked in the sense that they did confront the world as they saw it with a certain assurance. They had made enough sense of it to allow them to cope with daily disturbances.

The ideas they had were socially rooted, but rooted in an experience which cannot be categorised without doing violence to the complexity of their lives. Their experience was also historically rooted, in both a personal and a social past.

One object of presenting the two couples together is to make the point that conventional industrial sociology would have examined Tommy and Hugh's ideas at work. Community or family sociology would have looked at them at home. A sociology of women would have focused on Betty and Ann. What I have tried to do is to bring these perspectives together, and so highlight the difficulty of isolating aspects of peoples' lives.

Their family commitments made significant differences to the ways in which the men interpreted their work experience. The women were intimately involved, by what happened to their men. Both couples were part of Bedminster, of Hampers and of Britain in 1974. Yet what is more significant is the way in which the separate experiences of being men and women had cut across the process of constructing ideology from experience.

For the women, the lack of direct experience of their husbands' workplace was compounded by their refusal to learn from them. Their rejection of their husbands' position had buttressed an ideological stance that gave their position as *women* both dignity and substance. But it had also completely denied them the position learning experience of the dispute. We can see something of what this means in Tommy's ideas. He had been subjected to a profound, and in some ways, liberating, experience. But its effects on his radical consciousness were vitiated by the total separation of the sphere of work from the − to him equally important − sphere of the home. Daunted by Betty's opposition, he failed to extend his experience beyond the factory gates.

Alan and Gladys Hutchings: a case of miscasting?

The Hutchingses' home offered an immediate and striking contrast to the Turners' and the Davieses'. The houses in Bradley Walk had been built for £1,500 in the cheapest materials available just after the war. It was on the very perimeter of the city boundary amid a desert of amenities.

> The post office and the chemist are over a mile away. There are no clothes or shoe shops. You've got to go to Bedminster. I like to make wedding cakes − but I have to go to Knowle or Bedminster to get sugar, cake boards etc. *Gladys*

What neighbourly contact there was centred acrimoniously round the destruction of the few remaining trees and phone booths by the bored local youth.

Gladys was a small, fat, hard-eyed woman with stringy, permed hair and a harsh voice. Colin, the only child still at home, was a lean, pale boy, small for eleven, with a pinched face. His clothes were noticeably dirty and full of holes, and he was wandering round eating bread and marge. Alan was also small and pinched-looking, and he had a missing finger and a badly scarred arm.

The other two children, Brian and Carol (twenty and twenty-three), were married, with children of their own. Both had been sent to special residential schools − Carol for four and a half years in London and Brian for seven years to an ESN school in Yeovil. Already Colin had caused so much trouble at his primary school that the headmaster had threatened him with being sent away as well.

The family had had other contacts with the NHS and branches of Social Services. Alan had had a bad accident at a smelting plant, which involved extended treatment and kept him off work for six months. Gladys had had her bedridden mother living with them for three years, and Carol had had several problems as a child, including enuresis.

Both Alan and Gladys came from large families. Alan was the second child of thirteen brought up in poverty in Bedminster, and Gladys was one of six brought up in the St Pauls district. She seems to have been a sickly child and went to school for only five years (nine to fourteen). She still suffered from 'weak ears' which prevented her from doing factory work.

As a family they must have been well known to the local welfare, health and educational services, if not actually as a 'problem family'.[2]

On the other hand Alan was holding down a steady job, and apart from the six months after the accident had been in work since leaving school at fourteen. Seeing him at work, you recognised the steady, reliable employee and shop steward. Even when he talked about home and family he said nothing about difficulties there. It was partly that his response to any problem was to minimise it, but he simply did not tell you, for instance, that Brian and Carol had been to special schools. What he enlarged on was his hope that Brian would take up an apprenticeship to a skilled trade. But Brian was ESN and at twenty still could not read, let alone write, so that it would have been almost impossible for him to get any qualifications. It was not till I met Gladys that the full picture emerged. She had no sense that any of her problems were particularly unusual, or that the combination of adverse circumstances was worse than average. She merely related her experiences in a matter-of-fact way, together with her unfavourable view of the welfare services.

Indeed, she was liable to get much more angry when she thought something was 'wrong'. It was not easy with either of them, but especially with Gladys, to discover any *consistent* idea of how they *did* think things ought to be. Both of them embraced conventional rhetoric of various sorts. It was sometimes very reactionary, e.g. Gladys over family allowances or Alan over trade unions, and often plainly contradictory to other things they said on the same subject at the same time. On the other hand, given that they did *not* have a consistent, articulate ideology, and given the difficulties in which they often found themselves, their honest *ad hoc* responses may have been the best *available* way of coping with the world about them.[3]

The aspect of the locality that most affected them was the state of the green outside their house. Their responses to this, and how they apportioned blame, were illustrative. Here is Alan's version:

> The council does a good job — according to the difficulties they work under. Two years running they've planted trees — within a week there's only one left. There was trouble over football on the green on Sundays. The attitude of the council is 'Well, if you don't like it ...' They give you stupid answers like 'Collect fourteen signatures.'

Gladys was less bland.

> ... football on the green. It always seem to be us that create. It's always our garden they destroy. We've written three or four letters to the

council — all you get back is 'It's being looked into' — or 'discussed at the next meeting' — that was two years ago, nothing since.

So it was not likely that Alan was going to be involved in any protest about local amenities. He felt slightly guilty about it. 'All I'm concerned with is day to day — we don't concern ourselves enough.' Gladys, while realising clearly enough that things were not as they might be, saw no way of changing it. She perceived the possibility of organised protest:

> If the house was different it [the rent] would be fair. The houses are not very dear to build. You can't do a lot to bring rent down. People threaten — but nothing comes out. If it was abroad — they stand together and mean it — but English people are cowards. The council doesn't do repairs — or decorate, they don't even give you money towards it. We've got to pay for the ashbins now.

But she was helpless in her conviction that people 'won't stick together'. This was important in connection with women, because they were the group she saw as having the greatest potential.

> If only the women stuck together they'd have more power — but they won't stick together. They say they'll stand by you, won't pay rents — but just as the corporation comes round and says, 'If you don't pay you're out,' then they start paying their rents. Three-quarters of them back down.

> If all the women in the world stuck together — that's the biggest power anyone can have. It's the women that creates when the husband brings home the wage packet. Says he has to hand over more — and he can't. That's half the trouble with these strikes — it's the wives asking for more money all the time. You can't blame them. But they don't realise the men can't bring home more than they earn.

At other times Gladys seemed to have remarkably low expectations of what to expect when confronting authority or, in the case of this experience of hospital, expertise.

> There were very nice with Colin. I was very surprised when the surgeon talked to me in the ward, because I didn't think they tell you what's wrong. I never asked him. I was thrilled to bits. I thought, 'How nice.' When you ask some doctors they hesitate, they don't bother. He told me *just* what he had to do, about the operation.

She had been astonished and grateful to get the kind of explanation that Ann Davies would have demanded as of right. She had, of course, at least as much experience as Ann of the Welfare State in its various guises. Like her, she was critical, and like her she did not stop to analyse the system but went straight for the most obvious target — normally some junior official.

> My mother lived with us, her pension was £6·75; nothing from Social Security, so I wrote and asked for a grant and they refused, then this woman called. If I'd have been here I'd have chucked her through that door. [The official was snooping round while she was out.] I came back and had a right row with her, I'd asked for some knickers, etc. She said, 'If you've got two of each you don't need no more.' That turned me right off, that's why I won't pay full stamps.

Alan had little to say about all this; what mattered to him was the contrast with the time when it wasn't — in his impoverished past:

> I think the Welfare State is important. Yes. I can remember when I was young — a lot of things I couldn't have, and the Welfare could have helped. I was second eldest. There were thirteen in our family. Two sisters are abroad now, but all the rest are quite close. We get on pretty well. One time I had a coat — all our clothes came from the Salvation Army or were handed down — and it was white and furry. So my mum dyed it red. Then the first time out it rained and all the dye ran. I was covered with it, and the coat was pink. But I had to go on wearing it.

Gladys had a traditional working-class allegiance to the Labour Party, together with personal feelings of loyalty to Harold Wilson. Edward Heath, in contrast, was 'only a bachelor' (a common disqualification), and anyway he was too rich.

> With Heath, he's a bachelor. He don't know what poverty is. He's never been married, or had a family. Wilson does understand. I can't understand how Heath could buy yachts when there are still hungry children about. Why should he have all that? And its the same with the royal family. Where do they get their money from? I've got to say it — the Queen still gets Family Allowance. Heath didn't want to know it, when there was trouble. Wilson comes on TV and tells us. We was in the red after the Conservatives. Wilson brought it down. Our enemies — Japan — they wanted their money back.

> Wilson started off all right. Settled the miners, froze the rents and other things. He said, like last time — we've got to suffer, but we'll benefit from it. But last time he had two strikes on his hands. They didn't give him a chance. But now the unions have said their members won't

press — but its all coming on top. Nurses, Wills, Hampers, yet they said they wouldn't — this is like English people, they won't stand together. The unions let the country down by pressing. Only deserving cases should get it. Car workers get enough, so that's one out.

Yet, on at least one reading, the unions *were* doing just what she wanted and 'sticking together'. In fact Gladys made little attempt to cohere her ideas. Here she saw this; there she saw that. What she had *not* done was surrender to an apparently chaotic world.

We ordinary people have got no say at all. They don't treat the working class right. You want the right group of people — ordinary people, butchers, carpenters — that knows what poverty is, should run the country. Prime Ministers and MPs don't realise. They may think they do when they go round, but deep down working class people are fed up.

But without analysis, and without direction, where would this conviction lead? On the surface Alan's ideas sounded a lot more coherent than Gladys's. His priority was to impose order on the world. Thus he played down the difficulties with his children, with the neighbours or with the social services. On the other hand he showed a cynicism, and an absolute conviction that 'the truth' was hidden from him.

But there's so much distorted facts in the paper. No one comes up with true facts in the paper. We don't know the truth about anything. I wasn't surprised, really, at the election. I voted Liberal, for the first time. Usually I'm a Labour man. I was impressed with Thorpe. He seemed more straightforward — well, he's a politician. Wilson, etc., bicker like schoolchildren. Politicians aren't straightforward. If they told you like it is we'd all have different minds. There's a lot of covering up.

Alan's Liberal vote was an alternative that would not have been open to Gladys — whose vote was an act of symbolic loyalty to her background. Despite outbursts of cynicism, Alan never strayed far from his determined docility. And if things were wrong, then he took the blame, both as an individual and for the working class.

MPs should be independent. Quite a few understand — unless they're really rich. Quite a number are really interested. Like in Bristol, e.g. Tommy Smith — talks a lot of rubbish but ... ordinary people *could* have more say. I'm one of them, it's my fault. I could go to tenants' association meetings. All I'm concerned about is day by day. The future doesn't interest me. We don't concern ourselves enough. English people are sort of docile. They can be pushed and pushed.

Alan had worked at the smelting plant for thirteen years, and had moved to Hampers, which was more convenient, only when he felt he could drop the extra money as the children left home. Even so, he still did a great deal of overtime, twenty-four hours a week. Gladys had a substantial part-time job herself — domestic cleaning at a local authority old people's home. She made constant comparisons between her job and factory work, which she would have preferred because it was better paid and the conditions were better: 'You don't pick up infections from cardboard boxes the way you do from old people.' The reasons she gave for not doing factory work were 'her ears', which could not stand the noise (though she gave me no evidence of it), and 'I haven't the brains'. Factory work was invested with a superior aura because it had to do with machines.

In fact her refusal to work in a factory probably had more to do with her attitude to women working in general. Alan's deeply ambivalent views conceded far more than most men in the study did to women's rights and abilities — but he wouldn't like to see his wife do it.

> Equal pay — yes. I've always said that. Women in here work just as hard as men — harder, some of them. I don't expect them on big machines, but on stitchers, etc., it's just as hard work. And they're quicker, as well. I can't see why they should get £6 a week less. It's important for women to be in a union — not because I'm a shop steward, but we're fighting for them and they should be prepared to stand by you. I've always said this. I did a job with women alongside me. It was a very hard job and they did it along with me — taking turns — and people didn't know what you were talking about. But it's wrong. I'd hate to see my wife on those machines. Some women *can* do heavy work. This woman was as good as any man. Kathy, her name was. I used to have to turn the speed back a little ... Women are much quicker on the stitchers. Nine out of ten men couldn't do it.

And Gladys's natural energy and sense of fairness were tempered by a profound feeling of guilt at transgressing the 'natural' sexual division of labour.

> I work nine to three, six hours, only two hours off factory time, and its hard work in these homes. Factory workers have got it easy. Cardboard boxes is clean — no germs from them. I could do that. But domestic work is hard. I'd like to see money come up a bit — but for equal pay

I'd have to do a man's job. Like the handyman — cutting grass, etc. In one way I don't think women should get equal pay, because the man is the breadwinner. I shouldn't go to work by rights, because my husband is the breadwinner and goes to work to support the children. I go to work to help out. I've got to. I don't get Family Allowance for the boy. It costs a lot.

The Hutchingses' attitude to the position of women was important to them and they both stressed it. Both claimed that the demands of the *wives* of strikers were the crucial factor in causing a strike. This could work both ways, i.e. it could force the men to strike because the women needed the money, or it could force them back because they could not do without it. But they both had an unusually acute awareness of wives' influence as a factor in industrial disputes. Alan even suggested that the union had a direct responsibility to explain its action to the wives.

Well, if the men's out for silly things, and women steps in, then — well, good luck to them. If it's genuine, perhaps the union could explain to the wives. Perhaps it's too far-fetched to say unions don't explain enough to wives. If wives could be brought in a bit more. It's very difficult for wives and families at home. If it covers women they should be brought in. If I went home and said, 'I'm on strike,' and my wife said, 'What for?' and I said, 'Mind your own business,' she's be very worried. It *is* her business, in a way.

And while Gladys had rather traditional views on the role of women (in the home) she had actually worked outside it nearly all her life. She handled the household finances and had strong views on financial independence and the importance of what she did outside as well as inside the home.

Housework is just as hard, and it's hard doing domestic work outside. I'm getting fed up. It makes me evil to think that factory workers get more than us. At home I got my housekeeping, electric and gas, and TV. TV is my only pleasure, because I don't go out. If only I had a few pounds in my purse to go through the week. It's important to have money of your own. I think, if only I could go to a factory and earn good money, then Alan wouldn't do so much overtime. But I can't because of my ears.

Whereas Alan saw women as an important part of established processes, including unions, Gladys saw them as an unfulfilled potential force which could be 'the biggest power anyone can have', and *if* it did exist it would be qualitatively different.

> If women were in charge [laughs] it would be a lot different. I'd be
> soft-hearted. It might do some good — not take money from people.
> I'd give it all away, especially to children. It'd be fairer.

But there was no means of knowing how these vague formulations would
operate in practice, as she had no experience of women 'sticking together'.

An incipient bonus back pay dispute interested both of them. It was
Alan who had discovered the discrepancy but Gladys who was angry about
it.

> They only found out about the bonus through Alan. He brought it up.
> He's a steward, you see. He brought the scheme home. He said, 'They're
> catching us somewhere' — but he couldn't work it out. Then they found
> it, and the managers didn't know what to do — it's over twelve months.
> I say the men should make a clean break and come out. When a firm
> does that — robbing the men every week — these firms should be made
> to pay every penny. They gets their profits without robbing the men.
> Definitely I'd support it — when they robbed my husband. I'm very hot
> on my wages, I checks all me money up.

Exploitation was tolerable to her only if it was kept within strict bounds.
The moment an action was seen to go beyond this conventional Plimsoll
line it slipped suddenly from being 'the way things are' to being totally
and damningly wrong, as over the high salaries of some directors.

> £40,000, eh? Oh, isn't that wicked? Oh, that shouldn't be allowed. Oh,
> my God — no wonder they got disputes in factories. It don't make
> sense to me.

Of course the problem — which, as it happens, is well illustrated by these
two — was that the boundary came in different places for different people.
Why should £40,000 a year have been merely 'quite a lot' to Alan and
'wicked' to Gladys?

Alan had only been a SOGAT steward for about six months, although
active unionism was in the family. His father had been a keen member of
the AEWU, had never 'brought it home' or talked about it — as Alan was
not doing with his sons.

> My father was a blacksmith at the smelting plant. He was a strong union
> man — AEUW — but very quiet at home about it. He kept it separate. I
> do the same. I keep work at work. It's not fair on the wife. She doesn't
> repeat what happens to her. My boy is twelve and beginning to take an
> interest — but not in the union. The other boy asked about the job, but
> not about the union. Like other young men he's not interested till it

happens to them. My father always used to say there was no such thing as the union. The union should do nothing for you because you *are* the union — the members.

His convictions about 'not taking it home' had meant that he hadn't even told Gladys when he was made a steward.

The wife hadn't said a lot about it. She knew from someone outside who told her. There are meetings in the factory and chapel meetings once a quarter, but I always used to go before. But I don't bring anything home. She may say, 'It doesn't look as if you worked today,' and I say, 'No, I was sat in the office all day, or over the union,' but it's very rare.

Unlike wives such as Betty Turner and Ann Davies, Gladys *was* interested and quite prepared to be supportive.

I like him being a steward. He's doing a good job for the men. The union should get something done in a dispute — if it's worth it. The men are paying for it — out of their money. They get paid to do work for members, they shouldn't just sit back. SOGAT is very good, done a lot down there. When there was the dispute before, Alan's union got the rise for them. But when the trouble was on, Alan got his proper money every week — never got stopped like the other union. When Alan was telling me, I thought SOGAT was right. If it had done good they'd have gone out as well. So I said — that's it, they must be right.

Gladys had always been in a union and was currently in T&G. She knew exactly what she wanted of them *and* that she didn't get it. That she blamed on the male-dominated nature of unions. It left her a discontented, but still quite militant, member of a badly organised sector.

I don't know if women should be in unions. I suppose men expect women to come out with them. You do get unions who won't help you. We haven't got a proper steward at the moment. There's trouble at the home because we can't work the tools. There's a man steward. In some places like Wills's they do take up women's issues — but with domestics they don't seem to bother. We don't get told about new schemes, etc., until they're out. Unions should be for men, because they do more for the men.

Alan, like Steve Gray, had had the negative experience of not participating in the TWU dispute, although he had not been a steward at the time and consequently felt even less involved.

Last summer? At the time it didn't concern me — till it hit — then it threatened our jobs. It was a bit silly. They were always recognised. Maybe they were trying to prove a point. But they've got their rights [to strike]. The facts weren't known but I should say no. We shouldn't have gone out with them. If management had threatened them with a cut in pay, then yes, SOGAT should back them. But I didn't really get to the bottom of it. It shouldn't involve the whole factory. I never really knew. One moment they were here and the next day they were gone.

In fact, in the last resort, Alan was doubtful about the value of unions at all.

I shouldn't say it, but no, I don't think there is a need for unions. A better system would be a works council — men on the shop floor — maybe picked by management, maybe by the shop floor. They could be taught — it could be done quicker. Unions are too powerful. Works council representatives shouldn't have the same power. Who gave the TUC 25 million votes? I didn't. I never gave them a vote. They've never been round here. Unions should have no rights based on that.

Gladys was in no doubt. 'Unions are a good thing. There wouldn't be a chance for workers without them. They'd be forced back to work — either by troops or by the police.' So, as far as she could, Gladys held a much more consistently militant position than Alan — and while she could not practise it herself she was ready to support anyone who did. In other words, when she did see some possibility of action to redress what she saw as wrong she became instantly more coherent and consistent. She had an idea of conflict and a determined approach that left Alan sounding negative and weak. It was the opposite situation to that of the Turners and the Davieses. In all three cases the men were influenced by their wives but Alan, unlike Tommy and Hugh, was not fortified against the traditional conservatism of the women by a countervailing involvement in an active union. Instead *his* union was a conservative influence, and Gladys had not the institutional backing for her incipient radicalism to contend with it. Her sole connection with a tradition that was opposed to the hegemony — the labour movement — was through Alan. She neither wanted nor felt able to assert her views over his steady retreatism. The difficulties of the Hutchingses in developing a coherent ideology stemmed, in part at least, from a piece of miscasting. Where the forceful, militant partner is the wife and the husband is quiescent it cuts both off from the only support and experience that might be available to them in trade union activity. Alan may have been expressing a deeper truth than he realised when he called for the unions 'to talk to the wives more'. In this case, if Gladys had had direct access to some other source it might have helped both of them to develop a more positive response to a world that continually threatened to engulf them.

Sean and Mavis Gray: imprisoned radicals

It would be hard to present either Mavis or Steve as physically attractive. At thirty-eight Steve was a tall, lugubrious, gangly man who seemed much older. With his dark, greasy hair, centre parting and bad teeth he looked the standard spiv from an Ealing comedy. He was, as Mavis said, 'very quiet'. He was shy but anxious to be helpful. Before he spoke, he thought carefully, and it was clearly hard work for him.

Mavis, a year older, was also tall and had lank dark hair. Her everyday appearance conceded little to fashion: elderly 'separates' and laddered tights did her well enough. Although slightly deaf, she was the more fluent of the two.

They lived on Southmead estate, another early post-war planning disaster. They had four children (aged between two and thirteen) and had actually moved from a larger house because they couldn't afford the rent. As a result they were very cramped for space, which may have contributed to a high rate of childhood illnesses — bronchitis, chickenpox, mumps, etc.

Neither had been brought up in 'standard' families. Mavis's father died when she was four months old, and she was fostered, having no further contact with her own mother. She had a close relationship with her forster sister, who had recently moved to the United States, and she still saw her foster mother occasionally.

Steve 'never had' a father. His mother had one other child, a boy ten years older, and she had a hard struggle to keep them.

> I was unfortunate I never had a father when I was small. I never had much money — pocket money or presents. All I can remember is my mother going out to work to clothe and feed us.

As a result of their own childhoods both set considerable store by giving their children a better start than they had had.

> I try to make them a bit better if I can. Everyone tries to give their children a little better than they had.

Even so, Steve's aspirations for his children's careers were not high.

> My eldest son will get the same sort of job as I have. I'd like him to
> come to Hampers if he'd want to. I'd never force any of mine. I said
> I'll never do that.

Mavis, who in any case was more of a worrier, was concerned only that he
got a job at all.

> I often worry about the future. I wonder whether he [Rob] is going to
> get a job, and if he didn't, how it would affect him. I was told if he
> didn't get a job he'd have to go in the army — it's the only thing he
> could do. It's no good having a son around the house all day.

These responses (on a subject that both of them raised of their own
accord) illustrated a characteristic difference between them. While Mavis
worried constantly about everyday things like prices, schools, housing and
so on, and had the details at her fingertips, Steve declared that he was not
a worrier and lived for the present, but at the same time he restricted and
lowered his ideas of what was attainable. Both of them, in fact, were
imbued with a deep fatalism about the problems of the age.

The mainspring of their lives was their home and children, but these
created an immediate dilemma. Steve expressed the 'family man's' predicament when he said,

> Getting married was the turning point in my life — and when we had
> the family. The family is more important than work. But they go side
> by side. I can't stay home and see my family all the time if I haven't got
> no money.

So he worked a hard three-shift rota, and at least three four-hour lots of
overtime a week as well. Meanwhile, at home, Mavis accepted all that she
had to do.

> I think of it as a job that's got to be done ... when you're married you've
> got to do these things,

but she chafed against it.

> I hope to go back [to work] when the kids are older. I *would* like to.
> Once they're off my hands I'd like to go out to work. It gives you an
> interest. When you're home it gets very monotonous.

What Mavis and Steve were talking about was not an individual problem
that could be cured by some device such as 'role swopping' (even if Mavis
could earn anything like what Steve brought home) but the contradiction
that results from a capitalist-imposed sexual division of labour. The rigid

separation of, but symbiotic relationship between, the spheres of home and work forces incomplete and alienated lives on men and women alike. In this respect their fatalism was well grounded.

Their social life, such as it was, was also separated. The last time they went out together was

> last Christmas to the firm's dance. It's very rare we go out. We went to the cinema just after Christmas and took all the family.

Steve sometimes played skittles with the firm's team and was quite content, but Mavis was more sociable. 'I like company, I like to talk.' She relied on her women neighbours.

> Carol, the girl on the left, I get on very well with. Sometimes she comes in two or three times a week, sometimes only once.

> Jessica, who lives at No. 46, I go down the shops with her every night.

She accepted that her social life had to be confined to the daytime because of Steve's shifts, which meant that for two weeks out of three *neither* of them could go out in the evening. Mavis merely said,

> I've got kind of used to it now. I don't like night work, because it's awkward keeping the little ones quiet in the dinner hour when they come in ... I'm all right with him going out of the house [at night] because I've got the children, and you can always knock on people's doors if you need to.

The sexual division of labour was a conventional one. Schools, shopping, clinics, etc., were clearly in Mavis's province, and Steve refused to be drawn into discussion of this area. 'The wife will be able to tell better than me.' Bringing home the pay packet was his business. Mavis had worked at Hampers until she had her first child, but she still refused to discuss what Steve's work was like in any but the most general terms. She found her work at home far from satisfying.

> You're doing the same old thing every day. You get up, you do breakfast, wash up, and all that sort of thing. You don't meet many people when you're home, and it gets very monotonous, I think. I don't mind doing it, but if you go out it gives you an interest.

So, not surprisingly, she looked forward to the day when she could get back into the labour market.

> It's not *hard* work. It's not the same as going out to work. It's more

interesting going out to work — you meet different people, and you get a chance to change at work. I enjoyed going out to work.

So for her, it was the isolation and privacy, rather than the actual work, that she disliked.

On behalf of her family Mavis was also a fighter. If she detected injustice or a falling short of her entitlements she was not slow to act. She had, for instance, 'had a couple of rows up there' at the children's junior school.

Then Linda was on the coach, and one child screamed, and Linda was sitting by her and *she* was stopped going swimming *and* she was called a liar, so I goes round. I said to the teacher about why Linda was stopped; but not so much that, but why she was called a liar, because *I* don't call my children liars. He said, 'I asked Linda who was screaming and she said she didn't know, and she was sat next door.' And I said, 'Did it ever occur to you that she didn't want to split on this girl?' So he said she should have said, and we had a bit of a barny, like. And I said, 'OK, it's finished.'

Unlike Ann Davies or Gladys Hutchings, she would have preferred collective action to these individual campaigns. She felt a helpless frustration and fury about a whole range of issues.

We pay rates, and a couple of weeks ago the corporation refused to take the ashbins away unless we put them down on the road. I think it's disgusting. We pay rates but what do we pay for? People saw we can do anything, but there's not enough backing, like. It's the same about everything. People say individually — you say to your friend — 'What a shame we can't do anything about it.' But there's not the people behind you. Nobody says anything. Because in this country we're a quiet sort of people. It's the same going on buses — we don't say anything.

This explanation, based on a national psychology like Alan Hutchings's, did not satisfy her. Her experience in a trade union had pointed the way.

Women take more notice than me — it's a shame you couldn't get more people together. When you're at work it's different. You've got so much backing there. But housewives — who've they got with them? There's no one, really. You're on your own. If you could meet somewhere I think it would be a lot better, myself ... There should be a hall where everyone could meet. We never hear anything. The only snag is I'm home all day, with the children coming into tea and all that, and Steve on shifts — so you can't go to meetings. There's only one week to do anything (when he's on six till two), that's not enough if you had to go anywhere, and Steve can't, so you can't go to meetings ... There are no petitions I know of. I couldn't do anything about rents, anyway, because we're buying. I'd *like* to — for other people, but you couldn't ... But the ashbins are terrible for old people. It's terrible. It's not so bad for me.

So Mavis saw life in a capitalist society as a continual affront to her sense of justice; and she saw well enough that, at least for her, the locus of discontent and therefore of action was the 'community'. Yet, as she rightly pointed out, there were not even the most rudimentary means, e.g. places to meet and access to information, by which such a 'community' could express itself. What slight hopes there were were dashed by the devastating effects of the privatisation of domestic labour combined with shift working for the wage labourers. Nor was she going to get much help from Steve, who with a fundamentally similar analysis, and as much ground for anger, simply retreated behind the sexual division of labour.

I have heard of people who have gone to them [local councillors]. Whether they does enough for people I wouldn't like to say. Basically it's all run nationally, so it doesn't matter ... The bigger firms have a lot to say. It's not a good thing — and nothing can be done. This stems from people with money. If you've got money you can do most anything, you can't change anything locally — but the wife is more affected by shops and things.

Steve had been a steward ever since SOGAT first came into Hampers. 'Someone invited me in. I'm getting used to it now.' His account of the events leading up to SOGAT's introduction gives a good indication of his ideas and the care with which he came to his decisions.

It was mostly the three-shift workers who wanted to change. I didn't think what they [TWU] did was fair — because management wanted the corrugator to work three shifts, so they had all the factory over in the canteen to vote for two or three machines to go on three shifts. They said, 'If you vote for it, we'll give you a week's holiday.' Well, they had boys and women there. It weren't going to affect them, and they just wanted a week's holiday. Then management began talking about Continental shifts, and they [the men on the three-shift machines] thought they'd be sold down the river to do that as well — so we got SOGAT in.

For him the main job of a union was to fight management on behalf of the workers — not to be used by management to control them. And he saw his role as steward in the same light. 'If they can't handle it, they come to me and I go up to management.' He was well respected among the men he represented. As Arthur Rees said,

> He *will* have things put right. He won't mess around. He's straight on. He keeps his head, he don't just fly up and a lot of shouting and nothing come of it.

Although his everyday conduct as a steward was not so different from that of Tommy Turner or Hugh Davies, the underlying ideology was much more oppositional. He was a firm adherent of union solidarity, and supported the miners' strike.

> They deserve all they can get ... Heath only wanted a confrontation, only trying to get people's back up against the unions ... You see, I'm in a union, so I think they should get all they can.

In fact he was one of the few who saw a connection between different union struggles. 'The miners' victory would help others. It would get leverage to negotiate outside Phase Three. I'd like to think it would.' At the same time there were limits.

> We've got to try to help each other, and union solidarity is pretty good in this country, but sometimes it gets out of hand. I don't agree with that, for example when lorries were trying to get past [a picket line] and they were throwing things at them.

But when the TWU had initiated its dispute the year before, Steve had opposed them. As he explained it:

> TWU put in for a rise in June. Our wage claims are national. Every year we have a ballot for it. It goes through — throughout the country — and we abide by it. Our agreement ended on September 1st, so we couldn't press our case back to June. TWU had put in the June before for a rise — but this year they didn't want to wait fifteen months, i.e. till September.

It was, by the letter of the law, a watertight case — but what about union solidarity? He saw it purely as a duel between management and the TWU — with the odds on management.

> A lot of TWU members were moaning at their own union ... management weren't giving in. They let the foremen down a lot.

And when 'TWU said you ought to stand by us' he simply said, 'I thought we had a strong case: we should stick by the agreement he signed.' It was only later that he had had second thoughts:

> Management gave in in the end and paid everyone — our union as well. It did cross my mind that if we'd went in with them first of all we could have got it earlier, like.

Meanwhile what did Mavis have to say about the industrial situation, from which she drew her inspiration and of which she had had first-hand experience? She had rosy memories of Hampers:

> I was at Hampers, on the bottom floor — stitching. I loved it. I had to leave because I had Robert, otherwise I'd be there still. The money wasn't too bad — better than the pottery — at that time it *was* good money. I used to go up to Mr Milsom and get it sorted out all right. I always liked it there.

There was no mention of a union. As always, she 'sorted it out' by herself. She never seemed to have used the 'backing' that she later found so lacking in other contexts. Nor did she take much interest in Steve's union activity.

> He doesn't say a lot about being a steward. It doesn't make much difference to us. It's a bit more important, like. Men come to him and ask his advice. He feels more of a person — that's nice, really.

The failure to take up trade union attitudes appeared to reflect the real division in her world. Trade union politics did not have, and never had had, much relevance to her situation. What she wanted was an organisation like the unions, but in the community, that *would* be relevant. Over the dispute, Steve says he did tell her. 'I was telling her what happened. It was in the newspaper and I was saying "Well, they haven't got that right".' Was she interested? 'Well, yes, she was listening, like.' He didn't seem to have made a very good job of it. Mavis said:

> I didn't know a lot. Yes, he had to go to meetings. I said, 'How's it getting on?' and he said, 'Oh, they're on about this.' I said, 'What if they go on strike?' Steve's very calm, not a worrying kind. If we go on strike we do — being a union man, he has to. We'd have put up with it. But they gave in to them. I'd have been worried if they'd gone on strike for long. No one likes their husband to be on strike.

This concern with money — the essential link between her world and Steve's — came out more clearly when she talked about shift work. She could stand the inconvenient hours, and didn't think it harmed Steve's health. It made her task harder.

> I go up the wall. Steve says, once he's asleep he's asleep. But it's me. I feel I have to keep on [at the children] all the time, and it do worry me.

But it was the reason she gave for shift work that was significant.

> You get more money. You've got to look at that point. If you're going to get more money you've got to do these things.

Although Steve earned it, money was in *her* sphere. For the same reason, she was much more critical of the wage structure and hierarchy at Hampers than of any other aspect.

> Yes, they could pay more. They have a fair wage at the moment, but we're going to have to have more money or we can't manage. This is why all the trouble starts. The firms keep rising and rising the prices and then there's trouble in the factories because the men get so unsettled.

So that Mavis, despite a less sophisticated *analysis*, had arrived at a more militant position than Steve. In fact it was possible that Steve's lack of actual militancy stemmed at least partly from his detachment about his pay packet.

> I never worry about money. It's different for a woman – but I tell my wife not to worry. If we haven't got enough this week, that's it. Everybody, when they're married, worries a bit about money, and it's different now we've got our mortgage – we've got to watch it. But money affects the wife more.

In fact, far from a mortgage tying him down and making it harder for him to take industrial action, it was the first sign that he might be sufficiently 'worried' to precipitate himself into open militancy.

Money – or, rather, rapidly increasing prices – was central to Mavis's concerns.

> It's terrible, what's going on. Everything you pick up is 3p more than last week. I said to my husband that I'd worked out that biscuits had gone up from 6p to 11p in a year. One week I goes to Gateway and it's 5½p for peas. In one week it's up to 8½p. This is what annoys me – *everything's* going up. This shop had got a big notice – eggs 20p. They think they're giving you the world, but it's still high, really. And they're imported eggs – not like proper eggs ... My husband says we should only buy what we need. But I *do* only buy what we need. Like, I say we haven't touched a banana for months – they're over 10p to 11p a

pound. Even an egg's a luxury now to a lot of people. If they put the prices up, people with plenty of money stock up — fill their freezers — so when it goes up they're better off, because they can afford to do it in the beginning. The government doesn't understand ordinary people — and doesn't care.

At the time Labour was in power. 'It's much the same. You get poor people — same as before. There are still plenty of rich people.' But Mavis still loyally upheld Labour.

Labour government seems to be fairer.

I don't know a lot about politics but I felt they were more for the working people.

The only trouble is, once the Conservatives have got in it's an awful job for Labour to sort out what they've done because they can't just do it, can they? They get in a rut and they think, 'What can we do about it?' — if you think what they've got to sort out.

Again this, union action offers an inspiring example of *effective* action. Like Steve, she supported the miners' strike.

You can't blame the miners wanting more for their job. They should get it. Someone's got to give in, and I don't think it'll be the miners. They come out in '72. They've come out in '74. If they take what's offered they'll have to come out again in two years. It's the only way they can get anything done. I think it will be terrible if they *do* come out, mind — all the country will be in a worse state, but it's the only way they can get anything done.

Steve's analysis was based on similar conceptions of power and inequality. The fundamental difference between them was that, while Mavis's ideas were rooted in the Labourism of trade union ideology, she had also tried to take account of the real problems she faced in her experience of the world outside work: but Steve *remained* rooted in his (albeit well developed) trade union ideology. When occasionally he did extend his ideas beyond the familiar grooves he soon found contradictions that he was unable to deal with. Mavis went on questioning, if without much hope of finding a solution, but Steve had refused to take up the quest outside the limited arena of the workplace, and there the experience of *opposing* his opposite numbers in the TWU in their dispute had vitiated his radicalism. So, while his analysis did logically point towards confrontation, it was both the 'out-of-handness' and the translation of the economic war into the political arena that frightened him when he talked of the workers 'doing something drastic'.

> The present government is trying to cut wages down but they're not doing anything about prices ... They *could* stop the prices going up. It goes back to what we were saying about this management. Everyone's after more profit in every firm. One time or another the workers are bound to get fed up and do something drastic. I hope it never gets to that state, but sooner or later, if it carries on like this, it will.

He had a view of the world that was based on his experience of the inherited ideology of trade unions. But because he could not apply trade union ideas *direct* to political problems he ignored them or gave up in despair – 'Nothing can be done'. This was certainly exacerbated by his discouraging glimpse of trade union ideas in action at Hampers. Mavis, on the other hand, had a harder, clearer view of the world. For her there was no massive disjuncture between the two spheres. Nor had she been deterred from thinking about major issues and making connections. Even though she claimed, 'I don't know about politics,' she had a good idea of what was going on. Her problem was to find a target to attack, and a platform to fight from. Her realistic conclusion that, without solidarity, the working class could do nothing led her to a personal fatalism. Angry and alert, she could only launch individual tirades at the outriders of capitalism – small shopkeepers and teachers.

Her isolation deprived her of the same means of taking concerted action, but it had also deprived her of a general ideology that would enable her to form an overall analysis. Her thinking, therefore, was concrete and specific, but there was no way of linking her awareness to a political strategy.

In many ways Steve and Mavis made a good pair. 'He's very quiet, Steve is' – but thoughtful, and in contact with potentially useful ideas derived from his union allegiances. His failure to arrive at a radical position was at least partly due to the separation between his world and Mavis's. For Mavis could have provided the anger, the motivation and the drive for action had either of them been able to make the vital connections. As it was, their insights and experience served only to depress them, and imbue them with feelings of personal and political helplessness.

Notes

1   I have had no space to include here details of Ann's many protracted battles with the Housing Department, the Children's Officers, the schools and sundry other officials. Some are included in Chapter 5. She fought vigorously and often successfully on behalf of her family, but always on an individual basis. She was certainly the most militant of the four, and it is interesting to speculate what would have happened had she been in Tommy's position.

2   The notion of 'problem families' is used frequently and loosely in some social policy writing and within the social worker 'trades'. Sir Keith Joseph gave the term 'cycle of deprivation' a certain notoriety in his speech in Parliament in 1972. Whether used in concern or in derogation, these terms have the effect of distancing the user from the object. 'Problem families' are not people like the speaker. It enables teachers, welfare officers and so on to treat problems as symptoms rather than as difficulties within a particular situation. This process is, by its nature, incomprehensible to the recipients. Keith Joseph elaborated his position in K. Joseph (1974), p. 6, and there has been much subsequent discussion. See M. Rutter and N. Madge (1976).

3   There were real problems in dealing with the material the Hutchings gave me. Writing in this way about their ideas implicitly assumes that they did cohere in some way. It is difficult, therefore, to convey that incoherence itself can be a defence against an incoherent world. It also has to be admitted that some people are better at 'thinking' in academic terms than others. Gladys was not aware that she often contradicted herself, and even if it were pointed out to her she would continue simply to assert certain statement in certain contexts. But it has never been proved that the conventional academic stress on order, rationality, consistency and logic is necessarily the best way to deal with *all* the varieties of human experience. Gladys's interpretations are not invalid because they are not academic; but an academic response to them may be.

FOUR

MEN'S WORLD: WORK AT THE FACTORY

In Chapter 2 we discussed the impact of one event in the lives of some of the people concerned. The strike occurred within the men's world of work, and that was crucial in understanding the different responses of the men and the women. Now I want to explore some other aspects of the men's work experience. For it is not 'divorced' from the rest of their lives. Family responses to men's work, and the mediation of their experience to their wives, point to one set of contradictions that these men, like most others, had to work through, or live with.

Industrial studies abound which are couched in the perspective of the 'sociology of work', 'industrial sociology' or in the framework of a Marxist analysis. What all these studies have in common is an axiomatic acceptance of the separation of the productive process, without taking account of its implications. There is a relationship, albeit contradictory, between industrial work (and the consciousness it engenders) and workers' experiences of the rest of the world. There is also a relationship between the individual alienated worker and his family. This crucial link is frequently discussed within the context of the debate over the place of women's work in the reproduction of labour power, and especially in the context of the family wage.[1] The theoretical nature of the link is still under discussion, and how it was experienced in practice by these people may throw another light on the problem.

Working at Hampers

The work at Hampers was not very different from other industrial processes that have been amply described elsewhere.[2] The work was overwhelmingly semi-skilled, routine and monotonous. The vast majority of men worked a shift system — double day or three shifts. The pay was not good. It was a medium-sized company, and despite its recent expansion and absorption into a larger industrial complex it retained something of the character of a 'family firm'. It was also local — both in the sense of being long established and in the sense of being geographically near by. While its safety record was not good, the work was not especially dangerous. It certainly did not give rise to the kind of horrors associated with, say, coal mining.

It is a truism that the main reason why men worked at Hampers was the wage. There was certainly little intrinsic satisfaction. Faced with the non-choice, to work or to starve, Hampers was just one place where people 'chose' to work. Yet there *was* an element of choice. At the time, 1973–74, before unemployment became a major factor, they need not have taken a job in a factory, or in this particular factory. They could, for instance, have travelled to Severnside and bagged fertiliser for double the pay.

The reasons they gave varied according to their previous experience and their range of comparisons with other jobs, but mostly it varied according to their personal priorities — and these had to do with aspects of their lives away from work, mainly family considerations.

Here, for instance, is Arthur Rees, who left his job on the railways with considerable reluctance because it was

> ... a single man's job. It was poor money for the work we was doing ... There was the threat of redundancy, and we had to travel all over the country ... With prices rising I was only taking home £17 for permanent nights ... Here it don't compare with the railway — nothing ever will. Just the two of you on the footplate. You're your own boss. It's outside. It's a bit of a drag being inside. But that's what you got to do to get the money.

Some, like Michael Lee, left a skilled job as fitter or electrician to come to Hampers, either because the money was better or for the security. Some, like Don Grimshaw, who had worked in a number of unskilled jobs, or had been in particularly insecure ones — like the building trade — came because they were 'getting on', had a family and so needed a steady, reliable income. 'I was getting on: it was a steady job.' A few, on the other hand, like Alan Hutchings, had gone somewhere else for 'the money' (in his case the smelting plant) and then 'I came back to Hampers when I could afford it with the kids growing up'. Some had come quite deliberately for the extra money that could be earned on shifts and overtime. Others came in spite of that. Some came because it was handy, 'It's near home, I got fed up cycling to work.' Money *was* the single most important factor, but the men still struck some kind of balance between less money, on the one hand, and security, safer or pleasanter working conditions, convenience, or regular hours, on the other; or more money against boring work, shifts or less attractive working conditions. They all had families to support. It was the period in their lives when their financial commitments were likely to be at their greatest. Yet even under these conditions they had not abdicated altogether. They had refused to become totally enslaved to the wage. Instead, they had reserved the right to take other considerations into account and to come up with — if they could — a viable compromise.

So where men work, how much, and why, is indirectly affected by their family responsibilities. Yet the wives had rarely taken it upon themselves deliberately to influence their husband's choice of job. Their initial reaction was to stand back, to emphasise his autonomy and, with it, the separation of their two worlds. A few admitted that they had 'discussed' it together before their husband took his present job, although clearly it was 'his' decision. After all, as most of them said, he had to do the work. One (Jenny Steele) even said, 'If he wants a dangerous job he'll take it. That's up to him.' Later discussion revealed that there were some aspects of the men's work that were seen to affect the wives directly — such as pay, shift work and, to some extent, safety and security — and some that were not, such as supervision, working conditions and trade union organisation. Not surprisingly, the women had much more to say about the former than the latter. But they were inhibited about talking about *any* aspect of their husband's job because it was part of the 'man's' world, and therefore *not* of theirs.

But let us return to the work the men did and how they experienced it. As far as the actual jobs went, they had low expectations of the intrinsic reward, nor were they much surprised by it. 'It's monotonous, but you get used to it. There *are* no really better jobs' (*Hugh Davies*).

They assumed that the work would be boring, mentally deadening and physically hard. They stressed that, for them at least, any other job would be much the same and, in a sense, the less they thought about it the better. 'The worst part is coming in' (*Keith Thomas*). Some, like workers everywhere, clung to their 'dream' job. 'I'd prefer to be a TV engineer — out on the road — doing something useful' (*John Pollard*). 'I'd like selling or bookmaking. I nearly did it once, but I didn't want to chuck this job away' (*Paul Dixon*). But, on the whole, they stayed where they were, tied by lack of 'qualifications' and the overwhelming need to earn a regular wage. In fact, one of the noticeable features of this work force was its length of service. One man in the sample had worked at Hampers for thirty-four years, and the most recent recruit in the sample had been there five years. The average was just over twelve years.[3] In fact, what distinguished the work force was the *lack* of other work experience on which they could base comparisons.

For most of the men — and the women also stressed this point — the best thing about working at Hampers was what they called 'the atmosphere'. As Nigel Martin put it, 'it's *who* you're working with, more than what', and most men made reference to the workmates they liked. 'The blokes are fine' (*Fred Fletcher*); 'It's a good atmosphere, but by the end of the day minor irritations get you down' (*John Pollard*). It depended, by implication, on there being some opportunity to get to know and like other workers *at* work, which is by no means an automatic correlate of factory work.

The Hampers work force was not a militant one. Until 1973 there had been no industrial action that any of them could remember. Nor did they appear to resent supervision or management as much as, for instance, the workers down the road at Chemco did.[4]

Of course there was minor sabotage; there was satisfaction when an unpopular foreman or supervisor or even a manager got into a mess; they skived when they could — especially during the night shift. No one, in fact, was as committed to making cardboard boxes they were to making their dining-room partitions. They knew why they were there.

> They try to make us believe the common aim is to work for Hampers. I come here to earn enough money. I'm not interested in them. It's convenient. How can you expect a man on the factory floor to say, 'Be careful of that board?' He'd as soon kick it under the tubs.
>
> *Simon Steele*

Nevertheless they did work, and hard. Some of the irritants of Chemco might be muted at Hampers, but both sets of workers suffered the general degradation involved in selling their labour power and of losing control over themselves and the output, in circumstances where, as unskilled manual workers, they were 'pushed' to produce the maximum quantity.

As we have said, they endured it for the sake of the wage. In most work-based studies we never follow the wage out of the factory gate. This is important precisely because men do 'live' beyond the factory gates. They don't need money at work (except a few bob in the canteen): they need it at home, where they live. In fact the resilience of workers in enduring what they did at work, however degrading and however much they disliked it, depended on the realisation that the money they earned *there* enabled them to *live* elsewhere. They had invested other areas of their lives, notably their homes and families, with the meaning that explained and exonerated them from what they did at work. Wives at home were not threatened — at a conscious level — with the degradation of labour. They did see their husbands return white and drawn when they were on 'nights' (of which more anon) but it didn't diminish them in their eyes. Quite the contrary — bringing home the wage packet was one of the principal definitions of 'manhood' — and it was worth putting up with a lot to retain that badge. Like all workers, the men were trapped not just at the point of production but within capitalist society. Capitalist relations of production do not end at the factory gates — however much Hampers' workers wished they did. They penetrate every area of life and determine the lives of those members of the working class, such as the wives, who are not selling their labour power, quite as much as those who are.

The workplace and the wives

Wives rarely bothered to ask about work. None of the aspects of their husbands' jobs we have just mentioned was their immediate concern. Working conditions and management alike were simply part of what the men had to endure to bring home a pay packet. Their comments conveyed a massive indifference to the whole procedure (including the crucial issue of the men's resistance to the degrading nature of their work). 'He's a fool to stick it all these years' (*Ann Davies*). 'Ted's work? Goodness knows. I don't know, I've never been inside' (*Mandy Ferguson*). 'Well, he's never come home and said he's fed up, so he must be satisfied' (*Betty Turner*). Even more than the men, they expected the work to be boring and they emphasised this aspect. Many (contrary to the conventional assumptions about women liking repetitive work) said they couldn't stick the boredom themselves. Other than these few comments they soon passed on to matters of more immediate interest. Few had any idea about foremen or management, and fell back blandly on the local reputation. 'Hampers is a good firm' (*Ann Davies*); 'They were good during the floods — that's the only bit I know about' (*Betty Turner*).

But, as we have already indicated, there were aspects of their husband's work that they did feel qualified to talk about. These were most notably pay, shifts and overtime, which daily and directly affected home life, and safety, redundancy and promotion, which *could* affect it.

The wage packet

Pay, or rather the money in the pay packet, is, of course, the crux of the whole matter. Not only, as Marx pointed out, is the cash nexus the only bond between capital and labour but it is also the only direct contact between the family and the workplace. Assuming that the families were basically dependent on the husband's wage, they had to live on what he brought home. There were, naturally, differences in financial management, and there were differences in size of family and financial commitments (e.g. to a car, or a mortgage). Even so, there were limitations on how a family could live on Hampers' wages, and clearly they were not going to be living in architect-designed five-bedroom houses with a double garage and swimming pool. In fact, on the basic pay of £27·50 a man could not support a wife and two children in a council flat. Even with bonus it was not easy. All the men and both unions wanted bonus amalgamated with the basic pay, so that the regular, dependable weekly wage could be higher. Hourly-paid unskilled workers are highly vulnerable to fluctuations in their wage — illness, industrial disputes or simply lower production can make drastic inroads on what they take home. The ambition of all the families was to be able to live within what they could reasonably rely on. Overtime and other 'perks' could then be treated as pleasant extras. Aware of their vulnerability (and that their wages would not increase with age), these families opted for security. Time and again they expressed their disquiet at having to rely on something as precarious as overtime or bonus in order to live.

I do three lots of four hours [overtime]. I hate it, but it's the money. You should be able to earn a decent living wage — to get everything you need through a week — not luxurious, but rent, food and everything else that's necessary for a family. If you want a luxury, *then* do over-time.
John Pollard

He's got to put in a certain amount of overtime. I don't mind a certain amount, but it's bad when he *has* to do it.
Val Fennel

You shouldn't have to depend on overtime. You should get a good flat rate, and that's it. With bonus, you don't know where you are.
Cath Grimshaw

The pay's not bad — but he does a lot of overtime to get good money. It's wrong a man should have to work so hard for a living wage. We're only average. What people who're below average are like I don't know.
Mary Fletcher

While all the men and women in the sample expected that an unskilled workers in a capitalist economy their rewards would be barely adequate to their needs, there were considerable differences of opinion over whether the Hampers wage was adequate. They made reference to previous jobs which had paid better, or worse, or to neighbours or relatives who earned more, or less. 'Pay could be better. I resent the difference with the printers' (*Hugh Davies*). 'It's not too bad. We manage, we all moan' (*Tommy Turner*). 'This is classic, isn't it? If I was taking home £100 a week it wouldn't be enough' (*Keith Thomas*). 'My boy earns £100 on the buildings' (*Alan Hutchings*). 'If it wasn't for the bonus you wouldn't have anyone working here at all' (*Barry Young*). In other words, as Runciman (1966) has pointed out, comparisons were made with comparable jobs. They did not compare their wages to those of their manager (which they rarely knew), but they did compare it to those of car workers or printers, which they resented.

Opinions, and strengths of opinion, about the wages were more or less evenly divided between men and women, stewards and rank and file — with the proviso that the stewards, especially TWU stewards — had more details at their fingertips. What it did not relate to, surprisingly, was the material needs of the family as judged by quite crude criteria such as the number of children. For example, John and Sue Pollard, with one child, reckoned it was poor money and John did a large amount of overtime to compensate. They lived in a council flat and had no car. The Davieses were quite content, had eight children — five still dependent on them — were buying their house (at high interest rates because of Hugh's age), ran a car and did no overtime. The fact is that judgements about money were related more to expectations than to material circumstances. Hampers (if you included bonus and overtime) paid pretty near the average manual wage. Some people were prepared to accept it and some were not.

Working shifts and overtime

The key issues of shifts and overtime (that is, the time cost of the job) affected the wives almost as materially as their husbands. In many cases to do (or not to do) it had been a joint decision,

> We gave up. His stomach was bad and I was in a state.   *Jane Smith*

> I volunteered. It's a bit unnatural to sleep in the day. I talked about it with the wife, and she agreed.   *Steve Gray*

By and large, shift work was an evil that had to be endured.

> I don't like it, but I've always done it, for the money.   *Tommy Turner*

> I did shifts for three or four years to pay for the house. No one would do three shifts if they didn't need the money.   *Jim Smith*

> It's not good for any man to work three shifts — but the Continental system's worse.   *Keith Thomas*

I have to. I don't want to.   *Bert Hannam*

Among other problems were those of organising a household around irregular hours.

On six-to-two he goes to bed at nine o'clock because he's dead tired and gets up at four o'clock. On nights, everyone's tired. There's no one to call on when Nick isn't home.   *Felicity Skinner*

Many of the women mentioned the difficulty of keeping small children quiet while a man on night shift was asleep during the day.

I don't like night work because of keeping the children quiet. But if you're going to get money you've got to do these things.   *Mavis Gray*

Virtually everyone said that shift work interfered with their social life — as it obviously did. When you take into consideration things that are out of the question for shift-working families — like regular attendance at evening class, Labour Party ward meetings and PTA committee meetings, events which they rarely even considered — the effect of shift working seems even dramatic. Many people — especially the women — described the well known physiological side effects:[5] disturbed digestion, tiredness, irritability, etc.

I don't like two-to-ten and I don't really like nights. I'm not afraid, but to see a man on Wednesday or Thursday who's been on nights — well, it makes you feel strong about it. A man shouldn't have to work hours like that. Meals at different times. His stomach starts getting upset. His face goes white come Wednesday or Thursday. At holiday time it's drastic. It doesn't affect me, but the children won't see their father till tomorrow morning, and then only for two minutes. It's bad.

Jean Martin

However, there were compensations if you could endure it. While the 2 p.m.–10 p.m. shift was universally loathed, the 6 a.m.–2 p.m. was quite liked. Not only did the men get to see more of their children, and were able to help with the chores, but they could also get down to a proper, solid job of DIY or the like. On that shift, they felt, most of the day was their own. They had, for one week in two or three, won their day back from the factory.

Shifts make a difference. Jim notices the prices. But a man working eight to five won't, because he'll never see them.   *Jane Smith*

It upsets social life — and meals ... it shouldn't be a choice between shift work and money. It should be a real choice, because it agrees with some blokes — shopping and so on.   *John Pollard*

My aim is to spend as little time as possible to earn my living, and this is the way I can do it. It upsets the digestion, I can tell you that.

Mike Lee

I prefer three shifts. If I want to paper the house I can get it done now ... and I can take more part with kiddies and shopping and that.

Arthur Rees

By and large, men did not do shift work because they wanted to. The disadvantages far outweighed the advantages. They did it for the money (though this only applied to three-shift workers, and then only on nights) or because there was no choice. The prevailing attitude, especially of the women, was resignation. It had to be done, so their husbands did it, and they lived with the consequences.

I don't like shift work, especially two to ten. The nights seem very long stuck on your own. Nothing on telly. The day's never going to end. Six to two he's home soon.

Cath Grimshaw

Shift work's the worst part. But then, I wouldn't be able to get a job if he wasn't on shifts. (They do turn about.)

June Hannam

I get used to it. I'm not too keen on it. It's a good thing from the children's point of view, because he's home in the afternoon. When the children were very small I found it very tiring, because I was on the go the whole time. But it's good for the family.

Ros Neale

The common availability of overtime was often cited as an advantage. Exactly half the men did overtime — though it ranged from 'sometimes on Saturdays' to two men who did twenty hours a week every week. The balance between time and money was often a fine one. Some couples had laid down a basic necessary amount and the husband had to do — say — four hours' overtime a week to reach it. Such men (and their wives) particularly resented it, stressing the fundamental principle that a man and his family should be able to live on his basic wage. Part of this attitude stemmed from resistance to the idea that the employer owned all their time. While they accepted the sale of eight hours a day, the battle was fiercer at the boundaries.

For other couples the chance to get in a lot of overtime and consequently earn a lot of money was a big attraction. Of course, if you can choose, then you can regulate it. You can do a little extra for holidays or new furniture. In fact one of the chief resentments stirred up by the strike was that it *prevented* men doing overtime.

How safe is your job?
Redundancy was a nightmare vision.

> It would be awful, but what can you do?   *Jane Smith*

> Oh, my God, touch wood, he won't. If there's no work, there's no pay.
> *Diane Dixon*

Most people cited security as the main reason for joining Hampers, which was profitable enough to make redundancy seem a remote possibility. Those who had already experienced being made redundant were fairly confident about their ability to get another job.[6] The wives were less optimistic, but slightly more fatalistic. Few questioned that the firm had the right to make men redundant, even though some laid the responsibility for relocation on management.

> Management has the right, if work isn't available.   *Nick Skinner*

> It's one of those things you got to accept.   *Jane Smith*

> You've got to look at a lot of things — level of profits, ways of economising — but management should be responsible for finding other jobs.   *Max Fennel*

Hugh Davies felt more strongly:

> A man shouldn't just be cast outside the door because the firm doesn't want him.

It was the men who justified it in terms of the logic of capitalism, not the women.

One issue that people hardly ever raised of their own accord was that of safety. Hampers was not a 'dangerous' place to work. Nevertheless, machines have sharp edges and accidents did happen. A large number of men had had severe cuts or lost fingers (one nearly got blinded), or had suffered strained backs. In addition there were the long-term injuries to backs, and chest infections from the dust. Yet the wives seemed totally unconcerned about this aspect of their husbands' job. As far as they knew it was 'all right', and anyway that was his concern.

> They slip up sometimes.   *Jane Smith*

> You hear of accidents, minor ones. It's the tools — cuts, mostly.
> *Val Fennel*

> Pretty good, according to what he says.   *Cath Grimshaw*

> Safety? I've no idea. I'd bother if he was in a dangerous job.
>
> *Sue Pollard*

But when something did happen they changed their minds:

> It's not good. I feel quite evil because he slipped on some oil and slipped a disc and was home eight weeks. It's the second time he's done it. One man landed in Winford. Nigel put in a suggestion, and the manager screwed it up and put it in the bin.   *Jean Martin*

> I don't know they're very good. They tell you the things they should do, but they don't make sure you do. They're supposed to wear protective shoes — but Martin doesn't. He did try — but they hurt his feet. Things like that. Martin lost his finger in an accident at work. Lots of printers have lost fingers and arms.   *Ros Neale*

The men, on the other hand, particularly the stewards, were far were conscious of it as an issue. In the wake of Robens, unions were just beginning to realise the size of the arena as a legitimate union concern. There was an official safety committee, but it was considered a farce. Several men who had thought the issue through came to the inevitable conclusion that there was a fundamental conflict between profit and safety.[7] These same men were torn between their conviction that management *should* be responsible and their realisation that the unions would have to take a hand if safety was to be taken seriously.

While stewards were often involved in fighting compensation cases, and so were well informed about the detail and scale of accidents, the rank and file had a more casual approach.

> You take chances. But you have to. I don't worry. If you worried about it you wouldn't do nothing. You'd never do your job.   *Hugh Davies*

> The safety rules are not applied. Most people know the rules but the foreman doesn't push them.   *John Pollard*

> It's bad. Maybe they just forget. I don't know. If we just stopped work it would get done.   *Paul Dixon*

> There's things let slide — but then we do it ourselves.   *Arthur Rees*

> My truck's lethal because it's gas-driven and I'm always going on about slowing it down — but if you do you lose the object of getting loads as fast as you can.   *Barry Young*

Taking the white coat

'Promotion' meant being made a foreman — possibly a supervisor. The hierarchical ladder that is such an integral part of the professions and of management did not exist for these men, and they knew it. A few still clung to the Henry Ford myth (never as strong in England as in America) and proclaimed that anything was possible — though not for them. So what we are talking about here was the possibility of being given a little more pay, a little more status, a lot more responsibility and the metamorphosis from 'worker' to 'management'. For many that put it out of court. The white coat had too many disadvantages and not many compensations. It would alienate them from their workmates and lose them that 'atmosphere' which was the only thing that made work bearable.

You can't run with the hare and hunt with the hounds.   *Max Fennel*

I don't want it — I'd lose all my friends and worry. It's not worth it.
Paul Dixon

I know I'd be bound to change and go over to their way. You're just someone to be handed down to and you're at the bottom.
Bert Hannam

You've got to change, got to defer to management. You say you wouldn't but you would.   *Don Grimshaw*

Once you start wearing a nylon coat you're part of management.
Nick Skinner

About a third of the men would have welcomed the chance of promotion had it been offered to them, either because they didn't care about being cut off from their mates or because they believed they could still go on being 'workers', because real 'management' started higher up:

I'd like it, or I wouldn't have put my name down. It wouldn't change me. You've got to identify with management to a certain extent, but a foreman's not as wrapped up in management's points of view, like profit — that doesn't concern foremen so much. Not till you get higher. His job is to run his department to the best of his ability.   *Steve Gray*

The women, on the other hand, had no very strong feelings about their husband's promotion. They realised that it would not make much difference to them, certainly not in terms of the money that came home, and they were not much exercised by the dilemmas and contradictions of promotion. One woman, Ros Neale, a foreman's wife, did see it as a conflict. She had been surprised, and rather alarmed, by the change in

Martin since his promotion, and deeply regretted the severing of their social bonds with old work mates.

> I was surprised, because he's very — he's always been a union man — always sticks to the rules. Perhaps they respect him for it, or perhaps they think he's better on the other side. I was very pleased for him. He sticks to his principles. There was a lot of bad feeling when he was made up. He said it didn't bother him, but all the men he'd been friends with turned against him. There's one who never comes round now. He [Martin] wouldn't allow it, anyway. He says you can't socialise.

Some of the women realised that their husbands wouldn't welcome promotion, but most thought, vaguely, that it would be nice. Some went further and viewed it as a kind of tribute to their husband's work. These women were apt to be angry that their husbands had not been promoted even if, as was the case with Hugh Davies, he had refused it.

> I don't understand why he hasn't got it. I'd have liked it.   *Ann Davies*

> It wouldn't suit Max. If he was going to enjoy it it wouldn't affect me, but he wouldn't enjoy it. He's all for the workers.   *Val Fennel*

> I'd be pleased, but I haven't really thought about it.   *Diana Dixon*

> No. He wouldn't like promotion. I don't think *I'd* like it. *Jackie Young*

So the women had simply not concerned themselves enough to think about either promotion or safety. This was in spite of the fact that in theory it *could* affect them as much as pay or overtime did. Yet they *did* express ideas about other issues that seem, at first sight, to be more remote — such as profits or managers' salaries. But before we turn to these more general industrial questions let us look at some of the issues raised by the men's own workplace organisation.

The trade union bulwark

One-third of the men in this study were shop stewards in either the TWU or SOGAT. In order to act effectively as stewards, they had to accept the workings of at least one capitalist institution — the firm that employed them.

The achievements of both unions at Hampers had been considerable, at the ideological and at the material levels. Any of the union leaders could recall details of clever and fierce campaigns fought and won over such issues as safety, bonus and overtime. The stewards, as leaders, were an active element in the factory, with a separate identity, distinguishable from their own rank and file and from management. They were also the only organised defence the workers at Hampers had against the pressures of management.

It is worth noticing here the generally more critical stance on industrial and political issues taken by the rank and file compared with the stewards. This is no accident. After all, the stewards were men who voluntarily spent their off-duty hours doing things connected with work. The heart of the 'negativism' already referred to is simply the desire to get out and leave the factory behind till the next shift starts. So what were the stewards doing? We have already seen that they were not challenging capitalism, merely negotiating with it. It is not people who bang their heads against the system in frustration who become stewards. If you get too angry you look for other means or 'turn your hands upwards in despair in an age which advances progressively backwards'.[8] Stewards were men who, partly through temperament and partly because of historical tradition, believed that tradition offered a means of doing something, albeit of a limited nature. Their tragedy was, perhaps, that they had come to believe that the limited means was the solution.

In the discussion of all this, and indeed about the role of unions in general, there were quite clear differences between stewards and rank-and-file workers and between SOGAT and TWU members.

But the discussion was effectively limited to the *men* in the study. The women were happy to comment on general issues, and on specific points (such as pay) about their husband's jobs, but unions fell quite clearly and emphatically outside the category of what concerned them. They had all had jobs and some experience of pay and conditions. Few had belonged to a union at all, and only three or four had been members of an active union branch. It was only when they did have direct union experience — and not even then — that they would discuss the issues in detail. In fact, until the strike impinged on at least some of them, they were fully prepared to dismiss the whole area of union activity as irrelevant, and indeed alien.

The last point — and it was relevant to some of the men and all the women — is that the less you invest in work, the less you are likely to regard the unions as an effective point of action. The women's sheer indifference did not indicate political unawareness, but arose because they simply didn't care much what happened at work (neither did many of the men). The centre of their lives was elsewhere. Becoming involved in work and in the union meant that, in a sense, you lost your immunity, your ability to detach yourself from the system.

These men and women, then, had worked out their responses to and interpretations of the work situation, including the unions. When the dispute broke out, involving all the people in this study in different ways, it forced many of them to rethink their ideas and confront issues they had ignored. We have already seen some of the implications in Chapter 2.

What's it all for? Some general issues

Making fibreboard is not a glamorous business; nor is it the cutting edge of advanced technology, like chemicals or micro-electronics. If anything, it is the trailing edge of industrial production. Despite management's techno-logical jargon the men knew they were producing an outmoded product. Soon cardboard boxes would be replaced by cheaper (if ecologically disastrous) plastic containers. The machines they used were substantially the same as those in use fifty years ago.

So why make boxes at all? To make a profit, of course. The 'firm', that is, the directors and shareholders of Hampers, sold the boxes to other 'firms' (often in the same combine) for more than it cost to make them — including the cost of the men's wages. These calculations were carried out by 'top management' far from the shop floor, and by the 'top manage-ment' of other firms. 'Top managers' received high salaries for making these calculations — and for performing other 'functions of capital'. In addition the shareholders, directors (and managers in so far as they hold shares) received a share of the profits in the form of dividends and in-creased share values. The men were a part of the production process. If they could be dispensed with, they would be, and just as soon as they cease to contribute to the profit-making process they will be — just like any machines that became uneconomic. In fact machines were shortly to replace them. 'If you keep buying new machines, then unfortunate people will be out of work' (*Nick Skinner*).

All this may seem a laughably crude and biased introduction to socialism. But it is in exactly these terms that the men and women in the study — few of whom would claim to be socialists — saw the process of which they were a part and on which they depended. But their inter-pretation of, and response to, it did not follow the 'logical' socialist line. They came to terms with it in their own way, gleaned from a number of sources, but certainly not guided and informed by any coherent socialist ideology. They understood the forces at work — only too well — but they either found reason to approve of them or apathetically accepted them. A socialist response, by contrast, would require an alternative, so that the process could be questioned *and* challenged.

When they discussed topics such as profits or managers' salaries the women were drawn to respond as much as the men. Some men, especially the TWU stewards, knew a lot more factual detail about Hampers as a firm — but that did not necessarily lead them to take the same position on the same issues in a general industrial context. The women, clearly, knew less, but when they were provided with the information their response was much more likely to be applied to *all* other firms. Thus, because they were less caught up in the workplace, it was easier for them to formulate general views.

This was also the juncture when the material difference between groups of *men* — between the unions, and between stewards and rank and file at work — began to affect their views and point to some connections between experience and consciousness.

Making a profit

Few had any doubt that the firm existed to make a profit, and that this took precedence over every other consideration. The issues became clearest when they were seen in opposition to their own pay demands, or to 'conditions', such as safety or air conditioning. Equally, there was little question about which side managers were on and what their principal concern was.

> They care about the welfare of the men, about making sure they've always got a bit of money in their pockets — but it's a lot of crocodile tears. Until it comes into conflict with profit, and then it's a different story.   *Keith Thomas, TWU steward*

> There's lots of things they *could* do — like putting in air conditioning ... this air conditioning matters to me because of skin trouble. But they wouldn't accept it — they just want more money.
>   *Don Grimshaw, TWU production worker*

> No, they care about production. They care if you're still stood up at the end of the day, I think. You know, they don't want to see you carried out, but they seem more concerned — well — 'Get that out of the door' rather than 'Well, we'd better stop that machine and put that on in case you catch your hand in it.'
>   *John Pollard, TWU production worker*

> The ultimate aim of this firm is how much goes across the weighbridge. What happens to the stuff coming in the back door is incidental. It doesn't matter. It's a terrible thing.   *Michael Lee, SOGAT worker*

It is interesting how many of these comments — basically about profit — unmask the conflict with safety and welfare. In *this* context there were no illusions. Simon Steele (SOGAT steward) summed it up:

> At the end of the day it's how much work you've done, not how you've done it. There's always a line drawn between them and us. They try to make us believe the common aim is to work for Hampers. I come here to earn enough money. I'm not interested in them. It's convenient, that's all.

The unacceptable face of capitalism unmasked. Yet there is more to be said.

The men they called 'managers' were *middle* managers. They never saw *top* management — even of Hampers, never mind of the giant consortium that owned it. They recognised that these middle managers were also caught in a trap, that they were as vulnerable and dispensable as workers.[9] For some men this justified their actions.

> They're just worried about what the next man will think. They're insecure. They may not be able to get another job.
>
> *Dick Griffiths, TWU worker*

> We're just numbers. They deal with profits. That's their job. If it drops, they'll be out of a job.   *Don Grimshaw, TWU worker*

The women did not doubt that profit was the dominating concern, either. The difference between them and their husband lay in the context in which they noticed it. The dilemma of safety versus profit did not concern them — though perhaps it should have done — nor did the quality of management. They produced vague versions of their husbands' comments:

> Provided their [the managers'] pay packet's OK they're not going to worry about the shop floor. The only time they really worry is if *they're* in trouble.   *Jane Smith, wife of one of the most acquiescent husbands*

> If a worker has an accident someone can replace him.   *Gladys Hutchings*

> As long as they're turning for the machines all day. They try and kid the men they're doing the best for them, but all they're concerned with is their profits.   *Jo Lee*

> Management today is all profit. They'd get better results if they weren't like that. In smaller concerns where management *does* care.   *Val Fennel*

The 'small is beautiful' theme crops up again and again in the women's comments. To some extent it paralleled the older men's nostalgia for the small, personal units of the past, but it was stronger than that and reflected the fact that women, when they could, chose to work in small units, as also their hostility to unions — especially *large* unions. There was a kind of tired cynicism in their responses. It was noticeable that there was no difference in kind or strength of response between the different groups of wives.

Once past this apathy, the women were quicker to fasten on to the aspect that mattered to them, i.e. how it translated into inequality of money. Profit meant that they *could* pay the workers more, and, as Ann Davies said, 'Just more money — how much easier that would be.' They made direct comparisons with other firms, especially other firms in the same group. 'They should pay the same.'

> The firm could afford more — they're part of [the combine], and they make a bomb. Why shouldn't the workers get some?   *Mary Fletcher*

> If you look at [the group's] profits and then at the money your husband earns it makes you wonder.   *Jean Martin*

> It's not as high. They could afford more. They get plenty out of their profits.   *Jane Smith*

It was in this context, rather than in that of their husband's job, that they showed unanimous opposition to the principle of overtime. Men should not have to work overtime and they had no doubt that there were enough profits to pay them so they wouldn't have to. This meant that they laid claim to part of the profits their husbands created to improve the quality of their lives.

> He's got to work overtime and he shouldn't have to ... they definitely could afford to pay more, with all the profits they make there.
> *Mandy Ferguson*

> But it's not good unless you put in loads of overtime. I don't like overtime, and the firm could afford to pay more. The union are working on that now.   *Sharon Thomas*

> You could see the profits in the papers. It's a good amount and it doesn't go back to the men.   *Janet Griffiths*

> He does a lot of overtime to get good money. It's wrong a man should have to work so hard for a living wage ...   *Mary Fletcher*

The men rarely connected the question of overtime with that of profits. For the women the picture was quite different. They were not so concerned with the details of pay negotiations. What they were concerned with was the evident contradiction between their men having to work overtime to live and the size of the firm's profits. The implicit attitude was put explicitly by Janet Griffiths:

> It's not right. If they get over a certain amount [of profit] it should go back into the firm for a pay rise for the men.

And, in a toned-down version, by Gladys Hutchings:

> The workers made the profit. They'd be happy if the bosses gave them just a little extra.

And it was where the crunch came for Mavis Gray:

> They could pay more ... we're going to have to have more money or we couldn't manage. This is why all the trouble starts — because of the money.

The wages might, or might not, be good in themselves, but with one exception the women did not question that they *could* have been better. The snag was that no one knew exactly what Hampers' profits were. They were not published. They only knew what the group's profits were (published in shiny annual reports). Some of the men could work out figures based on the cost per box, the number of boxes per shift, the labour charge, etc.[10] This calculation was not open to the women, but they didn't care about details like that: they just *knew* the profits were big enough to have given them a substantial rise.

Despite their access to more information, the men were much more cautious. Some were not sure that the profits *were* high enough.

> I wouldn't like to say if management could afford more. If we were informed ... we ought to know. Why won't they tell us?
>
> *Vincent Flanagan, SOGAT steward*

> They could afford more. The dafty things you see built — money wasted, like the crazy-paving out the back. That could have been all flat. They built a lovely wall by the railway track, and then where we stick the trailers it's all loose shale, and you get all the dust in the summer and all the mud in the winter. Then if you go and ask for a 50p rise they just look down their noses at you ... Profit? No idea. I wouldn't like to guess.   *Barry Young, SOGAT production worker*

Some were cynical about the published figures. 'They said they'd publish profits, but when they do it's a lot of rubbish because they play fast and loose with the figures.' The stewards — especially TWU ones — had more idea of what the real dimensions of profit were. The point is that although the men were much better equipped with detailed information, they did not in fact make the clear *a priori* connection between wages and profits that their wives did.

The high rewards of capitalism

This whole concept of financial inequality in the capitalist system was symbolised by the high salaries of directors.[11] As might be expected, there was a clear division between the comments of the men and of the women — although there were also divisions between the men. What was raised here — albeit *sotto voce* — was the rationality of the whole capitalist system. If they protested, it is therefore interesting to note the grounds on which they did so. Neither the men nor the women — even the best informed men — had any idea of the size of really high salaries among chairman of the largest companies in the country. If they were told, the men took it more coolly, though the information sometimes rocked even well entrenched acquiescence.

That's not fair, because it's a team, the money should come back to the shop floor.
Max Fennel, TWU steward

No, *I* could sit at a bleeding desk all day writing. Do you think that's worth £40,000?
Ted Ferguson, TWU steward

They're not worth that — the more money you get, the less you do.
Paul Dixon, TWU production worker

No one's worth that money. It's not shared out fair enough. But it's like everything, isn't it? All the foods going up, but they're still making the same amount, or more, profit.
Nigel Martin, SOGAT production worker

Most of the men who reacted like this were rank-and-file workers, and usually in SOGAT, although there were two TWU stewards. But the majority accepted large salaries paid to top directors.

He's got a responsibility — he's got to be on twenty-four hours a day. It could make his health suffer.
Jim Smith, TWU shop steward

(This from a man whose health suffered so much on shiftwork that he had to be moved to form making when he was not yet fifty years old.)

It's not just prestige. You've got to work as well.
Don Grimshaw, TWU production worker

The men who held these views included a high proportion of TWU stewards. If they could accept this, then they were not going to have much trouble accepting shareholders, and for a good reason. But first let us see how their wives reacted.

> It's a difficult job. If they really worked hard they'd deserve it.
> *Betty Turner; husband, TWU shop steward*

> I wish I was getting it. Do they get much so they don't turn corrupt?
> *Jean Martin; husband, SOGAT production worker*

These were the *only* two women even remotely in favour of such high salaries. Others began by saying, 'Well, there's the responsibility,' but then soon negated it. The reactions of the rest ranged from cynicism through reasoned opposition to outrage.

> They can't be worth that much. That's where it comes — the rich and the poor. I expect the man on the shop floor works as hard as the manager. Obviously he's got the brains, but it's not what you know, but who.
> *Jane Smith; husband, TWU steward*

> It's the man that's actually doing the job should be paid a good wage, because they actually produce it and send it out. You say 'the top man' but I know in my place all he's doing all day is walking around, and at his say anything can happen — and yet he's not actually working on the floor with us, so he don't really know what it's all about.
> *Sharon Thomas; husband, TWU steward*

> When you think about it, they can't do any more work in a year than John does. He's got to work his guts out to try to get money to come home with, all they're doing is sit there. Fair enough, they're making important decisions, but they're still not doing very much.
> *Sue Pollard; husband, TWU production worker*

> I suppose so. (Pause.) That's £1,000 per *week*. No, they're definitely not worth that.   *June Hannam; husband, TWU production worker*

> Oh, isn't that *wicked*. It don't make sense to me.
> *Gladys Hutchings; husband, SOGAT steward*

Felicity Skinner, perhaps, should have the last word. 'They don't do anything to earn it. I don't believe in royalty, either. The money could be put to better use.'

In this instance both men and women had been presented with a straight fact — 'Some chairmen of large companies like ICI earn as much as £40,000. What do you think?'[12] — and this enabled the women to break through their initial feeling that it was none of their business. The quotations above show what they could do in terms of locating a *new* fact in their existing ideology. They also point to the nature of the ideology. It appeared to owe little *directly* to the working-class ideologies of trade unionism or labourism. But whatever its roots, it had enabled the women to come to a conclusion about an issue many of them had not previously considered, and their conclusion had, at the least, a class potential of some vitality.

Where did this vitality go when they considered one of the pivots of the system — shareholders? The men were divided in their views. Many — notably TWU stewards, but also others who 'knew about it' simply wished them well and would have liked to join in.

> Everyone should have a chance to invest — you'd work harder.
> *Paul Dixon, TWU production worker*

> Good luck to them.   *Hugh Davies, TWU steward*

> I don't know much. All I want is to win the football. I'd sit back then.
> *Ted Ferguson, TWU steward*

> Without their money the firm would pack up.
> *Tommy Turner, TWU steward*

> Best of luck. I'd do the same if I could.   *Keith Thomas, TWU steward*

They were basically adherents of the system. With their other attitudes — to managers' salaries and to the running of the firm — they gave the impression of knowing, in detail, what they were talking about and accepting the rules. They were not fools, nor did they intend to lose out, but when they fought it would be within the constraints of the system. They coincided, very largely, with the active union men. Not all, of course, accepted shareholders as natural and right — those who didn't were mainly SOGAT stewards.

> I don't quite agree with shareholders. Some profit should go back to workers who earn it.   *Steve Gray, SOGAT steward*

The women were on weaker ground. They knew little about 'shareholders' — sometimes they had not even heard of them. They were not encouraged to know, either by their husbands or by the prevailing culture. Hence they tended to comment palely and without enthusiasm.

> They're just ordinary people who've had a windfall. It's all right. It's like a bank.   *Cath Grimshaw; husband, TWU production worker*

> It's OK in a small firm. It's their money — they put it in.
> *Sharon Thomas; husband, TWU steward*

These comments show a strong contrast with their views of chairmen's salaries, where they were *given* the information. It illustrates the disability that sheer lack of information can be in the development of ideology.

Those women who did venture an adverse opinion were immediately overcome with helplessness.

> It don't seem fair. But then, what can you do, one person's views aren't going to alter it.
>
> *Jane Smith*

> Married women working — they're not concerned with things like that.
>
> *Val Fennel*

> I get so confused with all this kind of thing.
>
> *Sue Pollard*

The two most articulate summed up the women's position on this, and on their overall response to industrial capitalism.

> Some are making a lot of money without working for it. *Some* of them have saved money and invested it. Fair enough — but to make big fortunes out of it is a bit ... Still, I suppose it's the name of the game.
>
> *Claire Rees*

> I suppose you've got to have shareholders. They're usually moneyed people, because if you haven't got the money you can't become a shareholder, and they just sit back and wait for their profits to come in. Well, everyone *should* be equal. No one should have more than me, and I shouldn't have more than anyone else. So I don't really think it is right.
>
> (Is that possible?)
>
> Not really, not in this country. It's a pity, though. I mean, if the workers owned the factories they went to work in, there wouldn't be no strikes. They'd be happy to go in and work for themselves. But of course, you need money to buy shares, and if you haven't got money you've got to go and work for someone else.
>
> *Jean Martin*

Overall, it would seem fair to say that neither the men nor their wives liked the system under which they supported their families by working at Hampers eight hours a day, fifty weeks a year. They didn't like it in detail — shifts, conditions, pay, redundancy, management. It was not as bad as some jobs, but no one would choose to do it if they didn't have to. There were, as we have seen, differences in response between the different groups of men, but more striking were the differences between what the men said and what their wives said.

What unites those — the majority — who took exception to all or any of the aspects of capitalism that confronted them was their helplessness. Time and again — over redundancy or over shareholders — they resorted either to the inherent logic of the system or to straight fatalism. 'I don't think you can win, really.' 'They won't give you more.' 'The workers have got to lose.' 'It's just mad.' Both these kinds of response were open to the men, but women, because of their lack of information, had only the option of fatalism.

Faced with a system they dislike, women can distance themselves, can retreat into their own world. That their world was no less affected by the inexorable capitalist process is, for the moment, irrelevant. The point is, firstly, that they did express a more cogent and complete rejection — not so much of the details of the job, about which they didn't care, but of the 'rational' basis of capitalism; and, secondly, that because they could do nothing they retreated.

Some of the men also took this option: but for them there were two countervailing factors. One was that they had more detailed knowledge, and this, of itself, seemed to draw them into accepting the underlying logic of the system. If you are told often enough that you must be made redundant should the firm cease to make a profit, then you may accept it: if you face it once — when your husband comes home with his pay-off — the madness of it prevails. The second factor was that, provided you accepted the underlying rules, there was a format in which a *limited* challenge could be raised over *specific* issues. This is the trade union response, which the women, at least partly because of their exclusion, rejected.

In this chapter we have looked at 'men's work' in the factory from the perspective of the other world. We have seen how men take account of their homes and families in their working lives. The decisions they take and their response to work only make sense in the context of that other world — at home. Yet it has also been clear that women's exclusion from the workplace inhibits their discussion of it, even though they are clearly and closely affected by what their husbands do at work. It is also clear that the women's response had a clarity and a coherence that was not simply the result of negative exclusion. It was based on their positive identity, which was rooted in their world of work at home. It is to this sphere that we now turn.

Notes

1 See H. Land (1980), M. Barrett (1980), V. Beechey (1977).
2 E.g. H. Beynon (1974), M. Harastzi (1977), G. Palm (1977); R. Blauner (1964), T. Lupton (1963).

3 Length of service did not necessarily relate to age. Men in their twenties who had been there since they left school at fifteen had over twelve years' experience. Other, older men may have 'been about' and joined Hampers only recently. Breakdown of length of service by union: TWU stewards, 15·5; TWU workers, 11·0; SOGAT stewards, 12·5; SOGAT workers, 8·5; foremen, 12·0. Note that SOGAT workers had been at Hampers for a much shorter time, on average — and also that all stewards had longer service than their rank-and-file members.
4 Some useful comparisons can be drawn between Hampers and Chemco (Nichols, 1974, 1975; Nichols and Beynon, 1977; Nichols and Armstrong, 1976), which was a few miles outside the town.
5 See P. Kinnersley (1973).
6 In 1974, with virtually full employment, at least in Bristol, this supposition was quite realistic.
7 For a discussion of this point see T. Nichols (1975).
8 T. S. Eliot (1936).
9 The vulnerability of middle management is discussed in Nichols and Beynon (1977), chapter 3.
10 'They get £10 on every 1,000 *reject* boxes. Compare that with the Football Gate money — and that's only once a week' (*Paul Dixon*). 'We've got this particular "octobin" worth £3, and it costs only a few shillings to make. They paste the value of spoiled boards on the notice board so you get a good idea' (*Dick Griffiths*).
11 I could not discover what the salary of the chairman of Hampers was. At the time (1974) chairmen of companies the size of the parent firm were acknowledging salaries of £40,000. See *Labour Research* for periodic details.
12 As a methodological aside, this was the *only* occasion on which I provided the people I was talking to with any specific information.

FIVE

WOMEN'S WORLD: WORK AT HOME

The subject of our enquiry is the mediation and interaction of the worlds of men and women, which is both caused by and negotiated through the sexual division of labour. In the last chapter we looked at some of the effects on both husbands and wives of women's separation from the primary wage-earning arena. In this chapter I want to take up the other side of that separation — the aspects of women's experience which are allocated to them by the primary sexual division of labour. Here, again, I am interested in how men as well as women interpret what goes on in 'the women's sphere'.

The working class is characterised by its fracture into 'sections'. R. Hyman (1975, p. 178) has asserted that 'the immediate context of the world of work is necessarily sectional'. It is not, however, necessarily divisive. The achievement of capitalist ideology has been to ensure that 'sectionalism' is the bane of united class action. In this form the problem has exercised many students of class consciousness and class action. It is also generally recognised that *sexual* divisions characterise our society, but the connection between the two ideas has received much less attention. Here I want to develop the idea that working-class women constitute a 'section' of the working class; that their identification of themselves as women can be construed as a sectional ideology, and that it *can* have, but need not *necessarily* have, the divisive effects usually associated with sectionalism.

There is a sense, then, in which I am taking the experience of being a woman in a society dominated by sexist ideology as a particular 'case' of the mediation of experience and ideology.

Just as the strike at Hampers was an example of a *particular* experience, and Chapter 2 made clear the crucial divisions in consciousness that resulted from different experiences of the same series of events, what I want to suggest now is that the experience of being a woman and of doing 'women's work' is also a specific experience with effects on the constitution of consciousness, and needs to be explored as such. Women are not a class, but their specific experience as women has certain consequences for their *class* consciousness.

Doing women's work

Sexist ideology has laid down what constitutes women's work in the home, and none of the couples in the sample was in any doubt about what kind of activity that meant. The differences came (between the couples) over the allocation of particular tasks and responsibilities, and (within couples) over their response to these arrangements.

Designating an activity 'women's work' does not necessarily mean that it is reserved for women, any more than the fact that husbands were regarded as the 'breadwinners' prevented the wives from taking paid jobs. The sexual division of labour does not rest on sealed compartments of activity for each sex; it rests on the *responsibility* for the recognisable categories of, on the one hand, 'breadwinner' and on the other 'women's work'. There is no breakdown in the division of labour if a husband does the washing-up or even cooks his own supper. Conversely, even if a housewife *doesn't* do the washing up, she is still defined as having primary responsibility in that area.[1] The task is essentially to maintain, service and take care of the home, husband and children: in short to ensure the reproduction of labour power at day-to-day and generational levels.

'Women's work' fell into three main areas. The first was housework proper. The women all had husbands in regular employment, so they were not 'poor', but they had to manage on average or below-average money (depending on the size of the family). All had children. The houses or flats they lived in were adequate, but not spacious. Merely to contain the detritus of everyday living was hard work. They had the basic necessities for keeping the place clean, e.g. running water and electricity, but by no means all had vacuum cleaners or washing machines.

A second area of responsibility was feeding the family; shopping and cooking. Most of them, especially the ones who lived at Hartcliffe, were badly off for shopping facilities. Few had access to a car. They also had to cope with the complication of timing meals to suit the different schedules of children and husband, i.e. school times and shift times. Some tried to set a common meal; others just kept a running cafeteria. The day-to-day budgeting and shopping were the most direct connection with the capitalist cycle, via prices at the point of consumption.

The other main area of 'women's work' was the more diffuse but no less onerous one of psychologically and materially sustaining the children and, to a lesser extent, their husband. It encompassed a wide range of responsibilities: keeping the household running through the daily round of unfixed but inexorable chores,[2] looking after babies and pre-school children all day (and night), 'being home with the tea ready' when they were older, and for the husband after his shift, holding at least acquiescent views on the husbands' industrial action ... All these things meant subordinating their own needs and identity to those of the other members of the family.

At this point we can identify two aspects of the women's work that made it different from the work their husbands did at Hampers. An important feature of even the most boring hourly paid job is that it comes to an end. After the shift, or at five, the men can leave, and by coming home distance themselves from it. But a woman's work is always round her, except, possibly, when she goes out to a paid job. The other aspect is the social definition of it as relatively unimportant. Whereas the man's self-sacrifice, for the pay packet, is universally regarded as laudable, the woman's may be ignored or assumed as part of her 'nature'.[3] The fact that she is sacrificing herself to 'significant others' reinforces the loss of her *own* significance. As we shall see, the conventional disregard of 'women's work' does not wholly tally with how the people in this study saw it.

Conventional priorities would rate these tasks — housework proper, maintenance, renewal and sustenance — in ascending order of importance. Indeed, it was clear from other things they said that the care of the children *was* presumed to be the most important of the wives' activities. Yet 'women's work' meant, above all, housework.

> When you're looking after children, and trying to cope with your 'work', you can't do an outside job as well.   *Jane Smith*

> It's nursery helped me — you can get on with your 'work' better, can't you? You can't leave it, and you haven't time to sit and play.
>   *Felicity Skinner*

And discussion of whether it was a 'hard job' usually focused on aspects of *cleaning* — the physical demands it made, the boredom and repetitious nature of it all.

> When you're doing housework it's nothing — you can do it over and over again.   *Felicity Skinner*

> There's nothing to show for it. It's tedious on your own.   *Jo Lee*

It's so boring – you're stuck home all day.   *Don Grimshaw*

It was also the first objection mentioned to wives getting part-time jobs – their 'work' would suffer. When they said this both husbands and wives had in mind the meals and the children, but the concrete evidence was to be found in the unmade beds.

He wouldn't like to come home and find his bed unmade.   *Jean Martin*

What she does [part-time job] is ample, with the washing and ironing, etc., even when the kids grow up.   *Dick Griffiths*

She hopes to go back, but she realises she's got to keep the place clean and tidy.   *John Pollard*

It's all right provided what goes on in the home doesn't suffer.   *Michael Lee*

Maintenance was experienced mainly as shopping, especially by the women. It was this, rather than the cooking, that was felt to be a problem. It also had some claim to require skill, or at least special knowledge the men were not privy to.

They don't realise the cost of things, shopping – the cost of food. They don't realise what a woman's life is like.   *Cath Grimshaw*

Although cooking itself was not rated highly, providing food of any sort at the right times was a recurrent nightmare.

Now they [the children] come in at dinner and you give them a meal. Then he's on six-to-two, comes home at two – give him a meal; so it goes on. They come home at four and you've got to prepare another; probably he comes home at six and that's another. Seems to be all the time with meals.   *Felicity Skinner*

Renewal and sustenance, as the women saw it, involved two distinct responsibilities. One was to 'be home' when the children were small. The interpretation of this rubric varied widely. It could mean doing a fairly substantial part-time job before the children started school and gradually expanded it to a full-time one as they got older; or it could mean refusing to consider any outside work even when they were grown up because

she wants to be home with a cup of tea when they come in the door, because that's her job, not being out working, which isn't.   *Nigel Martin*

This was the aspect of 'women's work' that was most often mentioned as intrinsically rewarding.

It's a nice job with the children. The kids make it. The washing's hard, but when you see them going to school all nice it's worth it ... and when they say 'Mum, your bread pudding's marvellous.'   *Ann Davies*

The other responsibility was that variously seen as 'backing up' or 'standing by' your husband. Usually it was taken for granted but sometimes caused difficulties, and then it became explicit. During the dispute at Hampers some TWU wives hostile to the strike felt they could not interfere even to the extent of voicing an opinion, much less by opposing their husbands. Mary Fletcher said she didn't know about unions but 'it's just as well, really, or you'd only get into arguments with your husband'. Often the clash between their own feelings and the duty to support their menfolk was most clearly expressed when they talked about the car workers' wives,[4] who had expressed open opposition.

Oh no, it's not up to the wives. Men have got to please themselves.
June Hannam

I sympathise with their position, but they shouldn't shame their men in public.   *Ginny Sykes*

Even if I disagreed, I shouldn't advertise it.   *Mary Fletcher*

Those who did believe in voicing public opposition justified it on the ground that their primary responsibility was to the home.

I don't know — if they were desperate moneywise I'd have been behind them. If the family suffers their wives should have a say.   *Kate Wheeler*

With this brief review of the material reality of the wives' work at home in mind, let us look at some of the ideas the men and women had about different aspects of 'women's work'.

Aspects of women's work

Working around the house

I have pointed out that the lack of social recognition is an important aspect of women's work. At its simplest the argument runs: housework is not paid, therefore it has no value.

When I talked to the men about what their wives did at home, they told me first of all that it was 'hard work'. A lot of them even thought it was 'harder work' than their own. They based their judgement on its boredom and monotony, but particularly on the fact that 'it never stops'.

There's no holiday or rest. The wife was on all day yesterday with

Craig. I went home at ten o'clock and back in here at five, but she went
to bed at twelve and up again at four, and she was on the go all day.
Fred Fletcher

It's easier, but it's never done. She works at night, when I can sit down.
Nick Skinner

Most of them could draw on the experience of being left to cope with the
house and the children when the wife was ill or having another baby, and
it was a situation they were profoundly thankful to escape from.

When she was in hospital and I stayed home it drove me mad, being on
all the time, like.
Bert Hannam

It's far harder than I do in here. On Saturday she stayed in bed and I
worked harder than ever I do in here. It's murder.   *Don Grimshaw*

Several stressed that they couldn't do it themselves.

I don't think I'd like to do it all the time. Maybe that's why they go
to work.
Tommy Turner

At least one thought it could contaminate him.

I'd never do it. You can get conditioned if you don't watch it.
Nigel Martin

But most of the men[5] affirmed very positive evaluations of what their
wives did. Indeed, they stressed its importance, but they did *not* equate it
either with having a job or with their own work. It was simply not comparable: it was of a different order of activity. In fact, to ask them 'Is it *like* a
job?' was such an outlandish suggestion that most of them were hard put to
explain why it was not the same. They usually mentioned the conditions:
'You can do it in your own time' or 'It never stops'. More significantly,
they pointed to its *private* nature — 'You're lonely,' 'You're shut up on
your own all day.' Only one man (Alan Hutchings) mentioned the fact
that it was *unpaid* as a reason for its not being 'a proper job'.

Among the women there was a much less flattering assessment of the
work they did at home. Some liked it, but most didn't.

All women are the same. They get married — high ideals. It's going to
be lovely to wash the socks, cook the meals and all that for their
husbands, but after a few years the novelty wears off. It just becomes a
bit of a drudge. Not so much that you mind doing it, but it's the same
thing, day in, day out, all the time. You get stale yourself. I think —
well, if someone was coming for dinner you'd think, 'Oh, what will we

make for the meal?' and you pull yourself up to do something special —
but if it's just your husband you say, 'Well, sausages and mash, like
yesterday.' They don't appreciate it, anyway. If you put yourself out
they say 'What's this?'   *Jo Lee*

They thought it boring, exhausting, taxing, too much, not enough, complicated, lonely and endless. But on the whole they didn't go into great
detail. They shrugged their shoulders and got on with it. It was merely part
of life — not a very interesting or important part. Whether they liked it or
not was often less relevant than, firstly, whether it conflicted with a greater
desire to go out to work. In that case it was not the activity they objected
to but its *totality*. Secondly, some of them voiced feelings of duty and
obligation that overrode their personal preferences. By marrying and
having children they had denied themselves certain choices.

When you're married you've got to do these things.   *Mavis Gray*

It's my duty. If I didn't want to, I didn't have to get married, did I?
                                                          Jean Martin

In other words, you did it for 'love', whether you 'liked' it or not.
    They knew it was 'hard work', and most of them named a particular
aspect that got them down, but like the men they did not therefore
dignify domestic labour with the status of 'a proper job' (and *a fortiori*
none considered it comparable to work outside the home). It was too
mundane, too taken for granted, but, above all, it could not be called a
job because it was not paid. For the women, in contrast to the men (and
to the dominant ideology), this — not the conditions — was the crucial
difference between household work and a job. They did not even want
to be paid for what they did at home: that would have been to associate
it with the market place, to contaminate it.

Pay? No, it's your own house. It ought to be affection.
                                                       Cath Grimshaw

This is a clear example of the gulf that men and women alike saw between
the two worlds of 'home' and 'work'. Not only were they evidently of a
different order, but they should be *kept* that way. Behind this was the idea
of reserving some area for themselves which would not be degraded as they
perceived the workplace to be.
    Thus the husbands generally had a high regard for what their wives did
at home, but when I asked the women if they thought 'most men reckon
what their wives do at home isn't really work' they nearly all said 'yes'.
Some excepted their own husband but held it to be true of others — an

interesting parallel to the men who said most strikes were wrong but made an exception of their own. What the women seemed to be saying was that even though their husbands acknowledged it to be hard work and appreciated its value, it still did not have the stamp of approval as 'a proper job'. In a society where all relations are reduced to the cash nexus, value is simply not valid unless a monetary price can be put on it. That, at least was what many of the women felt, and as we shall see they were not just reporting a subjective phenomenon. Their reactions provided evidence of sturdy resistance to the dominant ideology, whether it was held by their own husbands or not, and a demand for more recognition of what they did.

> Men just go to work and come home and get paid, but a woman has to run a house and organise this and that.   *Diane Dixon*

> Sometimes old Don will come home and say, 'You don't know what work is.' They don't realise the cost of things shopping, the cost of food. They don't realise what a woman's life is like.   *Cath Grimshaw*

> Men don't realise till they have to do it themselves.   *Felicity Skinner*

> They seem to think you're home all day and it's a life of leisure. They don't realise there's cleaning to be done, and washing and ironing.
>   *Sharon Thomas*

Making ends meet

Inside, their homes varied more than the relatively small differences in take-home pay might have led one to expect. Factors such as the amount of overtime the husband did, the number and age of the children, and whether the wife had a part-time job, all varied the standard of living. More important were the financial priorities of the various couples — whether they put any *surplus* money towards a car, home ownership, new furniture or simply spent more on food. But in the end the determining factor was how successful they were — and that usually meant the wife — in stretching the money to cover as many necessities and 'luxuries' as possible.

Arrangements about money, and about how financial decisions were made, varied widely.[6] The men tended to be more forthcoming about the actual details of domestic finance — they also took good care to defend whatever the arrangements were. They were particularly defensive if the wife had no say in apportioning the pay packet or, conversely, if she was mainly in charge of money matters. A lot of the men pointed out that women had more to do with money: they spent it, and they tended to worry about it more. This led some of them to rely on their wives where money was concerned, but at the same time it made them feel incompetent — especially over prices. To others it was a relief.

> She pays the bills — I'm sorry to say, but she seems to enjoy it. Women are more adept at paying bills. She's been dealing with money all her life. A man buys his tea, but that's not the same as going shopping ... but my wife is a good manager, so I'm OK.　　　　　　*Barry Young*

Most of the financial arrangements involved the wife knowing at least her husband's average wage, if not the actual weekly amount. Only one, Jane Griffiths, had no idea what her husband earned. Usually the pay packet was divided between housekeeping money and 'his' money, but 'housekeeping' sometimes merely covered day-to-day incidentals while at others it included all the major bills such as rent and heat as well as food.

Again, while in all the households the husband had his 'pocket money' there was the world of difference between a situation where the husband could go out for a drink two or three nights a week, his wife counting herself lucky to save enough from the housekeeping for a pair of tights, and one in which both partners had the same (not very great) amount for personal spending. In the majority of cases, by the time the agreed 'necessities' had been taken care of there was little left over for luxuries of any sort. Underlying all these actual arrangements were the principles on which financial decisions were made — who decided if new clothes were needed, or whether to save for a colour TV. It mattered less who actually paid the bills if it was seen simply as a matter of convenience and not as a matter of principle. We shall see how the women felt about this in a moment.

Looking after the children

Arrangements varied here too, and the main burden of finding an alternative naturally fell on the women if they worked outside the home. A few couples (notably the Fennels and the Hannams) used the shift system to enable both of them to work. Sometimes it was the husband who 'went up' to the school to sort out problems or even took 'time off' work to take the children to medical appointments. Most men expected to do some of the household chores, and at least half had taken full charge for short periods. Virtually all expected to look after the children in some way when they were at home. Sometimes it only amounted to 'playing' with them while the wife got the supper. But others, sometimes unexpectedly, would launch into detailed accounts of battles at the dental clinic, or with teenagers over exam subjects or sex education. The amount of time and concern they devoted to their children was intensified by a common feeling that no one outside the immediate family should be involved in their care. It accounted for some reserve shown towards nursery places — the age of five seemed quite soon enough to hand children over to 'them'.

> I don't believe in nurseries. They're at school long enough as it is.
>
> *Janet Griffiths*

More important, a majority of the couples refused to allow anyone outside the immediate family to baby-sit in the evening. Usually this was restricted to one or other of the partners' 'mum'. Sometimes younger sisters were deemed suitable. Others would not even allow their mother to stand in for them:

> I never believe in baby-sitters. When the eldest was six weeks my mum baby-sat and she forgot the bottle. I've never approved of baby-sitting after that. We've had them; it's our place to look after them.   *Jo Lee*

With the men working shifts this meant effectively that some couples could never go out in the evening at all. A few men (Don Grimshaw and Norman Sykes) regularly went out for a drink several times a week by themselves, but by and large most couples spent the evening and weekend at home with the children and attending to chores — men and women alike.

One of the most interesting points to arise was the degree of variation in the arrangements that were made. At the same time both husbands and wives betrayed their awareness of a 'dominant norm', and if they felt they were deviating from it, as most of them were, they were careful to explain and excuse it.

The men, especially, were anxious to justify their own domestic arrangements in terms of the ideology itself. Women seemed less worried about 'conforming' as such than with establishing their own case as 'special': they were concerned not so much with justifying a deviation as with the feeling that there was a conventional norm of which they disapproved. We turn now to some key issues that arose from their experiences.

Economic dependence

Most recent writing on the subject has stressed that financial and economic dependence underpins the position of women in the home. In our case, the women themselves distinguished 'women's work' from a 'proper job' by the fact that it was unpaid. That, and the fact that they all depended for material existence on their husband's pay packet, make the issue of economic dependence crucial to their understanding of their position as women.

As so often, the whole family depended (primarily) on one pay packet, but the money belonged to one member — the male breadwinner. The husband does have a certain legal duty to provide adequately for his family with 'reasonable' housekeeping money, though it is difficult to enforce, short of a divorce settlement. Before that point is reached he is free to dispose of his income as he likes, not even necessarily disclosing how much he earns to his wife. The pay packet quite clearly belongs to the man, and that gives him power. He may or may not exercise it, but the relationship between husband and wife is still based upon the fact.

Custom and plain common sense decreed that in most cases husbands did hand over 'enough' money for housekeeping and that financial decisions were taken more or less jointly, so that the rawness of dependence was decently clothed. Indeed, the men seemed scarcely aware of it when they discussed economic dependence.

> You got to have trust in a family.   *Tony Wheeler*

> It's share-and-share-alike with us.   *Ted Ferguson*

> Most men ain't mean.   *Tomy Turner*

They were aware of the importance of money to their wives; they knew they worried if it was not there; what they did *not* realise was the significance to their wives of being dependent on them.

The women, on the other hand, were in no doubt at all about the issues and what their feelings were. Economic dependence — or, in its more positive version, 'money of your own' — was the feature of domestic labour that affected them most and their chief reason for wanting paid work. Only five had any reservations about the need to retain family allowances when the government proposed a different system.[7] The others registered strong and sustained reactions both to the family allowance issue and to having no money they could 'call their own'.

> It's wrong, really [to abolish family allowances]. It's the woman's bit of independence. You know you've got that money there — perhaps to last you the rest of the week; that you haven't got to go to your husband. Some husbands will make you crawl. It just gives you that little bit of independence.   *Clare Rees*

> ... if a woman hasn't got an outside job then she should have an allowance. She just has the housekeeping, and for the rest she goes without — or has to say to her husband, 'Have you any extra?' If you go to work you have your own bit of independence.   *Janet Griffiths*

He's worked for it, so I suppose he feels it's his, and sometimes I used to feel — not degraded, exactly, but as though I was getting a hand-out. Now, although I'm not earning very much, at least I earned it and it's my money to do as I want.

Jo Lee

It's not fair to take it away, because some men don't give their wives enough. I get £1·90 on a Tuesday, and that's very handy. Paul would give it to me, but a lot of men are quite mean. It's important to have money of your own because you need your independence.

Diane Dixon

In this case the political activity and media coverage ensured that all the women had heard of the government proposals, and knew it meant the end of family allowances. By and large they did not read newspapers or take any interest in politics. They had picked up the information because they regarded the issue as important and relevant.

They considered family allowances important only partly because of its practical benefits. Some did stress that even such a small sum helped to stretch the housekeeping, others that the payment on Tuesday (mid-week) made it especially useful. But its real importance lay in the fact it was 'a little bit of money of your own'. It was a touchstone for their feelings about their economic dependence. Few did not resent it, some found it galling at times, and some found it intolerable:

You can't say you've got anything for yourself. If I want anything in the way of clothes I've got to ask Nick to buy it for me. Whereas if you go to work you've got some money and you can get it yourself. If you have to ask for everything it makes a difference.   *Felicity Skinner*

These particular women were not so concerned about material deprivation. They felt deprived of something much more important — economic identity. They could see clearly that in their position as dependent wives they had no economic identity, except at second hand, through their husbands. This might not have mattered were it not for the fact that they lived in a capitalist society which operates quite explicitly through capitalist relations of production — which are mediated by, and expressed through, cash. Capitalism has outlawed all non-monetary relations. The women were therefore quite correct in equating their non-identity economically as spelling exclusion from the mainstream of society. In a very real sense, if you have no economic identity, you have no identity at all.

Women think independence is important. Men don't. I suppose because they don't ever lose theirs. That's important.   *Mary Fletcher*

Although 'money of your own' was of crucial importance, virtually all the women rejected any idea that they could be paid for the work they did in the home. The arguments have been well rehearsed in academic debate about 'wages for housework', but they needed no such preparation.

> Pay? No, because some people don't like doing it, so they'd rather be out at work.　*Jackie Young*

> How can you, really? Unless you get it from the government. You can't say to an employer, 'Look, I'm looking after my husband's children, you must give him £15 extra.'　*Claire Rees*

> You've to do it, anyway, even if you're paid.　*Mary Fletcher*

> You can't get paid. An employer won't pay you.　*Claire Rees*

'Money of your own' was vital. They discounted wages for housework and had little hope of a real increase in family allowances. It was, therefore, not surprising to find them determined to get it in the only practicable way — by taking a second job outside the home.

'Men's work'

Nearly all those who already had a part-time job (fourteen) intended to do more as soon as they could — most of them by working full-time. Of the remaining ten at least half were actively thinking about doing some paid work in the near future, despite opposition from the husband in many cases.

It was significant that this was an area where there was considerable explicit disagreement between husbands and wives. Some husbands didn't like their wives working even though they did. Some didn't think their wives wanted to go back to work, when in fact they had clear plans to do so, and didn't realise their wives intended to increase the amount of work they did. A majority reluctantly conceded that their wives did want to work, but would have preferred it if they hadn't. Only one, Max Fennel, actively encouraged his wife to work. 'My wife has always worked outside — she's done her utmost to pull her weight. The home should be run by the two of you.' All the others, if they allowed it at all, tried to limit and diminish their wife's job, convinced that her prime duty lay in the home.

> It's all right provided what goes on in the home doesn't suffer. She's doing a part-time job for her own pleasure.　*Michael Lee*

> Well, she can if she wants to, but she's enough to do at home. If she needs the money it's OK — but if she's just bored, well, it's greedy.
>
> *Paul Dixon*

> She has to work now because of the cost of living. I don't like the idea.
>
> *Nick Skinner*

> She wouldn't do the work she does if I had my way, because I think she's got quite enough to do at home. But I wouldn't want to tie her if a little job would do her good.
>
> *Jim Smith*

In other words, they had no idea neither of the strength of their wives' feelings about going out to work, or why they had such feelings. They accepted the sexual division of labour as it stood: but their wives, on this issue of economic dependence, challenged it quite fundamentally. Although all (more or less) apparently accepted the traditional 'woman's place', their rebellion against economic dependence created a tension that could not be accommodated within their ideology.

Even quite radical accounts of housewives with jobs have assumed that the paid employment *is* secondary to work in the home and that there must be a reason for taking it.[8] To imagine asking men (or women in China) why they work is to realise how deep the assumption goes. No one asks women why they stay home and look after the children, or men why they don't.

The reasons suggested as to why women go out to work tend to divide into the economic and the social or emotional. But this reflects a failure to recognise that money *itself* constitutes the main *social* reason. I have already argued that the *primary* sexual division of labour locates men in the market place: women at home. The argument in this chapter is that the separation of *labour* has become a separation of *spheres*, each with its own activities and its own ideology. Thus, when the women went out to work, regardless of what kind of job they did, they recognised that they were crossing some kind of boundary; that they were entering a world which was less their own. Yet their perception of what it meant to be economically dependent drove them to that solution.

They themselves declared that they saw their job as secondary to their main work *inside* the home and certainly thought about it in different terms from their husband's. All their jobs were in the traditionally female sector of the labour market, and most were working entirely with other women.[9] Even so, it was still seen as part of another world — the male one — and therefore essentially dominated by men. Their excursions into it were merely as migrant labour — almost as trespassers.[10]

All had worked full-time before they married, and most of them up to the birth of their first child. Very few had stayed on at school or taken other qualifications or apprenticeships. The vast majority had worked as unskilled labour in factories or small works. All their experiences had been in a rigidly segregated labour market. Even when they had worked in the same place as men, e.g. in printing works or at Hampers itself, their jobs, pay and conditions (opportunity to train, etc.) had been quite separate and different. Additionally, they had had very little *active* union experience on which they could build a labour identity. In fact many of them had either never been unionised, had been and didn't like it, or had no memory of it at all.

When their children grew up the women in part-time jobs wanted to step up their present work or take a full-time job. And most of those who were not working intended to do so at some point. Thus for most of them there were three separate phases of paid work:[11] before they married and had children; as workers with prime responsibility for young children; and, finally, freed of that responsibility when the children grew up. Only the first could have been a comparable experience to their husbands' — or any man's.

They clearly never considered the job they had before the children arrived as a life-long commitment, and this had caused them to be less than whole-hearted in their pursuit of either training opportunities or union representation. The second phase (the one they were in at the time) realised the most inhibiting factors of the first — both in terms of perceptions and in terms of material conditions. Their present jobs were noticeably lower-paid and with worse conditions than the earlier ones. Later, in the third phase, their domestic responsibilities reduced, it was clear that even though the time and energy needed to run the home would lessen, their and their family's view of its priority would not. Thus the third phase would simply be an extension of the second.

What I am suggesting is that, far from married women's part-time work being atypical and flanked by two periods of 'proper' work when there is no difference between their position and men's in the labour market, this middle and most inhibiting period is the defining one. Even when women are working full-time, unencumbered by domestic responsibilities, they still regard themselves — and are regarded — as not primarily in the labour market. It is this ideological 'fact' that is crucial in ensuring that their position at work is *always* different from men's.

The kind of jobs the women were in — cleaning, catering and shop work — and even the kinds of jobs they had had before, were all traditionally among the lowest paid. Few of them, in any case, did enough hours to bring in — at most — a quarter of their husband's wage.[12] Their jobs were marginal and supplementary, both economically and ideologically.

The 'two worlds' dichotomy is closely related to the workings of the capitalist system. The distinction between 'home' and 'work' was meaningless before the home became separated from production, with cash the sole connecting link between people, and 'consumption' a separate, apparently autonomous, sphere from 'production' and 'circulation'. This is not to say that capitalism *depends* on the sexual division of labour, or even that the sexual division of labour was an inevitable result of the development of capitalism. I am simply pointing out that women go into the market place to sell their labour power in a particular historical context. The transaction may appear similar when a man sells his labour power. But it is not. Women sell their labour power in a clearly differentiated market[13] at a lower rate and in poorer conditions. They also do it with a quite different consciousness of what they are doing. Employers are quick to make use all these factors, so that it is not simply the ideological that is in question but the interaction of the ideological and the economic. The women, like all others and in whichever phase of their lives, went into the men's world as women — which is why there is a sense in which all paid work can be referred to as 'men's work'. They crossed a boundary as real as the one a migrant worker crosses.

Unions and equal pay

The women were more openly concerned with their jobs simply as a source of money. Partly because of this, and partly because their experience of unions had been so negative in the past, they now regarded them with indifference. Mostly they were not in unionised jobs — but when they were it was tedious formality. The experience of Sharon Thomas was typical.

> Yes, I'm in the Bakers' Union, but not before this job. I was in TWU at Wills', but that was the only one. Everywhere else they haven't bothered, but this bakery was a closed shop when I went, so you had to join the union. To be quite frank, our union doesn't seem to have done a lot for us. You go to a shop steward with any problems. All the shop stewards are men ... I mean, if we've got a real grievance the best thing to do is go straight to our own manager — by-pass the union altogether. The only thing the union is good for is if you're off sick you get paid by the union — only a little bit, but still ...

And so it was not surprising if they often came to this sort of conclusion:

Men expect women to come out with them. But unions don't help women ... We've got a male shop steward. He doesn't bother.

Gladys Hutchings

So unions, strikes and even meetings were a distraction. They interfered with the simple business of going out, doing a job and earning money as quickly and painlessly as possible. The choice of work was limited. These particular women also had to face the logistical difficulties of finding time to fit in their work with their domestic ties. Their expectations of both the quality of work and the material reward were low.

I'm a shop assistant. I also look after a little boy, because he's always in the shop, and I clean the floors. It's 30p an hour. Everyone says I'm mad to do it, but I'm quite happy. It's local and the hours suit me. It's not much money ... I suppose I ought to, really. I've never made a stand for myself.

Joanna Lee

Well, on Sundays I go round the club and clean up. £2·32 for four hours — 39p an hour. I did question it, but it comes under catering, so I can't do anything about it. I don't know about a union. That's for full-timers, really.

Mavis Gray

Working part-time, they had no concept of united action or union solidarity. And in so far as they had experience of unions at all, it had not encouraged them to expect much. Even the most active and well informed (Val Fennel) would have preferred to work outside a union.

I work in Balham's. It's lovely. There are five of us and I'm in charge. We've all worked together before. We were in the union before, when we were up at the factory. I was a shop steward, but not now. There's no union, and no reason to have it ... it's the best wage we've had. That's a start when we'll need a union. They don't give way easily ... I got a couple of things done [when she was a steward] but I didn't want more. Not enough time to spare. When you have kids, working's enough. If women have families they don't take as much interest.

This was the most explicit reference any of them made to the fact that of having children affecting the way they thought about their work and union. It is, of course, the oft-cited reason why women are not so active in unions as men.[14] But from the general trend of what they said it was more probable the situation was the other way round. They had regarded their jobs as secondary and the unions as irrelevant long *before* they became part-time workers with children.

We have already seen that the husbands regarded their wives' jobs as secondary — both to their own, and to the primary responsibility of running the home. All the men (except one) drew a strong distinction between part-time and full-time work, a distinction not shared by their wives. What was crucial for the men was that *they* should remain the primary breadwinner. Part-time work could therefore be justified in terms of 'something to do', 'keeping her happy' and useful for the 'extra money'. But full-time employment — even though it would probably still not bring in more than half their wage — would alter the basis of the arrangement and, with it, their place in the sexual division of labour.

Consequently, the men found themselves in an awkward position when they talked about issues such as women in the unions and equal pay. Some were opposed to women taking part in unions, but a surprisingly large number said that once at work there was no difference between men and women. It was just as important for a woman to be in a union, and they felt rather more strongly than the women that they should get 'equal pay'. But this was 'other women', not their own wives. Several talked about the women who worked at Hampers, about how they should support their union, how hard their work was and how they deserved equal pay — but then went on explicitly to exclude their own wives: 'but I wouldn't like to see my wife do it', as Alan Hutchings said (see p. 70). In fact, like Keith Thomas and Steve Gray, he had expressly discouraged his wife from working at Hampers.

They seemed caught between a logic that regarded women as workers and a sexual division of labour that required them to be wives; and the two were, to some extent, incompatible.

The women's attitude to equal pay showed even more clearly that they did not see their work as comparable with their husbands'. Whereas the men were inclined to admit the principle (with the onus of proof on the women to show that they could do 'as much as a man'), the women supported it enthusiastically but within the strict terms of the formula 'for equal work'. This they took to mean *identical* work. So if women did *men's* work (and they always chose extreme examples like mining and referred to night work and 'heavy jobs'), then, and only then, could they expect the same pay. None of them regarded her own job as falling into this category. Thus although they would have liked 'more money' and felt they deserved it, they wouldn't claim 'equal pay'.

> But [paid] domestic work is hard. I'd like to see the money come up a bit — but for equal pay I'd have to do a man's job — like the handyman who cuts the grass and so on.   *Gladys Hutchings*

Not that a 'man's job' wouldn't sometimes be easier.

Well, there's our chargehand as a start. He does exactly the same as us — half the time he's just stood watching us, and yet he gets more pay than we do.
Sharon Thomas

In other words, the Equal Pay Act was for freaks, and did not affect them or the vast majority of working women. On the last point they were quite right.[15] What was more surprising was that they made so little fuss about the low rates of pay in the female 'ghettos'. Maybe the reason lay in the ambivalence, if not guilt, they felt about invading the men's sphere.

In one way I don't think women should get equal pay, became the man is the breadwinner. I shouldn't go to work by rights, because my husband is the breadwinner ... I just go to work to help out.
Gladys Hutchings

Here again, the sexual division of labour creates a chasm between two sections of the working class.

The sexual division of ideology

The fact that the women regarded their own paid work as of a quite different nature from their husbands' meant that they found it hard to transfer their own experience of work in 'imaginative extension' to that of their husbands. It was something they did not know about because they *could* not know about it, however much their husbands told them. When they talked about his work they would add the *caveat* 'but I've never done factory work'. Even if they had (like Sharon Thomas) they would say, 'but I've never worked at Hampers'. A few (like Mavis Gray) had even worked at Hampers and did concede that they knew 'what it was like there' though not what it was like to 'be a steward' or to do 'the men's jobs'. 'It's different for the men.' This made it almost impossible for them to identify with their husbands' position as workers, with all that that entailed in a class society.
The gulf between husbands and wives was not narrowed by the men's attitudes to telling their wives about their work. Very few — notably Max Fennel and to a lesser extent Hugh Davies — tried to involve their wives in their working life. Some thought they had no business to know.

I would say I try not to talk to her ... they're outsiders.   *Keith Thomas*

Most thought their wives wouldn't be interested,

unless it's someone she knew who's had an accident or died.
Barry Young

In any case, it was part of *their* survival tactics to keep the two worlds apart.

> Well, I could be wrong, but myself, once I go out this gate, that's it — that's work finished. I don't take it home. I don't talk about work at home. I like to forget it.
> *Tommy Turner*

Most agreed that their wives were interested when the pay packet was likely to be affected — but only then.

> If anything's going on — wages or unions — I usually tell her. I don't usually discuss it. I know the money I bring home interests her, so she has got an interest in the place.
> *Barry Young*

> I tell her if we're going to have a rise or a bonus.
> *Nick Skinner*

> A woman at home minding children — as long as she gets her weekly money she doesn't worry a lot.
> *Michael Lee*

So the women did not see her husbands' jobs as an imaginative extension of their own. They were expected to have only the narrowest economic interest in it, and no feelings of solidarity except those implied by marital duty. Any notion of *class* solidarity either between workers in different sectors or between people affected in different ways by the capitalist relations of production was completely absent.

We have seen how ideas about 'women's work' served to separate men and women. We have shown how the women's separation from their husbands' work experience acted as a limiting factor on both their and their husbands' ideas. Now it seems as if the women's *own* work experience, if anything, reinforced the separation between the two worlds. An illustration can be found in the small but significant incident of the car workers' wives. I have mentioned it already but now we must look at it in some more detail.[16]

Drivers at the BLMC Cowley plant struck on 3 April 1974. A week later the management withdrew 'normal facilities' from the steward A. Thornley. As a result, by 16 April nearly 12,000 workers had either been laid off or were on strike. On 23 April there was a small but vociferous demonstration by some wives outside the factory against 'the militants'. The episode was given star billing by the media, especially the more right-wing daily press. In fact the demonstration had little effect on the course of the dispute, and a counter-demonstration by wives in favour of the dispute was rather better attended. The response of the people in our study to that small incident as reported by the popular press and television shows what a monopoly the media have over such information, and throws some light on their attitude to women and real 'men's work'.

The women, especially, had obviously followed the affair closely. Like family allowances they *knew* about it, and their reactions were forceful. When they talked about their own husbands' wage they acknowledged that it was his because he earned it, and they were aware (and resentful) of their consequent dependence. But because it was connected with their role in the home this dependence gave them certain unspecified and indirect rights, and it was these they expressed when they talked about 'the Cowley wives'. They felt the women *did* have certain rights, and ones that were not usually acknowledged by the unions. They were entitled to the means to do *their* 'work'. If a woman's sphere of responsibility was imperilled by industrial action then they ought to defend it.

It's the women who determine whether the money's good or not.

Diane Dixon

If the family suffers, then wives should have a say.   *Kate Wheeler*

I think wives have a right to come out.   *Mandy Ferguson*

The wives were thinking about the household. You can only take so much.   *Val Fennel*

It's a good idea. It's the wives that suffer.   *Ros Neale*

It was seen in *immediate* terms. Unions in this case were a potential threat to next week's housekeeping, not a bulwark against next year's redundancy. Thus support for the Cowley wives enabled some of the women to express more clearly an active concept of a woman's rights over the pay packet *and* a deep-seated anti-unionism because unions denied those rights. The conjunction was powerful and, in terms of *class* consciousness, destructive. Unions were not seen as either useful or relevant to *women* inside or outside the labour force. Even so, many of the women retained their *class* loyalty to them, together with a general awareness of what life might be like without them (see Chapter 4).

They were only too clearly aware of the inexorable process that put money into pay packets on Friday, only to take it out of the housekeeping purse in the supermarket on Saturday. They caught a glimpse of the fact that they were an integral part of the process, but they did not see how they could intervene in defence of what they saw as their interests as women. Nor did they see those interests relating to those of the working class as a whole.

A surprising number of the men also supported the Cowley women's action. Essentially it was because they too recognised a woman's right to the financial means to do her 'job'.

> Well, a woman's got to manage.
>
> *Max Fennel*

> It's the women have to suffer.
>
> *George Roberts*

On the other hand most felt that the union was a man's affair and women shouldn't interfere.

> They hadn't any right to interfere.
>
> *Nick Skinner*

> It was a man's thing.
>
> *Barry Young*

> A wife expects more money. If a man is trying to get more she should bear with him.
>
> *Tony Wheeler*

> Most women don't understand unions, but they should take an interest in disputes. They should always back up their husbands, because they keep at their husbands — wanting more pay. So they should be prepared to back them up.
>
> *Nick Skinner*

Many men found themselves trapped by their own stated refusal (or dislike) of 'taking it home'. They could hardly expect unquestioning loyalty or support if their wives did not understand the issues. Yet they felt the women ought to give support because in the end that was how to get money. This was why so many of them said they only talked to their wives if some interruption to the pay packet was threatened — and by implication all industrial action would have to be explained in *financial* terms.

> It's definitely important to get a wife's support. Without it I couldn't come in so determined. It's natural for a wife to back you. A woman's got to manage — she's worried about the HP, feeding the kids. She's got equal rights — but she's spoiling the man's chance of getting extra money to give her.
>
> *Max Fennel*

This weak link forms one of the few bridges over the chasm between 'women's world' and 'men's world'. Men mediated their experience of the point of production to their wives in isolated bursts of explanation at best, and a wall of hostility at worst. Women's *own* experience at the point of production — whether as full-time workers or part-time supplementary earners — did not appear to bridge the gulf at all. The working class is split into two sharply defined and divided worlds. One is inhabited by men, the other by women.

The idea of two 'worlds' has been an important organising principle in understanding how both sexes understand 'women's work', and how the sexual sectionalism that develops prevents both from building a full class consciousness. The issue of the Cowley wives illustrates just this kind of impasse. At the same time the women's experience had given them insights into their 'real' position, e.g. as regards the need for economic independence which *had* contributed to their consciousness as women. I shall argue that this sectional consciousness has the same kind of contributory value as the men's trade union consciousness has for them.

To develop this idea, let us see how the men and the women regarded those areas of their lives which they *both* considered outside their sphere — the public world at the local and national level.

Notes

1 See P. Hunt's (1980) commentary on this in the context of the relationship between 'ideology' and 'social practice'; also her discussion of 'women's work', chapter 4.
2 See J. Tweedie, *Guardian*, 6 January 1975.
3 For related discussion of this topic see H. Gavron's old but still relevant study (1966), P. Hunt (1980) and A. Oakley (1974a, especially chapter 5, and 1974b) and much of the writing related to the domestic labour debate.
4 See p. 130 for a full discussion of this incident.
5 Only three particularly 'anti-feminist' husbands downgraded what their wives did at home. John Pollard thought it was 'less mentally taxing' than his (unskilled) work, and the other two just said, 'She accepts it.'
6 For a much fuller discussion of this point see P. Hunt (1980), chapter 2; also C. Bell and H. Newby, and A. Whitehead, in D. Barker and S. Allen (eds.) (1976b).
7 This was a live issue at the time because of the proposals embodied in the Green Paper, Cmnd 5116 (October 1972), to subsume the family allowance into a tax credit scheme. It would have meant replacing the weekly amount paid to every mother from her local post office with a complicated system that would pay the money (as negative tax) to the husband. Such was the outcry from a wide spectrum of interested groups that the proposal was dropped. All the women in the study were aware of the issue.
8 See A. Oakley (1974a, b), H. Gavron (1966), A. Feree, in *Social Problems*, vol. 23 (1974).
9 Seven had cleaning jobs, usually working on their own as local authority home helps, though some cleaned schools or old people's homes. One worked in a shop, and two more helped their parents who ran small shops. One worked in a dry cleaners. Two worked half shifts at Wills's, and another worked at the related firm of Marsdon's. One worked in a bakery and two were in catering. Only two were in a union.

10 See M. Porter, in J. West (ed.) (1982), for a fuller discussion of this material.
11 As Ann Oakley pointed out in 1972.
12 Only one woman — Val Fennel — earned more than a quarter of what her husband did. Even if they had worked full-time they would have been unlikely to have earned more than half their husband's wage. In April 1978 — four years after this study, and three years after full implementation of the Equal Pay Act — female manual workers still earned only 61 per cent of male manual workers' pay. (EOC *Research Bulletin*, 1979.)
13 See R. Barron and G. Norris (1976) and J. Rubery (1978) for useful discussion of the 'dual labour market' theory. While I would not want to accept that as it stands, I do concur with V. Beechey (1976, unpub., and 1978) when she argues that female labour is paid consistently and institutionally at less than its 'price'.
14 See P. Hunt (1980) and K. Purcell (1979). The latter article is (rightly) critical of the conventional assumptions about female lack of 'militancy'.
15 Given the discouraging number of cases won since its full implementation in 1975. See J. Coussins (1976) and EOC annual reports.
16 These details are taken from *Labour Research*, vol. 63, Nos. 6 and 7 (June and July 1974), supplemented by the daily papers at the time.

SIX

IDEOLOGY AND CONSCIOUSNESS: THE WORLD OUT THERE

So far we have been concerned to show the separated experiences of working class men and women — situated primarily in the factory and at home — and we have explored both the constitution of separate ideologies and their mediation between husbands and wives. But there are other aspects of the world that are neither 'at home' nor 'at work'. Among them are the indirect experiences of 'the State' and 'the community'.

In fact in these people's lives 'the community', in the sense of an independent local entity that included the individual families, simply did not exist. They were aware of a more or less attractive locality, measured in terms of amenities or 'atmosphere'. Indeed, most people had strong feelings about where they lived. But the most important aspects — schools, health and welfare services, (public) housing, even the buses and the roads were seen as the responsibility of an outside agency — the dimly conceived local council.

Equally, the people in the study, like people everywhere, were affected by national circumstances and decisions, sometimes even by international events. The remote officers who controlled — or purported to control — such things as prices, taxes, the situation in Northern Ireland, unemployment, national strikes and elections lay well outside the everyday world they felt they understood. It was, literally, the world out there — alien and incomprehensible to men and women alike.

In the course of collecting material I spread the net wide, unwilling to be limited to conventional categories. Having broken through the assumption that limited me to asking men about their jobs and women about their homes and families, I was eager to explore people's ideas about all the other areas of experience — especially as these had a clear bearing on their class situation in a capitalist society. The result was a wealth of information — about housing, about local amenities or the lack of them, about schools, clinics, rents, friends and relations, about the local council and local campaigns, and, on a wider spectrum, about national events, inflation, the media, corruption, the political parties and their leaders, and about people's own small contribution to the democratic process — voting. Obviously, it is impossible to cover more than a fraction of all this here. Yet by selecting a few topics we run the risk of once again pre-judging the issue of what is important for the creation of ideology in a class- and gender-divided society.

With this in mind, let us look briefly at three aspects of 'the world out there' which did appear to have significant effects on the people in the study.

The locality

They all lived in geographical areas to which they could give a name and which corresponded to certain lines on the map — postal districts, electoral wards and so on. The local facilities and amenities would make up an ambience — good, bad or indifferent — which would have an effect on their lives.

They did not discuss their district as an entity. They merely commented on the amenities — or, more usually, the deficiencies. Most people in the outlying areas complained of poor bus services, few and expensive shops, a complete lack of playgrounds for children or meeting places for adolescents, and of there being no cinemas, dance halls, cafés or other 'places to go'. There was no hospital, and the nearest library or swimming pool was in Bishopsworth. They also complained about vandalism and noise generally. Husbands and wives had much the same story to tell. Wives tended to go into slightly more detail — but not enough to support the contention that the 'community' was an extension of the 'home' and consequently part of their world.

Nor did these men or women feel they could do much about it — although the men, at least, felt that the *women* should do something about it.

> They've got to live with it. They're here all day, so they're stuck with it.
>
> *Nigel Martin*

or

> It just generally gets on their nerves.
>
> *George Roberts*

And the women admitted they tended to care more.

> Women are definitely more affected. All a husband does is go to work, come home and go to bed. He hasn't got to worry all day — like these

steep gardens, and kids, and the road ... women are better at organising. In fact I haven't known one man who has done anything. It's women that go to the councillors about houses and schools, etc. Women do the dirty work. Women councillors understand. A bloke will just listen to you, and say, 'Yeh.'
Mary Fletcher

It was noticeable that few people mentioned institutions such as schools or clinics. Instead they focused on the petty irritations of living in a particular place.

The men were divided as to whether women could and did organise or do anything to put right what they complained about. Those who, like Keith Thomas, dismissed the ability of women in the community to organise, often contrasted them with trade union activists in the factory: 'not enough of them step forward'.

It's no use moaning, you've got to collect together for strength.
Barry Young

Housewives don't belong to a union. All they can do is jog MPs.
Jim Smith

Some assumed that women *could* organise protests, and were puzzled as to why they didn't.

They seem to have a spirit that they want to do things, but there seems to be something a bit lacking when they do.   *Simon Steele*

I think so [they'll organise now] because of the way the prices are going up now. I mean if it was left to the men to buy everything, I think they'd more than have a go. But they don't worry about it so much as a man.   *Tommy Turner*

At the other end of the spectrum there were those who had no doubt that women could and did organise among themselves.

Women are better at organising, because they see each other up at school. Get a bunch of men together and they don't know who's who, or anything.   *George Roberts*

Women are much better at organising. They talk more freely among themselves. A group of women get together whenever somethings need doing.   *Tony Wheeler*

What is interesting about the positive views is that they depended on a specifically female institutional base — the school, shops or clinics, where women can meet and get to know one another. In other words, virtually all the men were, at some level, comparing community action with trade union action. It was a kind of parallel to their activity at work — and their evaluation depended, at least partly, on whether they could see comparable factors — leaders, meetings places, solidarity — in the community. One man's response raised another kind of parallel:

> Women can change a lot, but you want one to start it off. But a lot of husbands would stop it. Women feel more strongly about where they live. Most men just want a quiet life — they can't be bothered.
>
> *Dick Griffiths*

This was the other side of the coin to the one that showed wives resisting their husbands' industrial militancy even when they 'needed the money'. Here two worlds were in opposition: men and women had *separate* concerns, and far from supporting one another they would resist each other in order that their *own* lives should be undisturbed. I take up this point about how far women extend the boundaries of their world in the next chapter.

The only method of protest open to these people was 'pressure-group politics' — with all the paraphernalia of lobbying, petitions and fund raising. The working class has had its own armoury of protest, from food riots and poaching to 'boycotting' and rick burning,[1] and it is one that is at odds with the more incorporated practices of the middle class. The latter in turn are in marked contrast to the bargaining methods of the trade unions — particularly in that they depend on lobbying and influence, rather than mass intransigence. Not surprisingly, then, these people were not persuaded of their effectiveness.

What really attracted them was the idea of a rent strike. No one had ever taken part in one — indeed, none had taken place in Bristol. But they had read about them and often talked wistfully, while recognising that withholding rent in isolation would merely invite eviction. In this case they *could* see a parallel with union politics, and realised only too well that without a comparable solid and well organised body to back them any attempt would soon be defeated. As their homes were at stake, they felt they couldn't take the risk of failure. It says something for the achievement of unionism that similar 'risks' can be taken at work.

> People said we should have an action group when we had the rent increase. But I went through a lot, and I'm scared of losing a council flat. I'm not scared of a strike, but I would be of an action group.
>
> *John Pollard*

This failure to adopt the only politics available to them reinforced the realisation that the conditions they lived under were not of their making.

They could not be challenged or gainsaid or fundamentally altered. Because they ignore the overriding social structure, community studies sometimes give the impression that the intact, cohesive groups they describe could alter the circumstances in which they lived. But the miners in N. Dennis *et al.* (1956) could not eliminate the coal mines or even affect their operation.

The Hampers couples were just more aware of their helplessness. It was usually the women who talked about these matters, and who experienced most frustration.

> We tried for twenty-nine years to get a pavement, but apart from that we haven't bothered. You put petitions forward but they just get walked over. It's supposed to happen this year, but whether it will or not I don't know. I suppose if they listen to everyone's moans they'd get a plateful.
>
> *Mary Fletcher*

> Out the back they're digging the base for the South Bristol storm tunnel. All of a sudden these bulldozers and things moved in. Our lives were ripped apart. After three months we got together and made noises — and held a meeting and they stopped doing it at night — so that worked.
>
> *George Roberts*

His wife, Anna, was more specific and less sanguine:

> Well it goes back to the floods — a long time back, six years. It flooded Hartcliffe Way and Bedminster, and the idea is, the river which starts at Dundry — they'll take it from here to the General Hospital. But we went to a meeting about this, and they can't guarantee it will work — they tell you this after a couple of years of annoyance ... The letter didn't say we were going to be kept awake for two years. It just said it would be a nuisance.
>
> *Anna Roberts*

> People tried for years to get a hospital out there. It was squashed last year. No one takes any notice. Rent rises — it's ridiculous. You can't do nothing about it, and if you rebel they can just turn you out.
>
> *Simon Steele*

And as Nigel Martin observed:

> It comes down to signatures. They've got no authority. I suppose they could get something if they kept on about it — but the majority of people, if they want a thing changed, they want it *now* — not in two years' time.

Quite a few of the men who were active unionists drew a direct parallel between the effectiveness of union action as opposed to the vapidness of local protest — like Arthur Rees, who said, 'I've got more influence through my union,' and George Roberts: 'I suppose if you've got a weak union demonstrations are useful, to show people you really care.'

Here again is an absolute separation between the 'world of work' and the 'world out there'. They are both part of the capitalist world: the one concerned with the extraction of surplus value; the other with the reproduction of labour power (and with the consumption part of the capitalist cycle). Yet in the one there is a defensive organisation that has, over the years, made definite inroads into capital's absolute power over labour; in the other, individual workers and their families face capitalism alone, unorganised and virtually unprotected. The retreats that capital has made at the point of production have been more than offset at the point of consumption and in control over the conditions in which employees live all their lives, save for the working day.

This fracture in working-class experience affects men and women differently, and on the whole women are the losers. But everyone was affected by the total absence of identifiable working-class organisation in the local community. It made a difference to the quality of their lives, but in significant ways it also prevented them from making the connections between the experience of different parts of the capitalist cycle. For those who had no active union experience it reinforced a sense of isolation and helplessness. Those who had tended to concentrate on an aspect of their lives they knew they *could* do something about and ignore the rest, thus enabling capital to make substantial inroads without any effective opposition from the working class.

Nor, at this juncture, could the women see ways in which, from their vulnerable individual homes, they could intervene effectively.

The costs of reproduction

Housing is almost certainly the greatest cost of reproduction the working class has to bear. It was certainly a constant worry to all the people in our study. It is a commodity like any other, and should be considered as part of the discussion of prices. I have stressed that it is also where women do their 'work' and consequently has a greater significance for them.[2] Here I want to discuss the women's ideas about prices in general. At the time of the fieldwork, inflation had not reached its subsequent dizzy heights, but neither were people yet inured to the idea of constant increases, and it was a topic of great concern.[3]

The retail price of food, clothes and other consumer items represents the most obvious aspect of the consumption part of the capitalist cycle.

It is, and was, clearly seen as the obverse of the wage packet. Prices are also a kind of borderline area between national economic events and local experience; between politics and industry and between working men and their wives.

We have already seen where 'shopping' stands in the sexual division of labour. Prices in the shops clearly strike the women first and most powerfully. But, objectively, their husbands and the rest of the family will experience inflation — or rather the deteriorating relationship between prices and the net wage packet — just as much. The money simply will not stretch as far — though it was the women who had to try, and who had to explain their failure to their husbands. Some of their strong resentment derived from the fact that initially it *was* seen as a failure on their part. The husbands had kept their part of the bargain — the net wage had stayed the same — but *they* appeared not to have kept theirs. It was only gradually that both sides came to realise that prices were as little within the women's control as a wage cut (which is effectively what inflation is) would have been within the men's. In fact the women had even less control, because in the market place there was no equivalent of shop-floor collective resistance. Each individual 'housewife' paid separate prices for separate items in separate shops. The only visible restraint was the in-effectual 'price controls' imposed from above. Nor was the 'housewife' any freer not to buy than the worker not to sell his labour: both merely had a choice of evils.

Men and women alike saw a connection between wages and prices, and that they were in a sense analogous. As with rents, some saw that the only effective resistance would be a kind of strike, but that was impossible without the equivalent of organised trade union solidarity;

> We just accept them [prices], but we shouldn't. Something could be done by not buying. I do — certain kinds of meats I won't buy, and if we all did it together the shops would be forced to put the prices down.
>
> *Ros Neale*

Prices were an important part of the women's lives. It was a subject they would discuss at length and in considerable detail. The women would: husbands were rarely in a position to reel off the week's increases in the cost of groceries. Most accounts of shopping experiences were prefaced by expressions of anger — 'It's scandalous,' 'It's wicked,' 'It's disgusting the way they let them go up,' 'Oh, every day — it's like a cartoon.' Such feelings expressed anger and fear — both necessary ingredients of rebellion. The men simply stated the bald facts of inflation in measured tones. This difference was confirmed in the reasons they suggested for inflation. Both men and women felt they had to put forward some explanation. The problem of making ends meet had always been there — but the latest rise in prices was so dramatic that something more seemed called for. Various reasons were at hand, generously provided by the government through the media. They included wage demands (especially by car workers and miners), world prices (especially oil), and — from a section of the Labour Party — the Common Market. The men were noticeably readier to accept them than the women:

It's caused by world prices — oil. It was bound to happen. Oil prices were too low before.
George Roberts

The wages push the prices up.
Paul Dixon

It's a general trend in the world. We've had it easy for years, off our reliance on colonies abroad. Now we have to pay what others have to pay. What must it be like in India? They should have their fair share — like [tea workers] people that pick that live real rough. I wouldn't mind paying a couple of coppers more to see that babby live — if the money was going there.
Don Grimshaw

If you ask for more wages, the prices are bound to go up.
Alan Hutchings

The exceptions came from the SOGAT rank and file, workers, who introduced a note of scepticism bordering on downright disbelief.

They say it's world prices. But I don't know.
Fred Fletcher, SOGAT worker

Basically it's the government. It's a big con, because they say they'll put the prices up anyway.   *Nigel Martin, SOGAT worker*

If they can stop the wages, they can stop prices.
Arthur Rees, SOGAT worker

It was left to the women, therefore (and the SOGAT workers), to dispute the hegemonic explanation of price increases. Some found a convenient scapegoat in the Common Market, or in the introduction of decimal coinage.

7p don't seem nothing, but when you got it for 10*d* you knew.
June Hannam

When we went decimal the prices seemed to double.   *Jean Martin*

It's going to be hard to be level with France, where they can't afford fish and meat.
Anna Roberts

Much more significant, politically, were the number of women who blamed *profits*, or reversed the 'wages cause inflation' argument, declaring that wage demands were the necessary results of price increases. The importance of this belief should not escape us. Firstly, because it was an area the women felt was their own, they were prepared to offer decided judgements. Secondly, when they were roused, as they were over prices, their response was more radical than their husbands'. Although few of them saw anything they could do about it, they were certainly angry.

Well, those profits. That's always bugged me. They doubled their profits last year, but our wages don't double.   *Claire Rees*

It's all since the Common Market and decimalisation — putting it up to be the same as the others. It may benefit some, but it's a mistake for the majority, and some firms are making a profit out of it. Obviously when the workers see profits they put in for a rise. But the thing is to peg the prices. They wouldn't do it of their own accord — it would need the government to step in. It's not likely — they don't seem to go in for that. The people that make the money go on getting their way, and the government doesn't take any notice.   *Val Fennel*

Food's very expensive. You can't keep up, really. They say costs go up — but several firms made more profit last year than before. It's the public that loses all the time. The government should do something. They should cut down on profits.   *Mary Fletcher*

The apparently greater radicalism of the wives should not be overstated for often the husbands made the same criticisms of excess profits when they discussed wages rather than when they were talking about the less immediately relevant (to them) subject of prices. This was particularly marked among those husbands who were active unionists but unsympathetic to their wives' position.

The causes of inflation also raised the bewildering question of who really did hold the reins of power and how effective they were.

You've got to pay the prices, and that's it. If someone knew what they could be doing it would be sorted, but no one in government seems to. It just goes on and on.   *Cath Grimshaw*

I don't know how it works. I think investors put money in and want more out. I'd like to know, but I'm only an average person, so I don't know about inflation.   *John Pollard*

But a little later despair gave way to the observation that:

> They put a freeze on wages — but the bloody prices went up! Why don't they freeze prices?
>
> *John Pollard*

and then again:

> It's all beyond me.
>
> *Fred Fletcher*

> It's England lending too much, or giving it away and not getting anything in return, and all these countries wanting their independence ... well, something's bound to happen, because the working class just can't keep up with it. I don't understand it a lot, to tell you the truth.
>
> *Barry Young*

> Basically it's the government ... They seemed to stop the unions getting extra money — but they haven't stopped the big firms like British Leyland. They put their prices up last week. They made £13 million *more* last year.
>
> *Nigel Martin*

On the whole, then, the men accepted some version of the hegemonic explanation — although the ones with a clearly identified union affiliation did not talk about 'greedy workers' or blame strikes. The women remained entirely unconvinced, despite the blanket media bombardment of the time. Most of them attributed price rises to profits and blamed big business, but they stayed adamantly hostile to unions and industrial action.

The women revealed the fracture between their potentially radical response to what they could see happening and their generally conservative political stance. It was among them that retreat — 'Well, nothing can be done in a man's world' — was most likely.

Both men and women expressed feelings of helplessness in the face of spiralling prices. They located the problem and the solution at the national level. Consequently they looked to the government as the only possible source of action. I discuss their concept of power and government in the next chapter. The main point here is that they did not see themselves as in any way able to control what the 'government' did. This did not prevent them from being extremely critical of its lack of effective action, in particular the policy of freezing wages without any *effective* price controls to match. The government, a Labour government especially, *ought* to do something.

> Obviously when the workers see profits they put in for a rise. But the thing is to peg prices. They wouldn't do it of their own accord. It would need the government to step in — but not likely. They don't seem to go in for that. The people that make the money go on getting their way, and the government doesn't take any notice.
>
> *Val Fennel*

Profiteers should be stopped by the government. That's what they're there for.
Mary Fletcher

They stopped the unions getting extra money — but they haven't stopped the big firms, like British Leyland. They put their prices up last week and made £13 million *more* profit last year.   *Jean Martin*

The food subsidy is just vote-catching. Baked beans have doubled and they take 1p off bread!
George Roberts

Disillusion and hence cynicism were the most striking features of these efforts to grapple with patent contradiction. The keynote was despair and bewilderment rather than anger: vital components in British working-class ideology. The problaimed policy of both the Conservative and Labour governments of 1974 was to impose both a wage freeze and controls on dividends and prices. The plain fact, apparent to all these people spending the same wage in dearer and dearer shops, was that the former worked, while the latter did not. And while most of them accepted the logic of an overall standstill, they could not see that lower wages and higher prices were going to help them at all. Both at the time, and later, defenders of government policy put out propaganda to show how much progress was being made. The people in the study, however, were more persuaded by the evidence of their own eyes. This points to a massive failure on the part of hegemonic ideology. Coupled with strong feelings of anger, could it not have triggered mass protest, perhaps even the beginning of a real challenge to the established order? It did no such thing. Most people simply extended their own helplessness to the government. It was 'doing its best', but either the problem was too big or no one knew enough or — more significantly — the opposing power of big firms was too strong. To go further they would have needed the organised solidarity and alternative ideology that enabled the miners, in March 1974, to issue just such a challenge.

Living in the Welfare State

Since 1945 the concept of the Welfare State has ensured, in theory at least, that no citizen falls below a certain minimum level. The five major 'arms' — the social wage, housing, education, social security, personal social services and health — are organised in a coherent system. The families I talked to, like most of the population, had all had some experience at least of these aspects of the Welfare State. All had had contact with State schools and the National Health Service. The vast majority had lived in State housing. Some had sent their children to State nurseries or nursery schools. A few had encountered various other social services. A very few had been on social security or unemployment benefit, though many more had been able to claim rate or rent rebates, Family Income Supplement and other payments in cash or kind. All mothers with more than one child had received family allowances. These contacts constituted a large part of their experience of the 'world out there'. In fact much of what they had to do with in the community was actually the local expression of national policy, and paid for, at least indirectly, out of central funds. This included such crucial institutions as schools, the health service and housing.

The difference between social spending provisions and prices is that the former are legislated and organised at the national level, although they are actually provided by local intermediaries. Prices, on the other hand, are not legislated at any level — except by the market and a few governmental controls — nor are the retail outlets subject to statutory restrictions. Theoretically, then, as voters, people should have been more able to control this 'public' aspect of their lives than the 'market' aspect. Equally this area, like prices, has been seen conventionally as an extension of the woman's world. It was the wives who tended to go into greater detail, based on their day-to-day experience. But the husbands were not silent, and many of them had had just as much contact with schools or the housing authorities. As I shall argue, neither husbands nor wives felt they really understood what was being provided for them, much less that they had any control over it.[4]

People do not experience 'education', for instance. What they come into contact with is the *local* primary and secondary schools. These embodied the decisions and attitudes of the local authority, which in turn mirrored and were guided by central decisions. But people made judgements — which entered into their consciousness — based on these local manifestations. As we shall see, there was only marginal contact and no common action even between people who experienced the same things, e.g. parents of children at the same school, and who drew similar conclusions. For the purposes of this analysis the local apparatus — such as the council — can be ignored. Whatever its real power — and even its spending power is circumscribed — it is virtually invisible. Most people were aware of the local council only as the landlord, and assumed that all important decisions were made by central government. 'It's all done by Westminster.' 'Councillors just come and go.' So many opinions which *should* have been locally rooted were not, and instead formed the basis on which an interpretation of the wider society was formed.

For the sake of brevity, let us look at just two aspects of the Welfare

State as it affected these people — the National Health Service and the social services.

The health service
Despite the fact that all the mothers had had their children in hospital and were subsequently in contact with health visitors and clinics, all but a very few of the babies would have been born and stayed alive with little or no professional help.

Even so, there were fewer criticisms and more praise for the clinics, doctors and hospitals than for any of the other welfare services. This is less a full-hearted tribute to the medical services themselves than to the efficiency of the 'technical' smokescreen.[5] They didn't feel they *could* criticise something so far beyond their comprehension. Clearly they could not pronounce on the technical quality of the doctoring they got, but they could have pronounced on the quality of care. A few commented on a doctor's manner — 'He's a bit abrupt' — and a few more resented the interference of health visitors.

> I don't go to the clinic, because I got no joy — they contradict each other, and I don't think a baby should grow by the book. It worries you a lot more going to see them than stopping here and going by your own common sense. It's good to go if your parents can't help, but my mother's had five, and she could always tell me. And half of them [health visitors] haven't had children, so they're only going by the book.
> *Mary Fletcher*

But by and large both men and women made approving if vague comments on the attention they had received. Only when more direct and probing questions were asked — especially about the problem of getting information from medical staff — did an important deficiency came to light. Most of the women remembered some incident when they had been worried or frightened and had not been able to find out what was happening.

> It seems a bit impersonal in hospital. They gave me the impression I was a bit stupid. To me it was a big experience, but they just shut the door and say 'You're all right.'
> *Jo Lee*

> The doctors are never around, and the nurses won't tell you anything.
> *Kate Wheeler*

> Doctors aren't like they used to be. They're only pill-pushers now. They've no time to bother with you, and you feel you're a trouble to them ... I went to Southmead with a miscarriage. There was a shortage

of staff, and I hardly saw anyone. I've had four miscarriages — and I've got used to it. I had a hormone deficiency. They say you've got to have three mis's before they can do anything. That's bad, they should do it at the beginning. I got very upset, especially with the last one. I don't like the birth pill, but the hospital just put me on it. I had trouble with it and the hospital didn't bother themselves. It's terrible. You have to force yourself not to take babies [i.e. snatch them from prams]. They just let you get on with it. No one warns you. They ought to, because it's terrible. They don't worry — they just put you on a pill. You got to pull *yourself* together.

Cath Grimshaw

They took it for granted that they would not be given information; that they would have no choice or control over what was happening to them or their children once they were in medical hands. Indeed, they were pleasantly surprised when it was otherwise.

Colin fell on his skates just before Christmas. He had to go into the BRI for an operation. They said it was twisted gut — and he'd probably had it from birth. They were very nice with Colin. I was very surprised when the surgeon talked to me in the ward, because I didn't think they tell you what's wrong. I never asked him — I was tickled to bits. I thought, 'How nice.' He told me just what he had to do, about the operation.

Gladys Hutchings

Although most would have liked to know more about what was going on, they lacked the means to find out. Certainly there was no idea that patients or parents had any 'right' to know; rather, they regarded any human touch as a bonus to be grateful for.

This is a striking example of the way in which ruling ideology operates in real life. The capture of 'knowledge' is crucial not only to the control of the labour process, as documented by H. Braverman (1974). It is crucial to control in all spheres. Capital dictates — albeit in various historically specific ways — how we shall live, and hegemonic or ruling ideology tells us how to interpret the experience. These people *were* actually helpless in the face of the giant machinery of the State. They did not know what was happening to them, or why.

They were unable to challenge it effectively, not only because they did not have the organisation or the power, but because they had no information save that which was given to them. This is not to deny that welfare provisions have substantially improved the quality of working-class life. I simply raise this point as an example of how powerlessness is experienced.[6]

Essentially all the families spoke as the more or less grateful recipients of an expert service. Knowledge of and control over their own bodies had been removed from them by the NHS as part of the 'Ideological State apparatus'.[7] Several of the men had had industrial accidents. Yet none mentioned industrial safety in connection with the National Health services. They sometimes referred gratefully to treatment after an accident, but there was no idea that *preventive* medicine — encompassing industrial safety — should be part of the medical care they might expect. The two worlds were completely separated.

The medical services were valued far above education, the social services or any other branch of public spending. Furthermore, there was an expectation of survival, if not of perfect health. Although they worried about the future they certainly expected that all their children would live to see it. Women therefore did not have to bear extra children as an 'insurance', and in only a few cases had had children they did not want. This comparatively recent development is a revolutionary change in the pattern of life — for the rest of the family as well as the wife. Only one family had more than four children (and six of the eight were adopted), and eleven couples had two or fewer, whereas the majority of the parents themselves came from large families of six or more. Among other things it meant that the women would be freer of child-minding responsibilities at a younger age than their mothers were. And they would be likely to return to the labour force, particularly as their children would not be contributing economically until they were at least sixteen because of the raising of the school-leaving age. These changes affect women closely and crucially, but improved medical care has revolutionised the circumstances in which the whole working class lives. In the last fifty years it has developed vastly higher expectations of physical health. Raised expectations also extend to housing and education, if not quite as dramatically. The aspect which seems to have improved least is working conditions — that part of their lives most controlled by the market — and it is effectively symbolised by all those missing fingers, accepted as a 'normal' hazard.

Social services and personal benefits
The people in the study were 'respectable' working-class: they were not 'poor'. They did not need the 'safety net' of the 'discretionary' parts of the Welfare State. It was a matter of considerable pride, and also of vulnerability. People who were on the dole, or who claimed Supplementary Benefit, were regarded as inferior. As Betty Turner said, 'I should think if you were the sort to be always in and out of trouble you'd probably know' (about the social services). 'But we seem to just jog along normally.' Few couples had experienced unemployment, and the plight of elderly

parents was mentioned but not discussed, so that few had any experience of the 'helping agencies', social services or financial benefits — other than rent and rate rebates. Those who had, had a great deal to say — most of it extremely critical. All the families had, of course, received other payments such as family allowance and sick pay — but these were seen as different. You 'paid' for those with your stamp.

Six families had come into contact with what can be generally called 'welfare agencies'. Two had compound problems, two had a problem with one child, and two had had temporary problems due to injury.

These families, like most of the others, held strong views about 'scroungers' who used the services and claimed benefits illegitimately, although they all regarded their own claim as genuine, and indeed were outraged when they got less than they regarded as their due. Their experience did not lead them to question the myth of scroungers as a huge army of ne'er-do-wells and blacks. In fact it had reinforced it.[8] Those who had drawn social security harboured deep resentment against them.

It does happen that foreigners seem to have the ability to get more from Social Services than English people. The only amount I had was £7 10s for ten weeks — eventually went to a tribunal and proved my case. There's a bloke over there who's on Social Security. He's three times my size and looks as healthy as anyone. He's humping great pigeon lofts about, and he gets around £31 per week. Plus he was doing a spare-time job as well. I'm a bit disillusioned with Social Services. I never got anything out of it. It's like trying to get blood out of a stone.

Mike Lee

Outsiders are coming in and getting National Health. That I'd stop right away. People here are putting money in and you go down to Social Security and they just don't want to know. It happened to me, like. When my hand was bad. There was no money coming in — the wife wasn't working — and I went down. Three hours there — rent book, means test, the lot. In the end they said, 'Come back tomorrow.' Another two hours. In the meantime they went up to my home. And when I came back to work they stopped it out of my wages ... too many scroungers — and when you get a genuine case like me ...

Bert Hannam

The use of 'scapegoats' has effectively divided the working-class — and when allied with xenophobia and racism it is a dangerous brew.

In these supplementary benefit claims it was the men who spoke, but in all the other examples given above the husbands scarcely mentioned the incidents. It was the women who gave long, angry and detailed accounts of their experiences. Gladys Hutchings and Ann Davies especially had much to say. Here is Ann talking about school dinners:

Anyway, Paul wanted school dinners, so I goes down. 'Sorry, Mrs D. — only in exceptional cases.' So I said, 'Business people round here and their kids stay in to dinner.' Anyway, she wouldn't do it. I'm talking to a person who keeps Parks House, the pub. She said, 'I had a fuss, but look at the rates I pay.' I said, 'Jean, that cuts both ways — look at the rates I save having the children.' She was saying she was more entitled because she paid the rates. She said, 'That's your fault. What you ought to do is go in there and slam the money down and say they're staying and walk out. She can't do nothing then.' She said, 'You give me the money and I'll do it.' I said, 'I don't want anyone to do my dirty work.' I was a bit worried. Anyway, I went into the secretary and gave her Paul's dinner money, and he stayed in. Then I saw Councillor Sprachlin, because I didn't think you ought to have to go and demand it, because all the women that went to work just got it. The headmistress said she had too many. Sprachlin said anyone is entitled. I said, 'If you're full up you should give all children a fair chance. I goes down to the teacher, she really made me mad — the greengrocer is just stopping in to dinner and the woman in the pub is doing 200 dinners for students and says she can't do her own child's dinner. That's ridiculous. If she's entitled, so are mine.

Sprachlin has seen about me, but there are others. He doesn't care about the others, and it's still going on. There's one woman, she's massive and she has to go all the way down there every lunchtime. Poor woman, she had two others to bring down. You imagine, in the winter. So Sprachlin hadn't told her off that much?

Ann Davies was a natural fighter with a keen instinctive sense of justice. 'Black's black and white's white, and I'll be there.' Lesser women gave up and accepted what they got. It was each for herself. Jean didn't offer to go *with* Ann to the school — she offered to go *instead*. That may indicate friendship, but it was not the beginnings of solidarity.

Indeed, this individualism is at the root of working-class powerlessness, which we here already seen in connection with 'doing things locally'. What was striking was the number of articulate, forceful women (at least as articulate and forceful as the TWU stewards) who had waged protracted *individual* battles. There was not one case of collaboration, much less of joint protest. Faced with the impersonal monolith of the Welfare

State, they hurled their lilliputian force against it like so many little Davids.

These experiences point to a number of other problems. The first is the ambivalent attitude of the wage-earning 'respectable' working class towards the welfare agencies. They still carry the stigma of charity, and people would rather not have anything to do with them. Several mentioned that they or their parents had been sick or injured but said with pride that they had not claimed. They paid 'stamps' and recognised that they were entitled to some return. Instead they felt the money was being squandered on a vast band of underserving poor.

It was not so much the refusal of benefits that had infuriated the women, as the patronising attitude of social workers, bureaucratic ineptitude and what seemed wilful negligence of the needy. Yet they did not know of one another's existence, and even if they had they would have been unlikely to combine. Their response was also, essentially, a series of *negative* reactions to particular wrongs inflicted from above. They had had no hand in devising the system or putting it into practice, and they did not really expect to exert any control over it.

Nevertheless, while they did not act together, conflicts with welfare agencies had been instrumental in developing their critical perceptions of society, and they carried both their anger and their perceptions over into other areas. The women who had had trouble (either because they could not avoid it, or because they challenged it) with the welfare aspect of the State were noticeably less likely to accept government explanations of other issues such as price increases, wage freezes, strikes, public spending cuts, company profits or government policy.

> I don't say they don't care. They try to help everyone, but it always seems to be for the higher-class people.
>
> *Mandy Ferguson*

> Like everything else, it's promises, promises.
>
> *Diana Dixon*

> I think if Mr Wilson — my friend — hadn't frozen the rents there'd be trouble ... where does the Prime Minister get *his* wages from? ... the Queen still gets family allowance ... You find it's firms that makes the profits, but who makes it? Not the bosses. The workers. So why should the owners get all the profit?
>
> *Gladys Hutchings*

We can say, therefore, that experiences such as these had some potential in terms of causing people to question the *status quo*. At present the resulting more 'radical' potential remained imprisoned. Yet because these same women were much more ready to make connections between their own experiences and the social structure, arguably they might be more inclined towards remedial or defensive action (if not genuinely revolutionary action) than others who had not had those experiences.

The Welfare State has been the proud boast of the Labour Party and an important policy plank in its policy. It is therefore instructive to see how it was regarded.

Few people denied the continuing reality of poverty. Where they differed was over its extent, which social groups were affected and, most significantly, what caused persistent poverty. There was a fundamental difference of opinion, closely connected to conceptions of class structure, about the role of the State. On the one hand, if poverty was self-induced, then it was both morally and politically wrong for the State to intervene. People thought that 'help' in such cases would only perpetuate the problem by removing any inducement for the poor to 'help themselves'. But 'help' to the 'undeserving' also cut across their own interests as honest working-class. The State not only squandered their hard-earned wages but refused to help *them* when *they* needed it. They frequently substantiated their argument by accounts of 'scroungers'. The origins of such stories were usually second-hand and often patently mythical. They usually derived from popular press coverage. At the same time some people sympathised with the poor and unemployed and were disinclined to take the scrounger 'scare' stories too seriously even though they repeated them. These were also the ones with a more positive idea of and identity with the 'working class'. Some reflected a genuine confusion, like Anna Roberts:

> Well, yes. I went to the Welfare for myself but I don't like the way it lets men become layabouts. I agree with people who are genuinely sick getting it — but then, they're the ones who don't apply because it's charity — older people especially ... I think I should be able to go and get it without all these complicated forms that need A level maths — for something that's my right ... Poor people, lots of them, can't read. They haven't had a chance — or they haven't taken it. The government should do more. If you need £40 to live, then everyone should have £40 from somewhere.

Most, even if they did think the wrong people were getting it, were still prepared to defend the *concept* of the Welfare State, and especially of a health service.

> It saves a lot of money. Especially with children. We'd be at our wits' end. It's like renting a TV, you don't think twice about sending it down to have it repaired, but when the washing machine goes you do think twice.
> *Claire Rees*

It would be OK if they did help you. For instance, my girl, she was dirty and wet the bed and I just couldn't get help and had to pay for help like that hospital bed. There's enough help available. None of the family had any help when I wanted it. Social security: that's another crime. A genuine case like my husband can't get it. He only got £3 and it dropped to thirty shillings. Then you hear about people getting it with lots of lies. They lives on National Assistance, but they don't realise it comes out of working men's wages. The whole system is wrong. If benefits go up, the stamp goes up. The regular workers pay for it. There should be a system for examining out-of-work men to check in. Like my father, who was dying on his feet of cancer and they had the cheek to send for him to stop his money ... They're doing better at home with all the perks. They don't want to go to work. I've heard it.

Gladys Hutchings

It's important even now there's more money. Lots of kids wouldn't see school if they had to pay.

Val Fennel

I've been to hospital four times. I couldn't afford it except with social security.

Paul Dixon

Some people who supported the Welfare State pointed out that it wasn't actually 'free', because they, i.e. the workers, paid in taxation.

You pay enough taxes and things. But it would be terrible without it — like in the USA.

Jackie Young

Well, it's rather a point, because there's a lot that isn't free, like I take the pill and I've got to pay for the prescription — 20p.   *Sharon Thomas*

It's not necessarily free. The Health Service should be free, and I don't understand the dole, etc. It's not really free, because you pay in taxes. But I agree with it.

Kate Wheeler

These understandings of the Welfare State are important because no kind of working-class consciousness uses the moral weaponry of the ruling class to condemn large numbers of people who could also be called 'working-class' as lazy, scroungers or inadequate. Yet that is what at least some of the people did, while at the same time clearly identifying themselves as working-class.

On the whole the women had more difficulty in reconciling antipathy towards scroungers and inadequates with their own experience of trying to use the welfare services themselves. The result was often a cry of frustration. It also resulted frequently in a dangerous fracture between the 'respectable working class' — us — and the 'lumpenproletariat' (in Marx's designation) scroungers.

Yet the Welfare State is a substantial achievement, and many explicitly recognised it as such. It can be argued that it exists, at least partly, because capitalism needs a healthy, literate work force; but workers undeniably benefit.

In this chapter I have tried to illustrate something of the way in which working-class men and women respond to their experiences as working-class in relation to the capitalist State. In the next I shall be more concerned with explicitly 'political' ideas, but here we have looked at an area of experience which is not normally designated as political in the same way. It is also an area that is frequently seen as an extension of the home. Even in this brief account it should be clear that the description is less than adequate.

Experience of prices, housing, councillors, schools and Social Security did not persuade people that these were community matters over which they had some control. They identified them rightly as instruments of State direction, and they did not see the State as a neutral *deus ex machina.* They recognised the exercise of power in all such aspects of their lives and turned fairly quickly to consideration of who, ultimately, operated that power and in what interests.

The women were more closely involved on a day-to-day level with such institutions. Their concern, coupled with a greater ability to disregard media-purveyed explanations, had given them a real purchase on a rhetoric of anger and resistance. It was not part of their world, but the ideology of women's work caused them to resent their lack of control over issues which, they felt, bore directly on their success in doing women's work.

Yet men and women alike were helpless in the face of what they saw as an uncontrollable force. Whereas the men, at work, had been able to develop some strategy for voicing their dissatisfaction, and even, sometimes, for achieving change by means of the trade union structure, there was manifestly no parallel in 'the world out there'. The Labour Party, which might have filled the position, was viewed with detachment and disillusion.

Both men and women distinguished worlds over which they had some control — at home and at work — and the rest of experience, over which they had virtually no control. But the women, by-passing the limitations of the men's explanations, did formulate radical and cogent critiques. The resources of anger and confidence were there. What lay between them and action was the privatisation of the family and the failure of working-class organisation.

We must now follow some of these themes through, and explore the political roots of the men's and women's ideologies.

Notes

1 For a fine documentation of just one example see E. P. Thompson, *Whigs and Hunters* (1975).
2 See M. Porter, 'Near and dear? Working class women in the community', paper presented to the BSA Urban Sociology and Family and Kinship Groups, March 1980.
3 During the period of these interviews the retail price index rose from 10·3 per cent (November 1973) to 16·9 per cent (August 1974). The previous months had seen a steady rise from 8·2 per cent (January 1972), and this period marks the start of the period of intense inflation when the retail price index stayed at over 20 per cent for thirteen months (March 1975–March 1976), reaching a peak of 26·8 per cent (August 1975).
4 This complex and contradictory aspect of 'the State' has been usefully explored in *In and against the State* (1980). They make the point that while the benefits of the Welfare State are real enough, they are operated by the same capitalist state with the same priorities to preserve the interests of capital.
5 See B. Ehrenreich and B. English (1979) and D. Donnison (1976) for a full documentation of the 'capture' of medicine by male professional experts.
6 There is an excellent discussion of this aspect of class society in R. Sennet and J. Cobb (1978).
7 This valuable concept was developed by Althusser in the paper of that name in *Lenin and Philosophy and Other Essays* (1971). Although it has been much criticised (see M. Barrett, 1980), it offered both an impetus and a tool for examining the question of 'social reproduction'.
8 I am not denying that there are cases of fraud and 'scrounging', but the weight of evidence, especially that produced by Frank Field and his associates in the Child Poverty Action Group, has shown that they are far outweighed by the scandal of people who do not 'take up' the benefits to which they are entitled, or for whom it is made complicated and degrading. The 'myth', which frequently appears in the popular press, does have its effects — which are observable here. Many of these people would have forgone benefits rather than be tarred with the 'scrounger' brush, and when they did claim they blamed their difficulties not on the system but on the 'scroungers'. That the two subsequent quotations both come from men does not mean that the women were not equally imbued with the myth, although they did have more trouble relating it to their own experience as legitimate claimants.

SEVEN

WOMEN, MEN AND POLITICS

In the last chapter I tried to show that people's experience locally was essentially their experience of national policies, institutions and structures in a particular locality. Now I want to look more closely at their ideas about 'politics' and 'power', and whether gender had a significant part to play in their understanding. In particular I focus on the relation between gender consciousness and class consciousness.

We have already seen that the sexual division of labour in practice gives rise to an ideological separation of the two worlds of men and women. We have also looked at how 'sexual sectionalism' giving rise to women's consciousness has some parallels with trade union consciousness. Both act as fetters on the development of full class consciousness, but on the other hand both offer ideologies in which at least *some* experience can be interpreted and located.

All the men and women in the study conformed to the basic sexual division of labour — men at work and women at home — and they acknowledged the dominant sexist ideology that rationalises that arrangement.

However, on closer examination, it seems clear that many of the women, who thought that they had accepted the sexual division of labour, at the same time developed a consciousness of their position as women that questioned not the objective existence of a sexual division of labour but the social evaluation of it. It is the relationship of this redefined women's consciousness to ideas about power, politics and class that is our focus now.

Sexist ideology as an organising principle of perception establishes the separate 'worlds' of men and women. It also acknowledges the 'male world' to be the dominant one, and it was this aspect that was challenged by the women's consciousness. The male 'world' effectively encompasses all of what we might call 'the public sphere' — including trade unions and 'politics'. From this world women are excluded, or admitted only on special terms. The male world, in fact, contains all matters of 'importance', thus relegating the female world to the periphery. Significantly it is the male world that claims the right to define the boundaries and content of both worlds.

This represents a major cleavage within the working class. It means that working-class people organise their daily lives around their differences and not around their similarities. There would appear to be few ways of uniting the two worlds in common action for a common (class) cause. The sexual division of labour and its ideology are thus a massive barrier to organising women in traditional working-class or democratic (public) institutions, and a barrier to the development of working-class consciousness as such. The cleavage makes for difficulties in organising women, and points to certain tensions and contradictions that can inhibit men's full commitment to class organisation.

The world of women centres on the home, and neither the men nor the women in this study denied either the content or the separate nature of that world in terms which L. Davidoff *et al.* (1976) would immediately recognise.[1] But in fact nearly all the women offered some resistance to the consequent social definition of themselves as women, and some had developed a strongly felt and clearly expressed set of ideas that were at variance with it. This resistance was important in its own right — as a significant strand in their thinking. But it was also important because of the way their class consciousness was influenced by it. It seemed, at first sight, that this gender-based resistance was hostile, or at least negative, to traditional channels of working-class consciousness — such as labour or union ideologies — which were inevitably located in the male sphere.

To see whether this was so, or whether the relationship between women's consciousness and class consciousness was not more complex, it is necessary to examine more closely the way in which the women saw themselves — as women: to question whether and how they saw the prevailing social definitions of women as oppressive and, if so, whether and how they resisted them and what means they used to try to redefine their social position as women. More broadly, it is necessary to see how their response to these issues coloured the rest of their thinking. To gain a little purchase on these problems let us focus on one woman — Sharon Thomas.

One woman's experience

Sharon Thomas was forty-two when I met her. She had two sons — one working in Customs and Excise, and the other still at school but hoping for at least some O levels or CSEs. She was married to Keith, the vocal and militant branch secretary of the TWU. They lived in a council house in Hartcliffe. It was slightly larger than most others, but sparsely furnished. Sharon worked part-time in a bakery job that was very nearly full-time (7 a.m.–3 p.m.). She did 'finishing off cakes — that's creaming, jamming — everything like that, on a conveyor belt'. 'It's all right if you're allowed to move around, but then if you're stuck sometimes on the end packet you're stuck nearly all day long, and it can drag on. No one seems to come to relieve you.' Her work history was as fragmented as that of most of the other wives. Before she married she had had a variety of jobs, in a chocolate factory, as a cleaner and dinner lady at a convent school, and in a chain-store cafeteria. 'That was the one I enjoyed most. You was meeting so many different people there. That's what I prefer.' She had moved for the money, for convenience, or just as the fancy took her.

After she had had her two boys there was a long break when she had no paid work (until Peter was six) because 'my husband didn't really like me going out to work'. But when they moved to their present house and 'we needed the extra cash' she overcame Keith's resistance:

> It was either putting in for one of these or buying a new car. We put in and didn't seem to be getting anywhere, so we bought a new car and as soon as we had it the house came through — but we got over that by my going out to work.

So first she took an afternoon job at Wills's, then did five years at Gateway and finally moved to her present job. All the time she gradually increased her hours, and 'Keith doesn't mind so much now. He's got used to it. In the beginning he seemed to think he should be able to provide for all we needed, and of course it didn't work out that way ... I think we should both be able to go out and contribute together.'

But it was more than money for the increased rent and two growing boys that sent Sharon back to work in spite of Keith's opposition.

> When they were young I could just stick them in a pushchair, into the bus and down to see my mother. Well, then, when they went to school that was it. You was stuck in the house waiting for them to come home to dinner, then home to tea. You had no time for going anywhere, and housework to me is just a bore; I think it's just a boring existence staying home all day.

And hard work as well.

> At first it was harder [than working outside] but gradually it got so they were helping — and then my husband started helping which made

it even easier. He could see I was tired. Now when he's on two to ten he does cook his meal.

Even so she did feel her work in the home was not appreciated by the family. 'They seem to think you're home all day long and it's a life of leisure. They don't realise there's cleaning to be done, and washing and ironing. I don't like cleaning, I never have, but it's got to be done.'

There was no mention here of 'the satisfaction and virtues of running a home': it was just a drag. But she didn't challenge it, either. Even when she was working nearly a full day outside she was 'grateful' for the 'help' her family gave her, though it amounted to little enough.

The Thomases had a joint bank account, and they both talked as if Sharon's money was simply a supplement to the family budget. But it meant much more than that to her. 'It's important to have money of your own. If you don't work you don't have anything — unless you're given pocket money.' For the same reason she had signed a petition against the abolition of family allowances 'because there are a lot of unfortunate women who don't get enough from their husbands and they depend on that money to see them through the rest of the week'.

The fact that she was working, and had done for some time, had taken the edge off her feelings about economic dependence. She had got 'money of her own', but she saw it as vital, and looked with pity and understanding at women who suffered the full brunt of dependence. Her own dependence and indeed her contribution to the family income was still way below Keith's, but that she accepted. 'My wages cover household expenses through the week, but all the bills are paid from Keith's money, which goes into the bank.' So she was not looking for equality, or even full economic independence. She did, however, want 'equal pay' — of a sort.

Yes. I mean, we do jobs in there equally as hard as the men's. Well, there's our chargehand as a start — half the time he's just stood watching, and yet he gets more pay than we do. I don't think we've even started creeping up on their wages yet.

'Equal pay', yes, but not as a universal principle.

I don't think my husband thinks women earn it, to be quite honest. But then, I've never worked in his factory, so I don't know. In fact I asked my husband to get me a job there, but he wouldn't. He said it would be too hard for me ... very long boards you got to carry round, and the noise is deafening.

Yet substantial numbers of women (about seventy) did work at Hampers, and they didn't get equal pay, despite the fact that they had to carry round long boards in the same deafening noise as the men. What Sharon really wanted was simply *more* pay for what she did. Like many other women she either refused to take on her husband on his own ground ('I don't know about where he works') or cited extreme examples such as mining or dangerous chemicals to deny 'equal pay' as a universal principle. She divided the world of work into two quite discrete parts — 'men's work' and 'women's work' — and would not want or expect to enter the *men's* world of work herself. This is a crucial element in the women's argument.

When Sharon went out to work she was also looking for definition of herself other than as wife and mother, and a base from which to resist her family. 'Men think they know more — they're convinced of it. It all boils down that they think a woman's place is in the home, and that's where she should be, and shut her mouth.'

Yet this 'work base' was not 'organized' and certainly had nothing to do with traditional trade union institutions. In fact her experience of unions in her own working life had alienated her, confirming her impression that they were male-dominated and 'no part of a woman's life'. Most of Sharon's jobs, as one might expect, had been 'ununionised'. It was only at Wills and in her current job that she had been in a union, and she had not been impressed by the experience (see p. 126). But she had had personal experience of *individual* protest at work.

> Women just don't get the support that men do. I've found that in work, I might say. A couple of times they've tried to send us home at eleven because we've run out of work — the units to put the cakes in. I used to come home at twelve. The others go to the canteen. It's all right for them, but for me my time to come *home* is twelve to one, and I stick by that (to feed the boys). Couple of times I've stood up, and I've stood up on my own. A few have rallied round and said, 'We're not going either.' But the others have said, 'Well, if we've got to go, we've got to go' — and all that sort of attitude. They're afraid of sticking up for themselves, afraid of losing [because] they're women.

In this case anger and frustration erupted in individual action. There was no question of asking the union for support (they knew they wouldn't get it), but Sharon did expect support from other women, and blamed them when it was not forthcoming. Women were seen, therefore, as unable to generate the same solidarity and collective action as she could see men had in trade unions. This discouraging lack of solidarity, which can be explained more positively in terms of their lack of identification as workers, was nevertheless a common and damaging experience for the more actively inclined women.

Sharon Thomas's husband, Keith, was the secretary of Hampers branch of the TWU. He was deeply involved in the strike of 1973. At the time I saw his wife he was planning industrial action over bonus rates, and was constantly active in union affairs. His views reflected a well developed and thoughtful trade union consciousness. He had clearly learnt much, not only from his own experience, but from his contacts with full-time union officials and other well read union men.

For Keith the dispute was a crucial point in his life and in the formation of his consciousness. At the time he was wholly absorbed by it, and had learned a number of enduring lessons.

> The way I feel — if one of our members comes up to me I'd go the ends of the earth for him, because I know that that man — how can I put it — if I said to [the personnel officer] that I was going to do something with our branch he'd know full well that I *would* do it. In fact [the factory manager] did say our discipline was fantastic. I'm surprised they stuck it and backed us all the way. If we went and snapped our fingers and said, 'Climb the moon,' they'd do it. And I repay them the best way I can. I stick up for them and fight for their rights.

As well as this kind of union solidarity he had also learnt to deal with management, to control complex operations, to despise the dominance of the big holding companies over their subsidiaries and to scorn palliatives such as 'safety measures'. But despite the fact that he made some mention of equal pay for the women members of his union, and of the need to inform wives and ensure their support in an industrial dispute, he had clearly not relayed any of his work experience to his wife. Rather the opposite. He expressly discouraged her from getting a job there, and flatly refused to talk to her about his own experiences.

> I would say I try not to talk to her. She don't like the union, she wants me to finish with it because of the time ... I don't think women have any right to interfere, and I'm not saying that because they're women but because they're outside the problems that exist in that factory ... I should imagine if a bloke takes home his wage packet and the wife sees how little he's earning, that would put her on his side straight away.

But it didn't: Sharon was adamantly opposed to the strike.

> My husband went on strike, I think it was a week, but they were also on a go-slow for quite a while, and the money dropped and I kept on at him to get back to work properly: just carry on properly, because

they lose more money by striking than they get. I don't know the reason they strike — half the time it's just for more money, isn't it? The strike at Hampers was for more money, but the money we were losing was too much. It was quite a bit each week, because they lost it in bonus and overtime in any case. So wives should have a say, because it's the wife that has to run the home, and unless the money comes in they can't do it, can they?

In fact she viewed all Keith's union involvement with a jaundiced eye. It took too much of his time for too little reward, and

... it's the awkwardness of it — like Sunday mornings. It's the time when it overlaps in the evening. 'I've got a meeting.' 'What time will you be home?' 'I don't know.' So you're stuck there and you don't know whether to clear the table or leave it, and sometimes he'll come home at seven at night. 'Oh I don't want anything.' That's when you feel like picking up the table and throwing it at them.

On the other hand, better the devil you know:

He's got an interest in the union now, and he'd be lost if he didn't do that. I don't know what sort of interests he'd get up to them.

Not surprisingly, Sharon opposed other strikes too. 'I don't believe in strikes at all.' The AUEW One Day strike against the Industrial Relations Act 'was stupid', and the miners, 'They deserved the money, it's true, but I don't think they should hold the country to ransom for so long ... you've got to think of the old people who rely on coal.'

Sharon was anti-union, then, partly because her own experience had taught her that unions were negative and partly because Keith's positive experience was to her merely a frustrating inconvenience and ideologically bereft of any validity. For her, strikes simply hit at the weaker sections of the working class and were, in any event, an ineffective weapon.[2]

They can't go slow, can they? When they tried it it didn't do very much. They just had to go on complete strike — but strikes don't achieve much, either.

But before we reconcile ourselves to this apparent validation of conventional assumptions about the conservatism of working-class women, we need to put her views on industrial matters into a more general political perspective. While she railed against unions and against the activities of her 'militant' husband, in general political matters the position was reversed. Sharon voted Labour, although she had no illusions that they would actually do anything for the working class.

I think they'd understand more if they were forced to live, for two months, on an ordinary worker's wage. I think they'd come down to earth with an bump ... they're out for themselves. They *say* they're helping you, but half the time ... people with money. I think they have too much say.

Contrast this with Keith, who admitted that people with money had influence but 'I'd just like to be one of them' and who voted Conservative (when he bothered) because

I can't see any harm the Tories have ever done to the working man. I think the Conservatives are more lenient — more kindly disposed towards the working man — he's better off under a Tory government. I don't know why, but I always seem to live better under the Tories.

Keith's criticism stopped short at his *own* management. Sharon's was directed trenchantly at all shareholders and managers.

It's the man that's actually doing the job who should be paid a good wage, because they're actually producing it and sending it out. The top man — in my place, I know all he's doing all day long is just walking around, and at his say anything can happen, and yet he's not actually working on the floor with us, so he don't really know what it's all about.

She also had much to say about union leaders 'out for their own glory', the class structure — 'if you've got money you're important. If you've got nothing they don't want to know you' — about prices, local councillors and the media — all of it critical and well informed. She was certainly not as Keith described her disparagingly: 'It's no use talking to her, she can't pick up the evidence.'

Yet, at the local level, Sharon saw no alternative to the deficiencies in housing, clinics, schools or local amenities. Except for signing some petitions and discussing things 'up the school', she had *done* nothing. She had had no point of organisation around which to gather her anger, or generate solidarity with other women — either in the locality or, having rejected the union, at work.

She did see the lack of an institutional base at work as a weakness, but she did not blame the unions for failing to provide enough support and leadership. Instead she blamed other women. The same sort of individual battles as Sharon fought at work were recorded by women in connection with rent strikes, school dinners, school discipline or welfare officers. Whether they won or lost, they ended up feeling isolated and beaten, and their reaction was not to force their way into 'men's' organisation or take active steps to set up their own, but to withdraw into their shell and rail at other women.

Nevertheless Sharon resented her sex's exclusion from public life. She imagined the kind of world that would result from having women 'in power', and which would reflect her own priorities.

> Women would think of older people more, and children. Men are always thinking of working men's power. But children and old people, they just don't want to know. It would be better if women made the big decisions. I'd like to think it was the women ... they'd do more to keep prices stable. Men just don't seem to know that when wages go up, prices have got to rise. Some get higher wages and still give the same to their wives, so she has to manage with increased prices and less money.

Here Sharon embodies two common themes. One was the stress on consumption as against production. The other was emphasis on the human, 'caring' values.

Her ideas also show the complexity of the problem of trying to 'locate' her ideology It was constructed from 'contradictory' experiences, yet if we accept the centrality of her consciousness as a *woman* it gains an internal logic and consistency. In terms of relating it to her 'radical potential' we have to take account of the contradictory nature of her world. Her hostility to the labour movement derived from its neglect of her needs as a woman. Nevertheless she was also aware of the contours of a *class* society and her own position as part of the working class. Beyond the class 'loyalty' so many women expressed she was coherently critical of the fundamental structure of class society. Her lack of action simply reflected the lack of working-class institutional bases. Moreover, once away from the point of production, her experience as a woman had intensified her critical stance. Thus there was considerable 'radical potential' in Sharon's position, but the complex process of mediation between her experience and ideas as a woman and her experience and ideas as working-class make her final 'position' impossible to categorise in conventional single-line typology.

Women and the public world

We are now in a position to draw together some of the threads from Sharon Thomas's experience and from the themes that have emerged in the previous chapter. We are looking primarily at the relationship of gender consciousness and class consciousness. Pivotal to that is an understanding of how women construct a *specific* consciousness based upon and making sense of their specific experience of the world. Where this relates most obviously to the more usual concerns in the area of class consciousness is in the public world of national issues, politics, parties and events. The 'public world' in this sense is an extension of the 'world out there' that we discussed in the last chapter. There we saw that both men and women saw prices and schools as outside their control, and clearly outside their particular spheres of home and work. What I was concerned to demonstrate was that the separation of the home from the oft-vaunted 'community' reinforced the effective privatisation of the woman's work in the home.

The focus of this chapter is the understandings men and women have of the general concepts of power and politics. Here we are on contested ground. The men freely admitted that the working class, ordinary people like themselves, had no control over and little part in the government of the country, or even in the democratic process. And yet, as men, they claimed the whole area as part of their area of expertise. Thus they too found contradiction between their gender and their class consciousness.

It was quite difficult even to establish whether women had any concern in the 'public world' at all. A statement that women are 'not interested in politics' can be, and often was, simply a statement that 'politics' – as that was defined – was outside a woman's sphere of interest, or 'world' as *that* was defined. Although a number of men (eight) and a smaller number of women (four) refused to allocate 'politics' or 'organisation' to either world – regarding it as common ground (or equally alien) to both sexes – the majority were involved in the process of separating off areas of experience from one or other sex.

For example, there was general agreement that (at the local level) pedestrian crossings and schools, and (at the national level) prices, were an extension of 'women's work'.

> A few more women in the government would help, because men don't understand the shopping.
>   *Cath Grimshaw*

No one suggested that, if women had more say in running the country, foreign policy would be different, but they did say that prices would be lower;[3] nor did they see any connection between foreign policy and prices. Indeed, while prices were regarded as part of one world, and foreign policy as part of quite another, it was difficult to see how any overall analysis *could* be developed.

The men tended to agree that women were more affected than they by local amenities and conditions. 'They've got to live with it,' 'They're at home all day, so they're stuck with it' (*Nigel Martin*). The women had a rather wider and more explicit idea of 'their' sphere. Like the men, nearly all *did* think that there was a definable sphere in which women operated and were more affected by than men, and they generally seemed to accept that women *did* have more responsibility for the local community. The needs of the family were counterposed against the needs of the locality, often in contradictory ways, i.e. women were more concerned to fight for amenities because of their families, 'women *will* organise if it affects their family' (*Ros Neale*), but they were also prevented from organising by their family commitments. 'They get too tied up in their families (*Jo Lee*).

While most of the men were prepared to allow women an interest in their local community, they were less enthusiastic about their participation in public life at national level. Two thought it would be better if women had charge of prices, because they understood them. Any other husbands who voiced an opinion thought women had quite enough 'say' as it was, and matters would not improve if they had more.

The wives thought otherwise. They all felt that women should play a greater part in public life, and the way they talked suggested that it was something they had resented for a long time. There were some *caveats*; Cath Grimshaw spoke for one.

> A few more women in government would help, because men don't understand the shopping, but women do it, so they understand. Sometimes a woman can be more ferocious. But there shouldn't be a woman Prime Minister — that doesn't see right to me.

The same sexual division of labour that associated women with shopping, and wanted to reserve that sphere for them at all levels, also regarded the wielding of power and authority as outside it, however 'ferocious' women were.

Most of them stressed either the material benefits that would accrue from having more women in power:

> I think things could change if there was an all-women government; they'd put the wages up and the food down — if women did get in, the country would be a bit more organised. *Mandy Ferguson*

or a more tangible improvement in the 'quality of life':

> It would be better if women had the power. If women ran their homes the way men run the country there wouldn't be any happy homes. *Jane Smith*

> I don't think a man knows enough to run a country. Only a woman could — it's a woman that keeps the home together. *Janet Griffiths*

A lot of this depended on two unwarranted but interesting assumptions. One was that the point of consumption was of prime importance. They never mentioned production, or indeed any other aspects of capitalist relations. Again and again it was felt to be women's knowledge of *prices* that qualified them for public power.

> Even if they *do* get in they don't get much say. They're put in the Medical Department, or Roads; not in the top ones. It's the women who gets the stuff in and knows the prices and worries about money.
>
> *Janet Griffiths*

The other assumption was that women's sphere of competence included all Parsons's 'expressive values' — indeed, almost a monopoly of 'goodness'. They 'understood people' and cared for them; it was assumed that this personalised 'caring' would be carried over into public life. 'They'd be fairer, more soft-hearted' (*Gladys Hutchings*). 'It would be fairer. They know how things are ... they look after the old people more' (*Diane Dixon*). There are quite enough women in high places who could not be characterised as 'soft' or 'caring' any more than their male counterparts to expose this myth, but what we should notice here is that the idea amounted to a stance: it represents a *consistent* dissatisfaction with the prevalent analysis.

The men held the most familiar positions. Politics was an entirely male sphere, and women knew little or nothing about it. How could they, except through their menfolk? Eighteen of them stated this in varying degrees of intensity. 'She just isn't in a position to know. I don't know what women talk about when they got together — but I'm pretty sure it isn't politics (*Mike Lee*). They divided only over whether it was innate — 'women don't worry', 'women don't bother to listen' (*Keith Thomas*), 'they're just not interested' (*Steve Gray*) — or due to their isolated situation.

> I don't think we *know* more. We just hear about it — we talk about it here. That's the only reason we think we know. How many women have a chat in a café with thirty other women? They're cut off — have to rely on what their husbands say.
>
> *Don Grimshaw*

A deviant but interesting view (which defined politics as statecraft, not industrial issues) argued that because the atmosphere at work was so constricting women at home actually had *more* opportunity to discuss 'the news'. As John Pollard explained,

> In our case my wife is above me in understanding things. What slows me

down is coming into a job like this. Politics isn't mentioned at work —
at least, not till the last elections. It's mentioned more in connection
with the union. Real union men are more apt to be Labour. You only
get moans in here, not discussion. You can't have a discussion in a
factory like this. If you was sat down an hour discussing, you'd have
the foremen on you. You've got a sheet to hand in at the end of day.
You can't go round the factory just chatting here and there. My wife
meets a more varied conversation than me. Union, politics, jobs — that's
as far the scope here goes. My wife can talk about almost anything, and
she isn't controlled on the amount of time.

The woman's position was essentially a response to this male capture of
the 'political'. A few respected the male supremacy view that only men
knew about politics, and that made them superior because politics was
about 'important' matters. 'He tries to explain it, but I still don't understand' (*Cath Grimshaw*), 'I only know about the home and children' (*Ros
Neale*).

Some were 'collusionists': men just *thought* they knew more. 'Men do:
they like to *think* they do, but half of them don't go to meetings, and
don't know anyway' (*Betty Turner*). What lay behind these comments
was the idea that men — like children — lived in an imaginary world
where they *thought* they had the power. And women indulged them
because it did no harm and enabled *them* to get on with the really
important things — usually left undefined but centring round the home
and personal values.

Some women mentioned time as a luxury men had and women didn't.
'It's time — I haven't got time to sit down and read' (*Mavis Gray*).

There were also some counterparts to John Pollard, who reckoned that
women at home and had *more* time and opportunity to think and talk.

It's only in recent years I've taken notice. When you have so much time
you begin to think about things, ponder about things. Even when
you're over the sink you're not just thinking what's to be done in the
home. You're thinking about other things, like politics and what's
going on. When you're out at work you're in there all day chatting and
you're out at night. You've got no time to think.   *Claire Rees*

'Politics' is identified here with 'the news', parliament, foreign affairs,
Northern Ireland — not with industrial politics. Given that limitation, they
nevertheless had a point. If they can escape the disc-jockey, women not
only *do* have access to political information at home, but of a much
wider range. There was a tendency among them to hold a wider definition

of 'politics'. As Don Grimshaw and Claire Rees both pointed out, people in industrial production have neither the time nor the inclination to talk politics: 'You chat all day, and you're out at night.' So that although *theoretically* they are in a position to learn about capitalist relations of production at first hand, and to organise against them, it is easy to see why it so rarely happens. It is to precisely these young production workers and their experience that many socialist writers have looked for signs of working-class radicalism, and have been disappointed. What is, of course, lacking for women at home is an institution comparable to the unions that could mediate and interpret the information they do get. Even when they have an opportunity to talk together, e.g. 'down the shop', they are on their own against the prevailing ideology. So that 'I'm not intelligent enough. But I argue in shops, and I know I say sensible things' (*Gladys Hutchings*), but she had no confirmation except her own inner conviction.

But the majority of women — thirteen in all — defined politics simply as what men were interested in (with a stress on industrial politics) and maintained that the two spheres were incomparable, or that women's concerns were the more important. Both these positions involved a rejection of 'politics' as nothing to do with them. This kind of attitude was well represented by Mavis Gray:

> Men do, I think. They read a lot, and they're interested in politics and all that sort of thing. Women are interested in the cost of living and things like that.

And many of the others, having declared they knew nothing about politics and weren't interested, went on to say that what they were concerned about was things like housing, prices, welfare services, the care of old people and children, local amenities and sometimes even earthquakes or wars. These things were 'not political', and that left (effectively) industrial affairs and parliamentary politics: tidy exceptions to be sure, but of limited range.

What some of the most coherent seemed to be arguing was that there were two distinct spheres — and in so far as they were comparable they refused to regard the women's as inferior. If they were comparable, then the women's sphere *must* be better. They took strength in their opposition from a feeling of identity with other women. 'Other women understand.' So their response to what they saw clearly enough as an attempt to relegate them to the peripheral was to band together — not to invade male territory, but simply to define their own as what concerned them and to define it *therefore* as important.

What we have here, then, is both the motive and the means for the women to construct a consciousness based on their resistance to being defined as peripheral to any aspect to the world that *men* consider important.

Women's consciousness

What are the main elements of this 'women's consciousness'? Firstly, women delineated their world very sharply. There was little or no overlap with the 'men's world'. The majority of both men and women thought that the worlds were distinct, separate and, at least in some ways, in conflict. Anything which was defined as part of the men's world was therefore not part of the women's. For instance, it was common to define the 'political' as a male concern. Women don't know about politics because they are not men; though they effectively recaptured the ground by limiting the 'political' to parliamentary politics and industrial issues in the narrowest sense. This left prices, housing, education and so on as things they *could* be concerned about.

Secondly, women included in their sphere the whole area of moral values. Much of their condemnation of public life as it stood rested on what they saw as the neglect of such values: 'they don't seem to think of the old people'. For this reason many thought that if women had 'the power' it would result primarily in an improvement in the 'quality of life'. 'It would be better if women had the power. If women ran their homes the way men run the country there wouldn't be any happy homes.' 'I don't think a man knows enough to run a country — only a woman could — it's a woman that keeps the home together.' This aspect of the separation of sexual spheres also accounts for the rapidity with which they resorted to moral argument or — more usually — moral condemnation, where the men would, perhaps, use tactical points.

Finally, there was a marked stress on the point of consumption as the centre of interest, and of power. 'A few more women in the government would help, because men don't understand the shopping.' 'I think it would change if there was an all-women government; they'd put the wages up and the food down.' This, of course, was paralleled by the fact that women felt specifically excluded from the point of production. As I made clear in Chapter 5, even when they went out to paid work they did so on a quite different basis from men, almost as migrant labour, and consequently they had a different relationship to the production process. Whether the difference is economically 'real', as V. Beechey (1976, 1978) would argue, is less important in this context than the fact that it is real in its ideological consequences.

The key to the resistance the women expressed most forcibly was their dislike of the definition of 'housewife'. For them, going out to work did two things. It broke the absoluteness of their domestic role and it gave them 'money of their own'. None of them wanted to work in order to be part of the man's world as breadwinner, or to be more closely involved in trade union struggle at the point of production.

Most of them disliked the work they did in the home. In any event, whether they liked it or not, it was hard work, an important job, and it was grossly underrated. Some reacted by counter-claiming that running a home and family was *the* single most important social activity, to which production work must be subordinate. This element in their thinking is clearly in opposition to any Marxist analysis. But it should be remembered that the women, like their husbands, were not exposed to any Marxist analysis. What they *were* exposed to was trade union views, and these tended to an economic stress on politics at the point of production.

For most of the women the failure to organise was an Achilles heel that prevented a 'great power' from coming into being: 'if they stuck together, that's the biggest power anyone *could* have'. But only a few located the reason for this failure in the privatised home. In any event, although as women they wanted women in control, they were less certain of *what* they wanted to control. The gulf between women's world and men's world — with its claim to embrace the whole public world — introduced a note of unreality into their vision of what 'real power' would be like.

These, then, are some of the ways in which the women asserted their consciousness of being women. Some were more strongly 'conscious' of it than others, but there was an identifiable tendency to perceive their position as women in a particular kind of way and to react to it in the ways I have described above.

My attention had been drawn to these women because what they expressed in their consciousness as women seemed to cut across the development of their consciousness of themselves as working-class. It was largely an ideology of resistance; less: inchoate anger at being excluded from the mainstream of society and of being defined as secondary an essentially male world. Furthermore, they seemed to have accepted that strand in the dominant ideology which tells women to expect little or nothing for themselves. They tended to assume that nothing could be done to change anything. And as we have seen, not even the most positive of them tried to transcend the dominant sexist ideology, only to resist it.

Isolation was, of course, a key factor. There was no structured institution through which working-class women could develop or express an ideology as women. All the women *met* other women — at the shop, outside school, or among their relatives — and they had the common (but not shared) experience of isolation. They all had a network of female relations and friends with whom they spent a good deal of time. Sometimes they discussed issues such as prices, equal pay or family allowances and compared notes. But it was not the same thing as the shared experience of workers on the factory floor, because they actually *experienced* their position within the enclosed walls of each individual family home.

In addition, all the traditional means of organising, both in the labour movement and in democratic politics, have belonged to the 'public', male sphere and have therefore been out of their reach. They felt alienated by the very forms of organisation deemed appropriate to 'their concerns'. These were either middle-class-inspired 'protest politics' or individual action. There was a wistful note in their voices as they suggested other possibilities, such as rent strikes and food boycotts, that would relate more directly to their working-class experience. In other words, despite their rejection of the existing trade unions, and of union ideology they were actively seeking a class consciousness and a class action which would accord with their experience as women.

'Women's consciousness' and 'class consciousness'

The central question, then, is the effect of their consciousness as women on their potential class consciousness. We have seen that although it appeared that women's consciousness was hostile to trade unions and industrial action, in practice they were not especially opposed to class organisation and especially to the Labour Party. Class loyalty kept them faithful, and they would have welcomed an organisation like a union that could operate in their sphere.

There were, in fact, two distinct ideologies dominating the world in which the women lived. One was the overarching bourgeois hegemonic ideology; the other was the 'counter-culture' of working-class ideology — itself developed in resistance to hegemonic interpretations. It included both trade union and Labour ideology. Each ideology contained 'sexist' elements. These women consequently resisted both of them. In terms of the development of class consciousness, therefore, it cut both ways. They were equally critical of the institutions of the bourgeoisie — e.g. the media — as of those of the working class, e.g. unions. Untrammelled by the limitations of traditional working-class ideology they could, and often did, perceive and attack the fundamental inequalities in bourgeois society that the men tended to gloss over. Because they were less involved, it was all the harder to 'incorporate' them. Their vulnerability came in their acceptance of the moral 'caring' values as predominant, which inevitably led to isolation and a stress on the point of consumption at the expense of the social relations of production.

Ideology is born of experience. Although all the women were working-class, and had plenty of experience as such, they were deprived of institutionalised ways of transforming it into class ideology. This was not wholly a disadvantage. Freed from the fetters of trade union allegiance and ideology, their experience did generate a generally more critical response to the world they lived in.

They had a 'consciousness' of what it meant to be a woman. But their response reinforced the cleavage between the sexes, and the division in the working class. It was not yet a coherent ideology. They were therefore prevented from making sense of the world — including their class position — in ways that were significantly different from men's. The resources of anger and frustration tended, in the context, to be expressed negatively and in fragmented and isolated ways. If these ideas could be developed into a coherent analysis of women's oppression it must be within a general development of class consciousness.

The root of the problem was a fundamental sexual division of labour effectively dividing the working class into separate and possibly mutual antagonistic worlds. The result had been effectively to exclude women from such resources of ideology or institution as the working class had. Yet it had not driven them into mere apathy or conservatism: rather the reverse. Their general orientation towards class and political issues was more radical (in the sense of challenging the structure behind the appearances) and more class-'loyal'. But neither they nor their husbands saw this as a positive contribution to the development of a class ideology.

Women's 'class consciousness' was imprisoned in their 'women's consciousness' to the detriment of the development of class consciousness or class action either by men or by women. This then, is not simply a 'women's issue'. The sexual division of labour, and of consciousness, and the consequent chasm in the working class as a whole, has as much relevance to the analysis of men's consciousness as to women's. The gulf between 'men's world' and 'women's world' and the failure to take account of it constitutes a major barrier to the theory and the practice of developing a full *class* consciousness by either sex. The isolation of women in a separate sphere releases a huge potential of anger and criticism, and at the same time cuts them off from both the institutional and ideological menas to develop that potential any further. Equally, men too are living in a divided world. Their potential is vitiated by their inability to mediate it to the other half of their lives — their homes — and the other half of society — women.

The mediation of experience and the development of consciousness are a complex process, and the burden of this study has been to warn against resort to any mechanistic 'reading off' formula. Here I have simply developed another factor in the process — the consciousness that working-class women have of themselves. The effect which that has on the development of their class consciousness is both complex and affected by the specific social and historical conditions in which they live. Being a woman is one of those specific conditions out of which people construct their lives. Being an active unionist is another. Both are partial experiences and provide partial ideologies. The danger in our present (capitalist) society is that they can as easily vitiate as support one another.

Notes

1 There is a perceptive account of the ideas implicit in 'the home' as an ideal, and of their historic roots, in L. Davidoff, J. L'Espérance and H. Newby (1976). They make use of the term 'Beau Idéal' to describe the calculated construction of the domestic and moral idylls which 'separate women and family from public concerns and gave them their own sphere of social influence in the house' (p. 174).
2 The only study so far to have confronted this problem, especially in public service disputes, is *In and against the State* (1980).
3 Writing in 1980, under the first female Prime Minister, and with inflation running at record heights, this supposition has a certain irony about it.

CONCLUSION

I began this book with two problems. Firstly, how does the sexual division of labour structure experience for men and women, and how does gender-divided experience structure ideology? Secondly, how is specific experience mediated to ideology and to other people removed from that experience? Both involved focusing on the working-class family, an area still neglected by the theorists of class, and still a crucial theoretical problem for feminists.

Underlying these two problems has been a theme that emerged during the course of the study, and which I hope its structure has reflected — namely the possibility that women respond to their specific experience as women not just with a patchwork quilt of ideology but with a real consciousness of themselves, and that this must be related to their actual or potential consciousness as members of the working class.

I have taken as central the oppression and exploitation of both women and the working class within capitalist society. In other words, my political aims have been to locate the liberation of women within revolutionary socialist practice. Marxist categories of explanation have clearly informed my approach. While I have been primarily concerned with 'superstructural' elements — especially ideology and consciousness — I have taken as axiomatic economic determination 'in the last instance'. This is not spelt out but it is implicit in the care I have taken to describe the *material* limits on people's activity in terms of wages, standards of living, housing, educational facilities and the like. There are other indications that I have worked within general Marxist parameters. To name but a few, the over-arching perspective of a class analysis of a capitalist society has situated my micro-level observations. The fundamental and structural antagonism between capital and labour has provided the groundwork. I cannot here enter into the profound debate around these issues, but it does 'account for' why I should have been concerned with certain problems at a certain level; why I should have chosen 'working-class' people; why the men's work at the point of production and the women's relationship to it should have been taken as so central; why capitalist interests should have been identified with State hegemony and why the Labour Party and the trade unions should have been treated as 'defensive' working-class institutions. Furthermore, I have directed my enquiry not only towards understanding those facts in the dimensions of people's lives but towards altering them.

Before we conclude with the political implications I want to draw attention to an issue that was central both to the way in which the study was carried out and the way the book has been presented. I refer to a concern with 'consciousness', that is, the argument that the overthrow of capitalism and the establishment of the transitional stage of socialism cannot occur without the active intervention of a fully 'class-conscious' proletariat at a 'moment' when the specific conditions within the social formation of capitalism allow that intervention to be effective. I take my cue from those writers (e.g. A. Gramsci, E. P. Thompson, R. Williams and J. Berger) who have been concerned with the factors that accelerate or inhibit the *process* whereby the working class becomes an active conscious agent in the making of its own history. Yet how can the active agency of the working class in history be investigated without destroying the subject in the very terms of the concepts we have taken as central?

At one level this is the problem of the distance between and relationship of the 'intellectuals' and the 'masses' — a concern of both Gramsci and Lenin. At another it is the problem that confronts all historians who want to present process in the inevitably static form of the written word.

Like Berger[1] I have tried to present the people I studied so that they could speak for themselves within the context of their own experience. I wanted the problems to arise from the material and not from categories imposed upon it. I wanted, in any event, to convey something of the integrity, dignity, courage and intelligence of the working people I met. This kind of objective is manifest in many other studies (e.g. J. Berger, *Pig Earth*, 1979; R. Sennet and J. Cobb, 1972; P. Willis, 1978) and all of them have wrestled with the problem that Eagleton speaks of — how do you escape the 'inevitably partial consciousness of more or less faithful description without destroying the heart of the man or woman of whom you write?'[2]

It was in the light of this difficulty that I deliberately set the balance of my reporting on the side of description — as faithful as possible — of what I heard and saw. I tried to avoid glossing it too liberally with intellectual allusions. For one thing, I felt that to do so would be to introduce a grotesque imbalance. Who would listen to Tommy Turner of Hampers stumble towards a position that had already been gracefully articulated by Perry Anderson? Yet from a political view-point what Tommy had to say is at least as relevant as Perry Anderson's comments. But there is an element of fundamental dishonesty here. I did not simply act as a tape recorder. By my very choice of where I went, whom I talked to and what about, I was imposing my own problematic. Furthermore honesty compelled me to interrogate my own material. Apart from this I realised that simply 'to record' would be the equivalent of pickling in aspic — a procedure that subverts what should be eaten into a inedible showpiece. There are, therefore, some references either to comparable studies or to more theoretical works throughout the study. Even when I have not made the point explicitly it lies just beneath the surface.

So my attempt to study the experience and consciousness of these particular Bristol people in the specificity of their experience at a moment in time has forced me into an act of destruction. In particular the process of analysis has necessitated arresting process and dissecting totality. Yet the attempt was unavoidable. My solution has come, in the end, to a matter of judgement. At this point the people must speak for themselves: at that point what they say must be interrogated. It is not an entirely *ad hoc* empirical solution. Certain procedures have been evolved for collecting and interrogating material. There are certain common discourses, especially among Marxists. Yet sociologists (and they usually admit it) are still groping in the dark. All sociological knowledge is proximate. Do sociologists, then, give up the unequal struggle? The answer, I think, is that we cannot. Our task is too important to relinquish. I can, perhaps, leave it to that great apologist of the method, E. P. Thompson, to sum up the problem and the answer.

> In the end we also will be dead, and our own lives will lie inert within the finished process, our intentions assimilated within a past event which we never intended. What we may hope is that men and women of the future will reach back to us, will affirm and renew our meanings, and *make our history intelligible within their own present tense.* They alone will have the power to select from the many meanings offered by our quarrelling present, and to transmit some part of our process into their progress. [*Poverty of Theory*, p. 234; my emphasis.]

In the end we may be dead, but meanwhile we live. We assert 'values which we intend to enlarge and sustain in our own present'. We cannot afford to wait for future historians to 'make our history intelligible'. We have to confront 'our quarrelling present' and, aware of the difficulties that attend us, attempt to perform as 'patient and exact' historians in the present as we know it, developing and refining our techniques as we go.

The picture I have painted of the class consciousness of people in Bristol in 1974 is not an especially rosy one. Those I talked to were certainly oppressed, also sometimes angry — but more often puzzled, fatalistic and apathetic. Above all they were isolated. They were deprived of the weapons of solidarity and of protest. They were denied the theoretical and political means to analyse their situation. Even the men, gathered together in one workplace and backed by a union, could only attempt little ameliorative gestures. The wives were generally reduced to sporadic outbursts of individual indignation against a particular teacher or shopkeeper. Yet this *is* the case in England, today as in 1974. It can be a form of delusion to seek out assiduously those few incidents of mass revolt or isolated examples of genuine socialist solidarity. Certainly we should understand why, for instance, the miners' union is stronger than others, or how Corrie's abortion Bill was defeated. But it is also crucial to understand why the majority of the working class voted for the declared ultra-right government in 1979.

Moreover, the object of this study was not simply to paint a picture of unrelieved gloom, for that would not be correct either.

In the first place, although these people were cut off from any explicit socialist or even labourist analysis or influence, their own understanding of the world around them, rooted in their own experience, clearly rejected the media stereotype. They were not cyphers. They were strong, intelligent and independent. They simply lacked the theoretical and practical tools that they needed to go further. In the second place, many of the men had demonstrated to themselves — and to others — that labour solidarity and organisation could win small battles. They were well aware of the limits of what could be achieved through such organisation and of the constraints imposed by wives hostile to such activities. Nevertheless the dispute *had* been a positive experience. If those limitations were removed, especially the chasm of incomprehension between them and their wives, the possibility of genuine working-class action immediately arises.

And, turning to those wives, we have seen the potential shown by the women in the study. Precisely because of their separation from the incorporated tradition of unionism, they were able to declare a consistently more independent position than their husband. They were frequently more critical, angrier and more capable of imagining more appropriate alternatives. In each case they were imprisoned in their ideological and material isolation. But it raises the crucial question — what if that had not been so? What if there was, as so many of them wanted, an organisation *like* a union that was directed to their concern?

It was a small study. I have been at pains to point out the dangers of 'reading off' from experience to consciousness and of ignoring and specificity of people's lives. But if we are committed to revolutionary change that has the concerns of feminism at heart then we must, at least, pay serious attention to what the women were saying, for they were not silent and they could be very strong.

The working class is fractured by the sexual division of labour. Men and women alike suffer from gender-differentiated ideas which prevent them from working together to construct their own class history. That chasm must be bridged before the potential we have seen among these working-class women and men can be realised.

Notes

1 J. Berger, *Pig Earth* (1979), was a notable example of this kind of attempt.
2 T. Eagleton, review of *Pig Earth*, *New Statesman*, 15 June 1979.

METHOD

Method

I have already outlined, in the introduction, something of how I selected the topic for this study and how and why I gathered the material I did. This appendix is designed to fill in a little more detail, for those interested, and to discuss a few of the more interesting methodological points that came up. It may also give the reader some chance to evaluate the material I have presented. In a more statistical account tables could have come to my rescue, but in a qualitative study of this kind much depends upon trust — the trust the enquirer has of her informants, and they of her; and the trust the reader has in the writer.

My first loyalty has been to the complexity and integrity of the ideas of the people concerned. I have tried to reflect this throughout, sometimes at the expense of precision. I am still convinced that the only human-shaped boxes are coffins, and sociologists' concern to squash their human material into exact and measurable categories has destroyed them, like Procrustes, as people.

J. Westergaard has written, 'The real question is not the number of categories which people distinguish, but the nature of the relations which they recognise between them, and the basis of the differences which they see. Counting class labels is an easy and misleading substitute for the complex and sensitive analysis required' (in M. Bulmer, ed., 1974, p. 253).

Yet the language that we use in sociology, and the modes of thought within which we operate, place a heavy premium on rationality, and that relies for its operation on categories and classifications. It cannot, therefore, be abandoned without abandoning language itself. But it may be possible to counteract the deadening effects of categorisation by asserting other forces. One source for this resistance lies in the emphasis on process, dialectical relationships and historicity.

Another way is to welcome boundaries as things to cross, and categories as s source of confusion. Contradiction and confusion are not merely the results of conceptual untidiness. They are partly a function of our structures of expression and partly a reflection of social reality. At the same time the in-built strain towards consistency wars with the creative role of perplexity. The 'alternative vision' that Westergaard sought is thus as likely to emerge from creative confusion as from direct opposition to the capitalist hegemony. To welcome ambiguity, crossed lines and confused boundaries may, indeed, be to step outside the confines that have been set to keep us 'pure', but they may also be a way to a perspective that can see behind the categories to the sense beyond. It is also a cogent reason for seeking inspiration from a working class which is honestly puzzled by the apparently mad world about, and to try to reflect that complexity in the way I have written.

Gaining access

The original research design demanded an industrial firm that was large enough to provide the varied sample I needed and yet not extreme or unusual in its work processes. I needed free access to the factory, opportunity to interview the men in the firm's time and, above all, permission to approach their wives at home. I made simultaneous approaches to the management and to the relevant unions. Three firms responded favourably, including Hampers, which I chose mainly because a major dispute was going on there at the time. I was pleasantly surprised that this event did not preclude access, but on the contrary management seemed to imagine that I would be a soothing influence; and the unions, once convinced that I had nothing to do with management, were very willing to help. I needed the union's co-operation in particular in identifying couples who would fit my 'sample requirements'. Both management and unions stressed the difficulty I would have in gaining access to the men's homes. In fact it did not prove a problem, although a few men may have refused to take part because of it. Indeed, the wives were delighted to see me, and the men anxious to show off their homes. The cautious attitude of management and unions is some indication of the vested interest in the sexual division of labour they felt.

The fieldwork

The period December 1973–August 1974 was taken up with interviews, visits and chats with all the people involved, at home, at work, together and separately, together with the usual 'fact-finding' missions to union offices and personnel department. I had free access to the factory and consequently had other conversations as I made my way about, drank tea in the cafeteria and got the tape recorder mended.

My position in the factory was never made wholly explicit – except that I was not part of management. Most people knew I had 'something to do with the university' but cast me in the role of research *assistant* rather than research *student*, which was an advantage. Being a woman was also an advantage. The men did not regard me as a threat either to themselves or their wives. I was also seen as 'a bit dim', and consequently much time was spent explaining details of the mechanical operations in the factory, and of such things as the wage structure. In the course of this, men would express their views on a number of other issues. The wives were initially more cautious. Where they were unduly reserved I could usually mention my own children, and this, coupled with my evident first-hand knowledge of schools, clinics, hospitals, etc., usually put them at ease. If I was prepared, as I was, to help feed or bath the children they were more than happy to talk for hours, although much of this was like the men's, 'chat'.

One interesting difficulty that emerged was the difference when the husbands were present while I talked to their wives. I could never get them to relax and talk to me as freely when their menfolk were there. This was partly because in those cases the husband would introduce me, and as he had already met me was confident and friendly. The wife then felt 'outside' the relationship. On the other hand, the husbands wanted to be at home to show me the things they had told me about and were proud of — from their children to the new back boiler. And they were conspicuously more confident in their own home, often resulting in much longer speeches and much more critical opinions than they vouchsafed inside the factory.

I knew the shift system, so I could usually arrange for the husband to be there or not as I chose. Whenever possible I saw the wife first, alone, and then had a second interview with the husband present.

The questions

I carried with me a list of questions as an *aide-memoire*. They gave me general guidance on the topics I wanted to cover, and a starting point if ever the conversation flagged. Some questions I tried to ask everyone — but generally the conversation flowed freely, only occasionally directed back to the main topic. I also made use of current events — local and national as they cropped up.

The material I collected generally fell under the following headings:

1. Biographical detail: education, work history.
2. Work: work situation, pay, overtime, bonus, management, redundancy, shareholders, directors salaries, atmosphere at work.
3. Unions: stewards, role of unions — SOGAT and the TWU — the dispute, women in unions.
4. Issues: national strikes, inflation, national decisions, classes.
5. Wife's work: paid, unpaid.
6. The community: housing, amenities, social services, education, health services.
7. Local politics.
8. Change and the future: differences since their childhood.

The order was important. It was no use asking the women detailed questions about her husbands' bonus *first*. She would sooner tell you about the price of children's shoes and then how the bonus affected that purchase. More important, there were significant differences between what the men and women would discuss, given different leads. The men, for instance, discussed profits in relation to wages. The women ignored them in that context, but raised the issue quite spontaneously in the context of *prices*. How many studies that have limited what they ask have missed vital data because respondents do not 'categorise it' in the same way as the researcher does?

In conclusion I should add that I was more nervous of the tape recorder than the people I talked to, and much less adept as using it. The men, at least, took an active part in controlling it and neither the men nor women seemed inhibited by it.

Analysis

As everyone with tape-recorded material (and no secretarial assistance) knows, transcription and analysis are long and tedious. At times there is a danger of becoming too distant from the field experience. Faces fade and are replaced by colour-coded cards. Still, analysis must happen. I reorganised my material, imposed categories; I began to write.

I was aware of gaps in the material it was too late to fill. I was also aware that the fieldwork had a beginning and an end. I talked to all the people at a specific historical moment, both in their own lives and in the public history of the country. Much has changed since 1974, but more importantly I have been concerned with *process* and yet I have used essentially *static* material.

In the end I have written a tribute to the people who talked to me. I could not let them remain silent because of my failure to write. And indeed, if the women, and the men, in this study can speak to us they should give us confidence in the undying vitality of working-class people.

LIST OF PARTICIPANTS IN THE MAIN FIELDWORK

Shop stewards		*Number of children*
TWU	Tommy and Betty Turner	3
	Ted and Mandy Ferguson	4
	Hugh and Ann Davies	8
	Max and Val Fennel	3
	Keith and Sharon Thomas	2
	Jim and Jane Smith	2
SOGAT	Nick and Felicity Skinner	4
	Steve and Mavis Gray	4
	Alan and Gladys Hutchings	3
	Vincent Flanagan (wife did not participate)	4
	Simon and Jenny Steele	3

Production workers		
TWU	Bert and June Hannam	2
	Don and Cath Grimshaw	1
	Dick and Janet Griffiths	4
	Paul and Diane Dixon	3
	John and Sue Pollard	1 + pregnant
SOGAT	Fred and Mary Fletcher	2
	Nigel and Jean Martin	3
	Arthur and Claire Rees	4
	Mike and Jo Lee	3
	Barry and Jackie Young	1

Foremen		
	Malcom Watson (wife did not participate)	2
	George and Anna Roberts	2
	Martin and Ros Neale	2
	Norman and Ginny Sykes	3 + pregnant
	Tony and Kate Wheeler	2

I have included this list so that quotations can be located even when I have not specified what the union affiliation was.

BIBLIOGRAPHY

Allen, S., *et al.* (1974), *Conditions of Illusion.* Leeds: Feminist Books.

Althusser, L. (1971), 'Ideological State Apparatus', in *Lenin and Philosophy and other Essays.* London: NLTS.

Anderson, P. (1967), 'The limits and possibilities of trade union action', in Blackburn, R., and Cockburn, A. (ees.), *The Incompatibilities.* Harmondsworth: Pengiun.

— (1976b), 'The antinomies of Antonio Gramsci', *New Left Review,* November.

Ardener, S. (ed.) (1978), *Defining Females: the Nature of Women in Society.* London: Croom Helm.

Apter, D. (ed.) (1964), *Ideology and Discontent.* New York: Free Press.

Aronowitz, S. (1973), *False Promises: the Sleeping of American Waking Class Consciousness.* New York: McGraw Hill.

Barker, D. L., and Allen, S. (eds.) (1976a), *Sexual Divisions and Society: Process and Change.* London: Tavistock and BSA.

— (1976b), *Dependence and Exploitation in Work and Marriage.* London: Longman and BSA.

Barrett, M. (1980), *Women's Oppression Today.* London: Verso and NLB.

Barron, R. D., and Norris, G. M. (1976), 'Sexual divisions and the dual labour market', in Barker, D. L., and Allen, S. (eds.) (1976b), *Dependence and Exploitation in Work and Marriage.* London: Longman and BSA.

Beechey, V. (1977), 'Some notes on female wage labour in capitalist production', *Capital and Class,* No. 3.

— (1978), 'Women and production: a critical analysis of some sociological theories of women's work', in Kuhn, A., and Wolpe, A. M. (eds.) (1978). *Feminism and Materialism.* London: Routledge & Kegan Paul.

— (1979), 'On patriarchy', *Feminist Review,* No. 3.

Beharrel, P., and Philo, G. (eds.) (1977), *Trade Unions and the Media.* London: Macmillan.

Berger, J., and Mohr, J. (1975), *A Seventh Man: the Story of a Migrant Worker in Europe.* Harmondsworth: Allen Lane.

Berger, J. (1979), *Pig Earth.* London: Allen & Unwin.

Beynon, H. (1973), *Working for Ford.* London: Allen Lane.

Bland, L., Morrison, R., Mort, F., and Weedon, C. (1978), 'Relations of production: approaches through anthropology', in Women's Studies Group (ed.), *Women Take Issue*. London: Hutchinson.

Bland, L., Brundson, C., Hobson, D., and Winship, J. (1978), 'Women "inside and outside" the relations of production', in Women's Studies Group (ed.), *Women Take Issue*. London: Hutchinson.

Braverman, H. (1974), *Labor and Monopoly Capitals: the Degradation of Work in the Twentieth Century*. New York: Monthly Review Press.

Brooke, E., and Finn, D. (1977), 'Working class images of society and community studies' in W.P.C.S. 10, *On Ideology*. Birmingham: Centre for Contemporary Cultural Studies.

Brown, R. (1976), 'Women as employees: some comments on research in industrial sociology', in Barker, D. L., and Allen, S. (eds.), *Dependence and Exploitation in Work and Marriage*. London: Longman and BSA.

Bulmer, M. (ed.) (1975), *Working Class Images of Society*. London: Routledge and SSRC.

Burman, S. (ed.) (1979), *Fit Work for Women*. London: Croom Helm.

Caulfield, M. (1976), *Capitalism and the Family*. San Francisco: Agenda Publishing Company.

Central Statistical Office (1977), *Social Trends*, No. 8.

Child Benefits Now campaign (1977), *The Great Child Benefit Robbery*. London: Child Poverty Action Group.

Cockburn, C. (1977), *The Local State: Management of Cities and People*. London: Pluto Press.

Cohen, S., and Young, J. (eds.) (1973), *The Manufacture of News: Deviance, Social Problems and the Mass Media*. London: Constable.

Comer, L. (1974), *Wedlocked Women*. Leeds: Feminist Books.

Conference of Socialist Economists (1976), *The Labour Process and Class Strategies*. London: Stage One.

Converse, P. E. (1964), 'The nature of belief systems in mass publics', in Apter, D. (ed.), *Ideology and Discontent*. New York: Free Press.

Critique of Anthropology (1977), *Women's Issue*, vol. 3, Nos. 9–10.

David, M. (1980), *The State, the Family and Education*. London: Routledge & Kegan Paul.

Davidoff, L., L'Esperance, J., and Newby, H. (1976), 'Landscape with figures: home and community in English society', in Mitchell, J., and Oakley, A. (eds.), *The Rights and Wrongs of Women*. Harmondsworth: Penguin.

Donzelot, J. (1979), *The Policing of Families*. New York: Pantheon Books.

Delphy, C. (1977), *The Main Enemy: a Materialist Analysis of World Oppression*. Mardon: WRBC.

Denis, N., Henriques, F., and Slaughter, C. (1956), *Coal is our Life: a Study of a Yorkshire Mining Community*. London: Eyre & Spottiswoode.

Dromey, J., and Taylor, G. (1978), *Grunwick: the Workers' Story*. London: Lawrence & Wishart.

Edhlin, F., Harris, O., and Young, K. (1977), 'Conceptualizing women' in *Critique of Anthropology*, vol. 3, No. 9/10.

Eisenstein, Z. R. (ed.) (1979), *Capitalist Patriarchy and the Case for Socialist Feminism*. New York: Monthly Review Press.

Equal Opportunities Commission, *Research Bulletin*, No. 1, winter 1978–79, and subsequent issues. Manchester: E.O.C.

Foreman, A. (1977), *Feminity as Alienation: Women and the Family in Marxism and Psychoanalysis*. London: Pluto Press.

Fox, B. (ed.) (1980), *Hidden in the Household*. Toronto: Women's Press.

Gardiner, J., Himmelweit, S., and Mackintosh, M. (1975), 'Women's domestic labour', *Bulletin of the Conference of Socialist Economists*, vol. 4, No. 2 (II).

Gardiner, J. (1976b), 'Political economy of domestic labour in capitalist society', in Parker, D. L., and Allen, S. (eds.), *Dependence and Exploitation in Work and Marriage*. London: Longman and BSA.

Gavron, H. (1966), *The Captive Wife: Conflicts of Housebound Mothers*. London: Routledge & Kegan Paul.

Giddens, A. (1973), *The Class Structure of the Advanced Societies*. London: Hutchinson.

Goldthorpe, J. H., and Lockwood, D. (1963), 'Affluence and the British class structure', *Sociological Review*, vol. II, No. 2.

Goldthorpe, J. H., Lockwood, D., Bechnofer, F., and Platt, J. (1968a), *The Affluent Worker: Industrial Attitudes and Behaviour*. Cambridge University Press.

— (1968b), *The Affluent Worker: Political Attitudes and Behaviour*. Cambridge University Press.

— (1969), *The Affluent Worker in the Class Structure*. Cambridge University Press.

Gorz, A. (ed.) (1978), *The Division of Labour: the Labour Process and Class Struggle in Modern Capitalism*. Brighton: Harvester Press.

Gouldner, A. (1954a), *Wildcat Strike*. New York: Antioch Press.

— (1954b), *Patterns of Industrial Bureaucracy*. New York: Free Press.

Gramsci, A. (1971), *Selections from the Prison Notebooks*, translated and edited by Hoare, Q., and Nowell Smith, G. London: Lawrence & Wishart.

Harris, C. C. (1969), *The Family*. London: Allen & Unwin.

Hobson, D. (1978), 'Housewives: isolation as oppression', in Women's Studies Group (ed.), *Women Take Issue*. London: Hutchinson.

Hoggart, R. (1957), *The Uses of Literacy*. London: Chatto & Windus.

Hunt, A. (ed.) (1977), *Class and Class Structure*. London: Lawrence & Wishart.

Hunt, P. (1980), *Gender and Class Consciousness*. London: Macmillan, New York: Holmes & Meier.

Hyman, R. (1971), *Marxism and the Sociology of Trade Unionism*. London: Pluto Press.

— (1972, 2nd edition 1977), *Strikes*. London: Fontana.

— (1975), *Industrial Relations: a Marxist Introduction*. London: Macmillan.

Kalinzynska, E. (1980), 'Wiping the floor with theory: a survey of writings on housework', *Feminist Review*, No. 6.

Kinnersley, P. (1973), *The Hazards of Work*. London: Pluto Press.

Komarovsky, M. (1962), *Blue Collar Marriage*. New York: Vintage Books.

Kuhn, A., and Wolpe, A. M. (eds.) (1978), *Feminism and Materialism: Women and Modes of Production*. London: Routledge & Kegan Paul.

Land, H. (1975), 'The myth of the male breadwinner', *New Society*, 9 October.
— (1980), 'The family wage', *Feminist Review*, No. 6.
Lane, T., and Roberts, K. (1971), *Strike at Pilkingtons*. London: Fontana.
O'Laughlin, B. (1974), 'Mediation of contradiction: why Mbum women do not eat chicken', in Rosaldo and Lamphere (eds.), *Women, Culture and Society*. Stanford University Press.
Levin, V. I. (1963), *What is to be done?* London: Oxford University Press.
Lockwood, D. (1966), 'Sources of variation in working class images of society', *Sociological Review*, vol. 14, No. 3, reprinted in Bulmer, M. (ed.), 1974.
— (1975), 'In search of the traditional worker' and 'The radical worker: a postscript', in Bulmer, M. (ed.), *op. cit.* London: Routledge & Kegan Paul.
London Edinburgh Weekend Return Group (1980), *In and against the State*. London: Pluto Press.
Malos, E. (ed.) (1980), *The Politics of Housework*. London: Allison & Busby.
Marx, K. (1976), *Capital*, vol. 1. London: New Left Review.
Marx, K., and Engels, F. (1970), *The German Ideology*. London: Lawrence & Wishart.
McKenzie, R. T., and Silver, A. (1968), *Angels in Marble: Working Class Conservatives in Urban England*. London: Heinemann.
McKie, D., and Cook, C. (1974), *The Guardian Election Guide*. London: Quartet.
Mitchell, J. (1971), *Woman's Estate*. Harmondsworth: Penguin.
Mitchell, J., and Oakley, A. (eds.) (1976), *The Rights and Wrongs of Women*. Harmondsworth: Penguin.
Morgan, D. H. J. (1975), *Social Theory and the Family*. London: Routledge & Kegan Paul.
Molyneux, M. (1979), 'Beyond the domestic labour debate', *New Left Review*, No. 116, July.
Nichols, T. (1974), 'Labourism and class consciousness. The class ideology of some northern foremen', *Sociological Review*, vol. 22, No. 4.
— (1975a), 'The "socialism" of management: some comments on the "human relations" school', *Sociological Review*, vol. 23, No. 2.
— (1975b), 'The sociology of accidents and the social production of industrial industry', in Esland, G., Salaman, G., and Speakman, M. (eds.), *People and Work*, Edinburgh: Holmes McDougall.
Nichols, T., and Armstrong, P. (1976), *Workers Divided: a Study in Shop Floor Politics*. London: Fontana.
Nichols, T., and Beynon, H. (1977), *Living with Capitalism: Class Relations and the Modern Factory*. London: Routledge & Kegan Paul.
Nordlinger, E. A. (1967), *The Working Class Tories*. London: MacGibbon & Kee.
Oakley, A. (1972), *Sex, Gender and Society*. London: Temple Smith.
— (1974a), *The Sociology of Housework*. London: Martin Robertson.
— (1974b), *Housewife*. London: Allen Lane.
Parkin, F. (1967), 'Working class conservatives: a theory of political deviance', *British Journal of Sociology*, vol. 18, No. 3, September.

– (ed.) (1974), *The Social Analysis of Class Structure*. London: Tavistock Publications.

Parsons, T., and Bales, K. (1955), *Family, Socialization and Interaction Process*. Glencoe: Free Press.

Popitz, H., Bahrdt, H. P., Jueres, E. A., and Kesting, A. (1959), 'Workers' images of society', in Burns, T. (ed.), *Industrial Man*, pp. 281–324. Harmondsworth: Penguin.

Porter, M. (1978), 'Consciousness and secondhand experience: wives and husbands in industrial action', in *Sociological Review*, vol. 26, No. 2, May.

– (1978), 'Worlds apart: the class consciousness of working class women', *Women's Studies International Quarterly*, vol. 1, pp. 175–88.

– (1981), 'Standing on the edge: working class wives in the labour market', in J. West (ed.), *Women in the Labour Process*. London: Routledge & Kegan Paul.

Rogaly, J. (1977), *Grunwick*. Harmondsworth: Penguin.

Rowbotham, S. (1973), *Woman's Consciousness, Man's World*. Harmondsworth: Penguin.

Rowbotham, S., Segal, L., and Wainwright, H. (1979), *Beyond the Fragments*. London: Merlin Press.

Rubery, J. (1978), 'Structured labour markets, worker organisation and low pay', *Cambridge Journal of Economics*, No. 2, pp. 17–36.

Runciman, W. G. (1966), *Relative Deprivation and Social Justice*. London: Routledge & Kegan Paul.

Salaman, G. (1974), *Community and Occupation*. Cambridge University Press.

Seabrook, J. (1978), *What went Wrong: Working People and the Ideals of the Labour Movement*. London: Gollancz.

Secombe, W. (1973), 'Housework under capitalism', *New Left Review*, No. 83.

Sennett, R., and Cobb, J. (1977), *The Hidden Injuries of Class*. Cambridge University Press.

Spring Rice, M. (1939), *Working Class Wives*. Harmondsworth: Penguin.

Terkel, S. (1975), *Working*, revised edition. New York: Wildwood House.

Thompson, E. P. (1975), *Whigs and Hunters: the Origin of the Black Act*. Harmondsworth: Allen Lane.

– (1978), *The Poverty of Theory and other Essays*. London: Merlin Press.

Toynbee, P. (1967), 'The language of inequality', in Blackburn, R., and Cockburn, A. (eds.), *The Incompatibles*. London: NLR and Penguin.

Trotsky, L. (1973), *The Transitional Program for Socialist Revolution*, pp. 72–158 (first published in 1938). New York: Pathfinder Press.

University of Liverpool (1954), *The Dock Worker*. Liverpool University Press.

West, J. (1978), 'Women, sex and class', in Kuhn, A., and Wolpe, A. (eds.), *Feminism and Materialism*. London: Routledge & Kegan Paul.

– (1979), 'A political economy of the family in capitalism: women, reproduction and wage labour', in Nichols, T. (ed.), *Capital and Labour*. London: Fontana.

Westergaard, J. H. (1975), 'Radical class consciousness: a comment', in Bulmer, M. (ed.), *Working Class Images of Society*. London: Routledge & Kegan Paul.

Williams, R. (1961), *Culture and Society, 1780–1950*. Harmondsworth: Penguin.

– (1976), *Keywords: a Vocabulary of Culture and Society*. London: Fontana.

Willis, P. (1977), *Learning to Labour: how Working Class Kids get Working Class Jobs*. London: Saxon House.

Wilson, E. (1977), *Women and the Welfare State*. London: Tavistock Publications.

Wilson, R. (1963), *Difficult Housing Estates*. London: Tavistock Publications.

Women's Publishing Collective (1976), Papers on the Patriarchy Conference. London.

Women's Studies Group (ed.) (1978), *Women take Issue: Aspects of Women's Subordination*. London: Hutchinson and University of Birmingham, Centre for Contemporary Studies.

Young, M., and Wilmott, P. (1957), *Family and Kinship in East London*. London: Routledge & Kegan Paul; revised edition, Harmondsworth: Pelican, 1962.

Zaretsky, E. (1976), *Capitalism, the Family, and Personal Life*. London: Pluto Press.

Subject index